INTERNATIONAL SOCIAL WORK RESEARCH

Issues and Prospects

Tony Tripodi and Miriam Potocky-Tripodi

OXFORD
UNIVERSITY PRESS

2007

OXFORD
UNIVERSITY PRESS

Oxford University Press, Inc., publishes works that further
Oxford University's objective of excellence
in research, scholarship, and education.

Oxford   New York
Auckland   Cape Town   Dar es Salaam   Hong Kong   Karachi
Kuala Lumpur   Madrid   Melbourne   Mexico City   Nairobi
New Delhi   Shanghai   Taipei   Toronto

With offices in
Argentina   Austria   Brazil   Chile   Czech Republic   France   Greece
Guatemala   Hungary   Italy   Japan   Poland   Portugal   Singapore
South Korea   Switzerland   Thailand   Turkey   Ukraine   Vietnam

Copyright © 2007 by Oxford University Press, Inc.

Published by Oxford University Press, Inc.
198 Madison Avenue, New York, New York 10016

www.oup.com

Oxford is a registered trademark of Oxford University Press

Library of Congress Cataloging-in-Publication Data

Tripodi, Tony.
International social work research : issues and prospects / Tony Tripodi and Miriam Potocky-Tripodi.
p. cm.
Includes bibliographical references.
ISBN-13 978-0-19-518725-0; 978-0-19-518726-7 (pbk.)
ISBN 0-19-518725-3; 0-19-518726-1 (pbk.)
1. Social service—Research—Cross-cultural studies.   2. Social service—Research—International
cooperation.   I. Potocky-Tripodi, Miriam.   II. Title.
HV11 .T745 2006

361.3072—dc22   2005036619

9 8 7 6 5 4 3 2 1

Printed in the United States of America
on acid-free paper

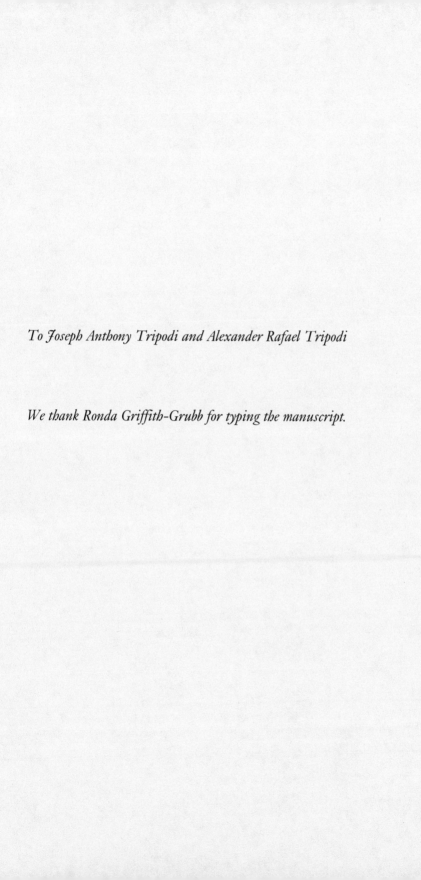

To Joseph Anthony Tripodi and Alexander Rafael Tripodi

We thank Ronda Griffith-Grubb for typing the manuscript.

CONTENTS

INTERNATIONAL SOCIAL WORK RESEARCH

1

INTRODUCTION

What Is International Social Work Research?

RATIONALE FOR THIS BOOK

During the past one to two decades, two parallel developments have occurred in social work: first, an increasing emphasis on research knowledge, as seen in advancements such as evidence-based practice, and second, growing awareness and appreciation of the importance of international issues in social work. The United States National Association of Social Workers (NASW) has remarked:

> As it becomes more obvious that the world's problems are everyone's problem, it is likely that more and more social workers will play a part in world affairs. Indeed, more American social work departments see the enormous need for social workers in the international arena and are adding specialties in this area. (p. 1)

Social workers' expanding roles in this arena include "researching international issues with a focus on improving people's quality of life and addressing injustices" (NASW, 2004). Yet, curiously, the social work literature has not addressed directly the nexus of these two streams.

In the nineteenth edition of the *Encyclopedia of Social Work*, Midgley wrote "International and Comparative Social Welfare," an article in which he discussed the interdisciplinary nature of social welfare research with respect to comparative studies of social need and of social policies and human services. He believed that

> a major direction for future activity in the professional domain requires the fostering of greater *mutual* collaboration among professionals in different parts of the world. The unidirectional transfer of professional ideas and practice methods from the industrial to the developing countries must be replaced by reciprocal exchanges in which professionals in many different societies learn from each other. (Midgley, 1995, p. 1496)

However, he did not distinguish international social work research from research in other disciplines, nor did he discuss specific issues in the conduct and utilization of international social work research.

3

In our summary of new directions in practice research (Potocky-Tripodi & Tripodi, 1999), we did not discern any trends regarding international research issues at a conference of the Society of Social Work and Research. In addition, in the 2003 supplement to the Encyclopedia of Social Work Research, there were no articles on international research in social work (English et al., 2003). The research articles in the Encyclopedia focused on empirical research, evidence-based practice, empirically based interventions, and the history of social work research in the United States.

There has been social work research in numerous countries for many years. Journals such as the *British Journal of Social Work* and *Social Work* are increasingly reporting research from other countries. To illustrate, the April 2004 issue included research studies in England, Israel, Scotland, and Hong Kong. Moreover, there are recent international collaborations such as the Campbell Collaboration, which is an international organization that compiles and disseminates systematic reviews of intervention studies. However, there has been no systematic examination of issues involved in conducting and utilizing such research.

It is our belief that social work scholars and students should be sensitive not only to the need for knowledge exchange between countries but also to issues involved in obtaining and utilizing such international knowledge. The perception of this need, which forms the rationale for this book, is based on international exchange of information and ethical considerations. It is quite evident that there is an increasing exchange of international information by modern technology. Further, many social problems transcend national boundaries, such as the plight of immigrants and refugees, human trafficking, domestic and child abuse, mental and physical health, drug commerce, and so forth. Thus, social work practitioners and researchers can enhance the likelihood of effectively addressing these problems through international collaboration and information exchange.

Such international knowledge sharing may be seen as an ethical imperative. In accordance with the policies of the International Federation of Social Workers, there are international, ethical principles and standards for all social workers. Several principles and standards are relevant to the rationale for this book: principle, "Social workers have the responsibility to devote objective and disciplined knowledge and skill to aid individuals, groups, communities, and societies in their development and resolution of personal-societal conflicts and their consequences" (Healy, 2001, p. 282); standard, "Apply relevant methods in the development and validation of knowledge" (p. 285); and standard, "Promote and share opportunities for knowledge, experience, and ideas with all social work colleagues, professionals from other disciplines and volunteers for the purpose of mutual improvement" (p. 286).

PURPOSE OF THIS BOOK

The purpose of this book is to present a perspective on international social work research, issues involved in the conduct and utilization of international research, and examples of international research studies. The book is intended to be a sequel to basic research texts in social work (such as Rubin & Babbie, 2005; Grinnell & Unrau, 2005;

and Yegidis & Weinbach, 2001), and a supplement to texts on international social work (Healy, 2001; Hokenstad & Midgley, 1997, 2004; Lyons, 1999). It aims to sensitize the reader to the prospects and potential for international social work research.

There are five subpurposes that are unique to this book and will be discussed in this chapter as well as throughout the book:

- The two social work streams of international social work and social work research are juxtaposed in international social work research.
- We provide a broad definition of international social work research. We define it as research that involves the use of literature from two or more countries to frame the research problem, and specifies implications of the research for two or more countries. International social work research involves different languages, customs, traditions, and emphases in using social research methods to develop knowledge for social work.
- We present a unique typology of international social work research to serve as a guiding framework for assessing and conducting such research. Our typology encompasses some concepts already in existence, but goes further in providing a new perspective on what international social work research is, how it differs from national research, and how it may be classified. The commonality in all international research is the extensive use of literature from two or more countries and the development of implications for two or more countries. Within that umbrella, we typologize international social work research as *supranational*, *intranational*, and *transnational*, subdivisions that will be defined later in the chapter.
- We focus on social work research as distinguished from social science research or social work practice. In this chapter, we expand on this definition of social work research: the use of social research methods for producing and disseminating knowledge that is pertinent to policies and practices that affect and/or are implemented by social work organizations, practitioners, and educators.
- We present in-depth examples of international social work research studies from various sources to illustrate and explore the relevant methodological issues. We draw upon social work journals in the United States such as *Social Work* and *Social Work Research*, and other countries, such as the *British Journal of Social Work*, as well as international social work journals, such as *International Social Work*, *Social Development Issues*, and the *Journal of Social Work Research and Evaluation: An International Publication*.

JUXTAPOSING INTERNATIONAL SOCIAL WORK AND SOCIAL WORK RESEARCH

International Social Work

Contemporary forces leading to international social work are: the increasing involvement of society and social work in international activities, that is, internationalism; and globalization, or global interdependence, with its positive and negative consequences for society and social work.

Internationalism

Midgley, in discussing the challenge of international social work, noted that

> a great deal has been accomplished over the last century and . . . many more social
> workers now have an appreciation of international issues. Many social workers travel
> to meet colleagues in other countries to learn from their experiences. Student ex-
> changes are also much more common than before. Attendance at international con-
> ferences is high, and the number of social work books and journal articles dealing
> with international issues has increased. Many schools of social work now have co-
> operative agreements with counterparts in other countries, and many more social
> work educators are involved in joint research and training projects with international
> colleagues. (2004, p. 2)

Nevertheless, Midgley points out that many critics believe that much more needs
to be done for social workers to truly adopt an international as opposed to a domestic or national perspective; moreover, "unlike many other professions social work
has neglected comparative research and relatively little has been done to replicate,
test, and adapt practice innovations from other societies. This has disadvantaged
the profession, which can improve its effectiveness and relevance by learning from
other societies" (p. 3).

Among the sources of increased international involvement are: national and international organizations, task forces concerned with international issues, international conferences, publications, and educational exchanges and student field
placements. Healy (2001) has provided an excellent, comprehensive discussion of
governmental and nongovernmental international organizations that are sources of
social work international activity. These organizations, such as the United Nations,
the Red Cross, the Department of Health and Human Services, and so on, deal with
a variety of social work problems, including world health, disaster relief, international exchanges, migration and refugees, international adoptions, and so forth. Healy
(2001) discusses four key international social work organizations: the International
Association of Schools of Social Work (IASSW), International Federation of Social
Workers (IFSW), International Council on Social Welfare (ICSW), and Inter-
University Consortium for International Social Development (IUCISD). The
IASSW includes 2,500 educators from 80 countries); it "supports the development
of high quality social work education and training, curriculum development, exchanges of academic staffs and students, and research projects" (Global Social Work
Congress, 2004, p. 8). The IFSW is active in human rights and social work ethics,
and "promotes social work as a profession through international cooperation, supports national associations, facilitates contacts between social workers globally and
establishes relations with the United Nations and other international organizations"
(p. 8). Along with IASSW and IFSW, the ICSW sponsors the journal *International
Social Work*; it serves "as a forum for exchange on knowledge on social welfare and
social development" (Healy, 2001, p. 59). Membership is comprised of national
committees, national organizations, and international organizations such as the International Federation of Red Cross and Red Crescent Societies, the International
Federation on Aging, the Salvation Army, and so on. The IUCISD is "an interdisciplinary organization founded by social work educators to promote social devel-

opment" (p. 53). It includes members from industrialized and developing countries, exchanges knowledge from research, theory, and practice in international conferences, and publishes the journal *Social Development Issues*.

Organizations, national and international, often develop committees and task forces that have the aim of increasing international involvement among social workers. A task force of the U.S. National Association of Deans and Directors is illustrative of the desire to increase international involvement. Led by Alberto Godenzi, dean of the Boston College School of Social Work, and Kay Davidson, dean of the University of Connecticut School of Social Work, the task force has developed a proposal to obtain data on approaches to international social work education that include information regarding current activities in these areas (Godenzi, 2004, p. 2):

- International field education opportunities
- International student exchange
- International students enrolled in U.S. schools of social work
- International faculty exchange in teaching, research and service
- Infusion of international content into curriculum
- Funding opportunities for international activities
- Building reciprocal and sustainable alliances with international partners

It is the first step in obtaining information about current activities among American schools of social work to develop new initiatives to continue to foster the development of international activities and collaborations.

There are many interdisciplinary as well as social work international conferences. In recent years there have also been international conferences regarding research in social work practice. Moreover, attendance at these conferences continues to increase, allowing for a greater possible involvement in international activities. An example is a recent Global Social Work Congress involving the IFSW, the IASSW, the Australian Association of Social Workers, and the Australian Association for Social Work and Welfare Education, held in Adelaide, Australia, in 2004. The congress involved perspectives on social work education in the United States, United Kingdom, Europe, Asia, and Africa; and it considered comparative international developments, with speakers from Hong Kong, Canada, Ireland, England, Norway, Finland, and Australia. The overall theme of the Congress was "Reclaiming Civil Society," particularly with respect to the role of social work in the context of armed conflict, globalization, disaster, famine, and other contemporary social problems.

Books, newsletters, and journals are another source of potential international involvement. Greif (2004) reviewed articles in seven major social work journals for a 10-year period, 1991–2001, to determine the extent of authorship of those living outside of the United States. Thirty-seven of 448 articles (8.3%) were authored by persons living outside the United States, and six (1.2%) were coauthored by a U.S. and a non-U.S. author. The non-U.S. authors were primarily from Canada, Israel, and Australia. The point of the article was to illustrate the fact that there is international involvement, but much more remains to be done to internationalize the knowledge base as reflected in American social work journals.

We conducted a content analysis of article abstracts appearing in social work journals from 1995 to 2004 using the search term "international social work"

(Potocky-Tripodi & Tripodi, 2005). We found 279 abstracts. In order to determine salient topics for social workers, we classified the articles by subject. The majority (64%) of articles were devoted to these topics: social work education (16%), social work practice (13%), child welfare (7%), international social work (6%), poverty/development (6%), women's issues (5%), and mental health treatment and services (5%). Thus, there is a wide range of social issues that are internationally relevant for social workers.

Still another source of international involvement is that of student and faculty exchanges, study-abroad programs, and lecturing and research through such auspices as Fulbright scholarships. There is activity in these areas, but data have not been systematically gathered and distributed. One survey of international field education is illustrative of the extent of possible student involvement. Panos, Pettys, Cox, and Jones-Hart (2004) conducted a survey of 446 accredited social work programs in the United States. They were especially interested in studying the extent of international field practicum placements that were used for master's and baccalaureate students. They found that in 1997–2002, 665 students were placed by 94 social work programs in 55 countries. Twenty-one percent of the accredited social work programs placed students internationally, with the largest numbers placed in Canada, the United Kingdom, Mexico, India, and South Africa. Seventy-five percent of the total number of placements was in English-speaking countries. The authors concluded that there has been a significant drop in placements since 1988, but there is also an increase in social work programs developing continuing and long-term placements.

It is apparent from this brief review that there is some internationalism in social work, but it may include only a small fraction of students, faculty, and practicing social workers. However, it can be argued a greater proportion of social workers, if not all, are affected by globalization or global interdependence.

Globalization

According to Healy (2001, pp. 2–3),

> global interdependence has created significant areas of international responsibilities as well as new opportunities for social work impact by reshaping the social work environment in four important ways: (1) International social forces and events, most dramatically the movement of populations, have changed the makeup of social agency caseloads and affected domestic practice in many countries, including the United States. . . . (2) Social problems are now shared by both more and less economically developed countries far more often than in previous decades, making mutual work and exchange more desirable. . . . (3) The actions of one country—politically, economically, and socially—now directly and indirectly affect other countries' social and economic well-being and the overall social health of the planet. . . . (4) Finally, there are enhanced opportunities for international sharing and exchanging made possible by rapidly advancing technological developments in areas such as communications.

Healy points out that interdependence is essentially the sensitivity and response of one nation to the forces arising from other nations and from within, including such dimensions as environmental pollution and degradation; cross-cultural influences in music, folklore, language, foods, and so on; economic influences such as the price and supply of oil, unemployment, trade and trade barriers; national and international security, safety from terrorists as well as from worldwide epidemics such as AIDS, influenza, mad cow disease, and so on.

It is quite apparent that there are positive and negative consequences of global interdependence. For example, migration can be positive for those who leave one country for another to increase their standard of living, education, and access to employment; but it can be negative in that the migrants can continue to be in poverty and even in slave status. There may be positive aspects of a war against terrorism, but the negative aspects of the problems of street children from war-ravaged families can be daunting.

In general, globalization tends to be depicted as a force that can lead to negative consequences. Dominelli (2003, p. 7) argues that globalization in addition to economic interdependence,

> has become a social geo-political system that has spread into every aspect of daily life and has touched every region of the globe. Despite its integration into the interstices of daily routines, globalization has failed to enhance the quality of life for all. In this context, social workers as the professionals charged with promoting well-being have a key role to play in ensuring that its progressive elements become accessible to all.

Dominelli (p. 7) defines globalization as

> the organization of social relations in ways that promote the penetration of capitalist forces of production and reproduction into arenas of life hitherto deemed sacrosanct from market-driven imperatives. Globalization involves the global spread of capitalist social relations and their integration into every aspect of life—the social, political, cultural, economic and personal, and the consequent reordering of social relations in all these spheres.

Polack (2004) discusses how the global economy leads to injustices and inequities in the distribution of resources. He argues that many business practices, having their roots in colonialism, have led to a debt crisis in the global South. Sweatshop labor abuses and inadequate wages for meeting basic human needs are seen as a negative consequence for the poor, marginalized, and disadvantaged. Correspondingly, many business practices have increased profits as a result of outsourced jobs. The obvious challenge is how to increase both profits and the meeting of basic human necessities for all people. Polack suggests that social justice issues should be included in social work curricula, and he believes "social workers have the potential, especially when working collectively and in coalition with other groups in the United States, to influence federal policy conducive to remedying or mitigating the growing inequities in the global economy" (p. 288).

What global interdependence has produced is the possibility of internationalism without leaving the country: work with refugees and immigrants is increasingly appearing in social work caseloads, and the need for cross-national and cross-cultural knowledge is a definite responsibility for social workers within any country. In contrast to globalization, internationalism with respect to social work involvement is typically assumed to be beneficial. As Hokenstad and Midgley (2004) indicate, we can learn from social workers and others in countries other than our own. We may discover good ideas for programs geared to ameliorate identified social problems, and we may learn effective practices that can be incorporated in our work. We may learn that we need to collaborate with other social workers and other disciplines to devise strategies, policies, and practices to cope with worldwide problems.

Definition of International Social Work

We subscribe to Healy's (2001) definition of international social work: "international professional action and the capacity for international action by the social work profession and its members. International action has four dimensions: internationally related domestic practice and advocacy, professional exchange, international practice, and international policy development and advocacy" (p. 7). Internationally related domestic practice includes working with refugees and immigrants, international populations, international adoptions, and so forth. Basically, it refers to work in one country that deals with at least one other country, for example, working with a Mexican immigrant in a U.S. city, with all the cross-cultural and cross-national implications that social workers should consider in their practice. Professional exchange involves communication of knowledge and sharing of experiences, as are involved in internationalism as previously discussed. It also involves social workers within one country communicating by e-mail across countries, reading social work and related journals from other countries, participating in international conferences, and so forth. It is evident that professional exchange does not necessarily require the social worker to travel to other countries. Although American social workers tend to be provincial when it comes to communication in other languages, typically only knowing English, social workers and other professionals abroad often know two or more languages, for example, Chinese and English in Hong Kong; Italian, German, and English in northern Italy; French or English and indigenous languages in parts of Africa. There is no doubt that knowledge of idiomatic expressions in other languages is basic to transnational and cross-cultural competency.

International practice involves direct work in international agencies. Social workers practice in relief and disaster work as well as in social development, working in either governmental or nongovernmental agencies. Social workers may be involved in assessing social needs and in the evaluation of social programs. As a result they may be instrumental in developing social policy and in advocating for basic changes.

These practices and policies point to the international social worker's need for knowledge of social work research. The international social work practitioner utilizes basic research knowledge in at least three ways. First, the social worker should be able to understand and utilize the results of research, particularly the assessment of evidence that is basic to international social work practice; that is, studies of evidence-based practice. Second, the social worker is often involved in needs assessment, especially in the use of small surveys and focus groups for developing programs. And third, social workers can be involved in the evaluation of the effectiveness of program and practice strategies. Knowledge of social work research is vital for international social work practitioners, enabling them to make decisions based on previous studies that might be available and on data they collect. But what is social work research and to what extent can it be differentiated from social science research?

Social Work Research and Research Roles

Social work research eclectically employs a wide variety of research methods from the social and health sciences. These methods, depending on the social work problem under investigation, may include cost-benefit and cost-effectiveness analyses from economics, survey techniques from sociology, participant observation and participatory research from anthropology, epidemiological methods from the health sciences, experimental and quasi-experimental designs as well as single-subject designs from psychology, data analytic techniques and graphic methods from statistics and mathematics, qualitative methods and case studies as well as instrument construction from the social sciences and related professions such as sociology, psychology, psychiatry, nursing, public administration, and so forth. Research methods are also utilized from interdisciplinary modes of investigation such as program evaluation and evaluation research. In essence, research methods are utilized from a variety of sources and adapted for developing social work knowledge.

There are several possible research roles for social workers: the practitioner's role in employing notions of evidence-based practice and practice evaluation; the evaluator's role, focused on program evaluation and the aggregation of data from single-case studies; and the researcher's role in developing and testing theories about social problems, social work interventions and programs, and social policies.

In regard to the practitioner's role, Gibbs (2003) provides a conceptual definition of evidence-based practice: "Placing the client's benefits first, evidence-based practitioners adopt a process of lifelong learning that involves continually posing specific questions of direct practical importance to clients, searching objectively and efficiently for the current best evidence relative to each question, and taking appropriate action guided by evidence" (p. 6). Thyer (2002) traces the historical development of this modality from evidence-based medicine, succinctly specifying principles of evidence-based practice for the development of treatment methods in social work. The practitioner's role in utilizing research methods is to critically appraise available research evidence and to evaluate practice effectiveness (Tripodi, 1994, 2002). Blythe, Tripodi, and Briar (1994) specified how social workers can use social research methods in their direct practice. They indicated that direct practice research utilizing single-subject designs and other social research methods has the following characteristics (p. 2).

- It is conducted by practitioners in social agencies and human service organizations.
- It is integrated into the worker's other practice activities.
- It contributes to empirically based practice.
- It can employ a wide variety of research techniques.
- Its basic goal is to provide information that is directly helpful to practitioners.

The social worker as evaluator employs methods of data analysis and techniques of program evaluation, which is "essentially the application of social science research methods to assess the planning, implementation, and outcome of social programs and interventions" (Smith, 2002, p. 757). The social work evaluator also employs other methods for assessing social needs and evaluating programs that address those needs; for example, qualitative research (Padgett, 1998), participatory and stake-holder research (Gutierrez, 2003) and survey methods (Rubin, 1995).

The role of social work researchers is to use rigorous research designs to develop and test theoretical models for informing the design and development of social work practices and programs and social policies. Theory development is an inductive process that typically entails the use of qualitative methods. Once a theory is developed, it must be tested to determine whether it is supported or refuted by empirical evidence; this is a deductive process typically entailing quantitative methods. Some of the classic texts that inform these theory-based research processes include Glaser and Strauss's (1967) work on grounded theory and Popper's (1959) work on theory falsification.

For the development of direct practice interventions, Thomas (1981) provided a methodology distinctive to social work research in his discussion of developmental research. The classic text on experimental and quasi-experimental design by Cook and Campbell has formed the basis for many research and evaluation efforts in social work and related fields over the past 25 years (Cook & Campbell, 1979). In addition, pertinent to international social work research, Estes (1984, p. 1) defines the field of comparative social welfare, indicating that a variety of social research methods are drawn from disciplines other than social work:

> Comparative social welfare is a discrete field of research inquiry aimed at understanding national and international patterns of social provision. The patterns that are of greatest interest to comparative researchers are those public and private systems of social care that emerge in response to recurrent human needs; that is, recurrent human needs that exist in all societies regardless of their particular forms of social, political, or economic organization.... Comparative social welfare is also an interdisciplinary field of inquiry that draws heavily on the knowledge and specialized methodological bases of researchers trained in many areas of the social and behavioral sciences.

Definition of Social Work Research

Social work research is the use of social research methods for developing, producing, and disseminating knowledge that is pertinent to policies and practices that affect and/or are implemented by social work organizations, practitioners, and educators. It aims to describe and explain phenomena relevant to social work (Tripodi, 1974, 1981, 2000). Social work research is distinct from, yet related to, social science research and social work practice. Rubin and Babbie note:

> [Social work research] is social science methodology applied to social work.... [Unlike traditional academic researchers], social work researchers ... aim not to produce knowledge for knowledge's sake, but to provide the practical knowledge that social

workers need to solve everyday practice problems. Ultimately, they aim to give the field the information it needs to alleviate human suffering and promote social welfare. Thus, social work research seeks to accomplish the same humanistic goals as social work practice; and like practice, social work research is a compassionate, problem-solving, and practical endeavor. (2005, pp. 4–5)

Social research methods include all of those procedures and conceptual approaches for obtaining credible, reliable, and valid observations for specifying concepts and relationships among variables, and for making inferences and generalizations about social phenomena (Tripodi, 2000). A variety of concepts, techniques, and procedures are employed in social research such as the following: research designs for case studies, surveys, correlational studies, and quasi and true experiments; participatory research, action research, and ethnographic field studies; qualitative data gathering and analytic techniques; single-subject designs; statistical techniques such as multivariate and bivariate analyses; graphic techniques and the development of mathematical models; instrument construction techniques for generalizing causal inference (Shadish, Cook, & Campbell, 2002); and so forth.

Related to social work research is social work evaluation, which is the use of social research methods that are focused on obtaining information about the programmatic and practice needs of social work clientele and about the effectiveness and efficiency of social work programs, policies, and interventions that are designed to stabilize, reduce, or eliminate problems presented by the beneficiaries of social, health, and human services. Social work evaluations may include needs analyses, goal setting, monitoring of program and practice implementation, specification of costs and outcome measures, and the development of information systems for tracking clients. In essence, social work evaluations can be considered a subset of social work research, utilizing social research methods that focus on "these interrelated foci: the need for services, the costs of services, the quality of care provided by the services, the extent to which services are actually implemented, and their effectiveness and efficiency" (Tripodi, 2000, p. 7).

Social work research has these knowledge objectives (these objectives are modifications of knowledge levels presented in Tripodi, 1974, 1981):

- Development and operationalization of concepts
- Qualitative and quantitative descriptions of concepts
- Formation of hypotheses
- Testing of correlational hypotheses
- Testing of cause-effect hypotheses

Concepts and their operationalization are basic building blocks for the development of variables. Social work research can seek to identify the existence of qualitative, interactional relationships among concepts, such as the relationship between corruption in local government and the documentation of human sex trafficking among illegal aliens. Social work research can also aim to yield quantitative descriptions within variables, such as can be observed in census data, for example, the percentage of persons in U.S. geographic areas whose second language is English. Theories and their derivative hypotheses can be formulated as the result of studies seeking emergent data from qualitative relationships among concepts. And social work research can seek to test correlational relationships among variables, such as a predicted relationship between education and income among U.S.–born as opposed to foreign-born residents in a specific geographic area; and causal relationships among variables, such as a predictive hypothesis that those substance abusers who receive a psychoeducation intervention are more likely to reduce their abuse of substances than those substance abusers who do not receive an intervention.

Social research methods are designed to satisfy criteria of achieving knowledge objectives under investigation. The criterion for achieving the development and operationalization of concepts is *concept translatability*, that is, the extent to which concepts can be defined nominally and operationally so that they can be employed as variables in subsequent research. The criteria for appraising qualitative descriptions are *the production of evidence documenting the existence of qualitative* (e.g., narrative or interactional) *relationships that are credible to social observers*; while the criteria for achieving quantitative descriptions are the *measurement accuracy* of variables and *their reliability and validity*. To assess the formulation of hypotheses, one assesses the extent to which the hypotheses are researchable (hypothesis researchability), that is, the extent to which they can be tested in subsequent research. Correlational hypotheses are tested by statistical techniques indicating the strength and direction of relationships among variables that are reliable and valid. And causal relationships are supported when there is evidence for a correlational relationship and when it can be demonstrated that one or more independent variables are the cause of observed changes in one or more dependent variables. Evidence of causality would include the time-order relationship between independent and dependent variables and the control of extraneous factors, that is, control of threats to statistical conclusion validity, internal validity, construct validity, and external validity (Shadish et al., 2002).

A variety of social research methods are used to provide evidence for achieving knowledge objectives. Some typical uses of social research methods are as follows. To provide evidence for the development and operationalization of concepts, case studies, participant observation, and techniques of instrument construction can be employed. Qualitative methods, nonparticipant observation, and participatory research can be used to formulate theories and their derivative hypotheses. Census, survey and epidemiological methods are used to form quantitative descriptions and to test correlational hypotheses. And quasi-experimental and experimental designs are used to test causal hypotheses.

SOCIAL WORK RESEARCH TRENDS IN SELECTED COUNTRIES

Social work research trends in selected countries have been studied for the decade of the 1990s. Although not a comprehensive accounting of social work research studies in the world, analyses of research in the following countries serve to indicate the vast scope of the need for research and the types of studies that have been conducted: China, Australia, Israel, England, the United States, Canada, and Sweden.

In a special issue of research on social work practice in Chinese communities, Shek (2002) made these observations:

- There appear to be few studies in Hong Kong and in Chinese communities that are focused on the effectiveness of social work interventions, and evidence-based social work practice is in its beginning stage of development.
- This special issue includes articles that are based on the collaboration of social workers and academics.
- There are three articles based on assessment. Two of the articles examined measures of psychosocial functioning that were translated from Western countries, and it was concluded that Chinese social workers should validate those measures in their own communities. The third article provides evidence that Chinese researchers are also developing indigenous scales for research in their own communities.
- There were articles that focused on the evaluation of the effectiveness of social work interventions, especially illustrating the integration of Western interventions with Chinese concepts and the collaboration of social work practitioners and academic researchers. It was observed that the one group pretest-posttest design was commonly employed rather than true experimental designs for evaluating the effectiveness of interventions. Essentially, at best, the researchers were able to provide correlational knowledge regarding changes associated with the introduction of interventions.

Crisp (2000) reviewed the history of social work research in Australia and made these observations (pp. 189–190):

- Changes in the funding of human services in this country mean that organizations can no longer afford to treat research as an optional extra in social work practice. Increasingly, evaluation is expected from community agencies receiving public funding to provide health and welfare services.
- On one level, the requirement of greater accountability has been embraced by many social workers. The Victoria branch of the Australia Association of Social Workers (AASW) has a practice research specialist interest group, and research workshops for social work practitioners are well attended. Nevertheless, rigorous empirical evaluations of social work practice remain somewhat rare, and a preference for qualitative rather than quantitative evaluations is quite apparent in Australia.
- Although program evaluation will undoubtedly become a focus of social work research in the years ahead, an exciting development over the past decade has been an emergent academic research program dedicated to the development and evaluation of innovative practice methods.
- A further recent development in Australian social work practice research has been the growing collaboration between social work academics and government departments in large-scale program evaluations.

Auslander (2000) reviewed 600 research articles from Israel published from 1990 through 1998. The authors were primarily faculty members at Israeli universities; 88% of the authors were Israelis. A small group of articles (11%) were written by Israelis in collaboration with authors from other—usually English-speaking—countries, that is, the United States, Canada, Great Britain, and Australia.

The articles covered a variety of social work fields of practice, from corrections to migration. The top four areas were, in order, health, military and war, mental health, and families. Auslander classified the research designs of the studies and reported that 54% were associational (or correlational); 19% quantitative-descriptive; 17% cause and effect; and 10% qualitative. The use of true experimental designs was rare, and quasi-experimental designs were usually employed for evaluating the effectiveness of interventions. Auslander noted the following trends affecting research.

- There is little time available for social work practitioners to be engaged in research.
- There is a language problem, in that most researchers publish in other languages, and Israeli researchers often spend a great deal of time in translating and validating research instruments developed in other countries.
- University libraries have been collecting translated and validated study instruments.
- There is a growth in doctoral programs, and several universities have developed research centers.

Kazi (2000) reports his work with social workers and other practitioners at the Centre for Evaluation Studies at the University of Huddersfield in developing evaluation strategies that can be incorporated into practice. He and his colleagues have been remarkably successful in establishing the use of single-case evaluation by social work practitioners. He attributes this success to (p. 103):

- Establishing a partnership between practitioners, managers, and academics to meet the needs of practice evaluation
- Encouraging the use of single-case designs even if the practitioners are not happy with standardized measures
- Emphasizing firmly the fundamental requirement of measuring outcomes and enabling the types of single-case designs to fall into place naturally

Kazi and his colleagues indicated how they were able to be more effective evaluators by using multiple research methods: single-case designs, surveys, needs assessments, focus groups, and other qualitative methods.

In her review of social work research and evaluation in the United States, Bronson (2000, p. 125) says:

Social work research and evaluation in the United States today is more methodologically sophisticated and accessible than at any other point in the history of American social work. Several social work journals dealing with research and evaluation have appeared recently, and articles in those journals reflect the increasing extent to which social work researchers are using complex statistical analysis methods and research designs to add to social work knowledge. Funding for social work research and evaluation is increasingly available, and social workers are better prepared to engage in research and evaluation activities. In spite of these significant advances, serious questions about the role of research in social work, the relevance of research and evaluation for practice, and how social work research and evaluation should be conducted remain the focus of considerable debate in the United States.

Bronson points to several factors that contribute to advances in social work research and evaluation: the increased availability of research funding at local, state, and federal levels of governmental sponsorship; increased forums for presenting and discussing the results of research in conferences, journals, associations, and interest groups; requirements in social work education for students to learn how to evaluate their practice, and an increased emphasis in doctoral education for the preparation of students for conducting scholarly research; and increased demands from funders of social services and the public for accountability and evidence of effective programs and interventions. Among the problems in research and evaluation in the United States, Bronson emphasized these: confusion about the differences between research and evaluation, particularly as discussed in debates about the scientist-practitioner model, empirical social work, and evidence-based practice; and the paucity of useful intervention research and the failure of research and evaluation to guide practice.

Nutter and Hudson (2000) reviewed 169 research and evaluation reports in Canada from 1996 to 1998. Topics addressed in the research dealt with social issues and social policy, theory and practice, the social work profession, and areas of service. The types of research most commonly used were survey (86%) and quasi-experimental designs (11%); only one study employed experimental methods. Nutter and Hudson (p. 56) concluded that

> approximately equal proportions (one-fifth each) of the reports were produced by social work academics and consultants, and nearly one half were done by social service employees. . . . Social work academics submit relatively few research proposals to the major Canadian social science and humanities research funding body and their success rate is half that of non–social work faculty. . . . The Board of Accreditation Manual of the Canadian Association of Schools of Social Work pays relatively little attention to research and evaluation.

Jergeby and Soydan (2000, p. 59) observe that in Sweden there are two traditions regarding the relevance of research to social work practice: "research in and about social work, and evaluation of social work practice." They indicated that there is little evidence-based practice, and there is increasing interest in evaluation and quality assurance of social service programs: however, there has been relatively little evaluation research until recent years. Research in social work departments tends to consist of "theory-based, descriptive and explanatory descriptive studies" (p. 61). The authors consider a number of problems and prospects for research in Sweden, and they indicate that some experimental designs are employed in evaluative studies. They conclude their review with future challenges for social work research (p. 69):

- Making social research and evaluation more responsive to the needs of clients and professionals
- Developing forms for fruitful partnerships between researchers and practitioners
- Developing methodologies of evaluation of social work practice for production of generalizable knowledge and in the meantime producing knowledge that practitioners recognize and find useful in everyday practice with clients
- Developing measurement instruments for outcome studies

- Broadening understanding of ethical aspects and dilemmas of social work research and evaluation (the research interest) and of the integrity and autonomy of clients (the client interest)
- These are crucial issues seen from a Swedish perspective. It seems, however, it could also be the perspective of other nations

A DEFINITION AND TYPOLOGY OF INTERNATIONAL SOCIAL WORK RESEARCH

Our conceptualization of international social work research builds on definitions of international social work and social work research; it has been stimulated by the variety of international studies that have appeared in journals in the past five years. Recalling that social work research is the use of social research methods for producing and disseminating knowledge that is pertinent to policies and practices that affect and/ or are implemented by social work organizations, practitioners, administrators, and educators, *international social work research can be considered socialwork research that is relevant to international social work.* It aims to develop knowledge that is pertinent to any of Healy's (2001, p. 13) four areas of action: "internationally informed domestic practice and related policy advocacy, participation in and utilization of international exchange, international practice, and international policy formulation and advocacy." The knowledge sought for international social work depends on the state of current knowledge available for the social work problem under investigation, and the research methods employed depend on the knowledge objectives sought, financial and ethical considerations, the sociopolitical environment, and expertise in the use of research methods. We conceive of the commonality in all international research as the extensive use of literature from two or more countries to formulate research problems and objectives, and the development of implications for two or more countries. International social work research is distinguished from national (or noninternational) research, in that national social work research is research concerned with native populations within a country with no attempt to utilize literature from other countries to frame the research problem, or to discuss implications for international social work.

Within the broad umbrella of international social work research, we typologize three types of research: *supranational, intranational,* and *transnational* research. *Supranational research* is concerned only with research and research participants from one country. It may be focused on research in any country. What makes the research international and distinguishes it from national research is the use of literature from two or more countries, as well as the development of implications for two or more countries. *Intranational research* occurs when a population from another country is studied within a country, and literature from both countries is used with implications also made for both countries. A typical study of this type involves the study of immigrants, refugees, and/or seekers of political asylum. This may, for example, involve study of Hmong, Vietnamese, eastern European, and other populations who have resettled in the United States or Canada, as well as in other countries; Pakistanis in the United Kingdom; Italians in Argentina; Albanians in Italy; and so forth. Finally, *transnational research* is comparative research between populations of two or more countries; literature across populations is used, and implications are made for each population. This is the type of research called for by Midgley (1995) and by Estes (1984), that is, comparative social welfare research.

This typology encompasses some concepts previously used by other researchers and writers, such as "cross-national" and "cross-cultural" research. Cross-national research that compares populations from two or more countries would be equivalent to transnational research, as long as literature and implications are considered for the countries that are being compared. Cross-cultural research can take place within one country as well as between countries; therefore, it does not necessarily denote transnational or cross-national comparisons. These and other concepts are often used interchangeably and without clear definitions. We believe that our typology provides at least three benefits to social work researchers. First, it broadens the scope of what has traditionally been considered international research, which has been limited to what is our category of "transnational" research. As such, the typology should encourage social work researchers to undertake more international research, particularly those who may previously have viewed their research as noninternational. Second, our typology provides a clearer and distinct means of describing international research, thus avoiding problems of overlapping and ill-defined terminology. Finally, our typology provides an organizing framework for identifying and assessing methodological issues, incentives, and barriers in conducting and utilizing international research.

Figure 1.1 illustrates and summarizes the juxtaposition of international social work and social work research into our new conceptualization of international social work research.

According to this conceptualization of international social work research, the following observations are noted:

- Research conducted in any country is national, unless it uses international literature to develop the research problem and discusses implications for social workers that can be considered to be international. Therefore, the publication of a study in Hong Kong published in an American journal, or research in the United States published in an Indian journal, or research in Israel published in a British journal, and so on, is not necessarily international. This does not mean, as discussed by Hokenstad and Midgley (2004), that one cannot learn and develop hypotheses pertinent to international social work from national studies; however, it is up to the reader of such studies to formulate implications for international social work, rather than from the author's objectives of knowledge development.
- The three categories of international research are not completely pure types, that is, there can be some overlap among the categories. This will become evident as we provide examples of these types subsequently. Nevertheless, they can be used reliably. To determine this, we independently reviewed and categorized four years of 36 articles published in the *Journal of Social Work Research and Evaluation: An International Publication* (2000–2004), and we achieved a percentage agreement of 89%, which is a sufficient degree of interrater reliability (39% of the articles were supranational, 47% intranational, and 14% transnational).

International social work

International professional action and the capacity for international action by the social work profession and its members. (Healy, 2001, p. 7)

Dimensions:
- Internationally related domestic practice and advocacy
- Professional exchange
- International practice
- International policy development and advocacy (Healy, 2001, p. 7)

Social work research

The use of social research methods for developing, producing, and disseminating knowledge that is pertinent to policies and practices that affect and/or are implemented by social work organizations, practitioners, and educators.

Knowledge objectives:
- Development and operationalization of concepts
- Qualitative and quantitative descriptions of concepts
- Formation of hypotheses
- Testing of correlational hypotheses
- Testing of cause-effect hypotheses

International social work research

Social work research that is relevant to international social work.

Supranational "beyond borders"	Intranational "within borders"	Transnational "across borders"
• Research with native-born population(s) within one country • Research problem is framed with literature from beyond one country • Implications are made beyond one country	• Research with international migrants within a country • Literature from both countries is used and implications are made for both countries	• Comparative research between populations within two or more countries • Literature across populations is used and implications are made for each population

Domestic social work research

Research concerning native populations within one country.
- No attempt to utilize literature from other countries to frame the research problem, or to discuss implications for other countries
- May include cross-cultural research within one country

Figure 1.1. Conceptualization of international social work research. The data in the first chart are from *International Social Work: Professional Action in an Interdependent World* (p. 7), by L. M. Healy, 2001, New York: Oxford University Press. Copyright 2001. Reprinted with permission.

Brief Examples of the Typology

National Research

We provide the following example of national research: "Investigating the Differential Effectiveness of a Batterer Treatment Program on Outcomes for African American and Caucasian Batterers" (Buttell & Pike, 2003).

Buttell and Pike evaluated an intervention program designed to achieve changes in psychological variables related to domestic violence perpetration. A domestic violence inventory was administered to 61 participants before and after the intervention. The participants were arrested in Tuscaloosa County, Alabama, in the United States and were ordered by the court to participate in the intervention program aimed to change psychological variables related to domestic violence. The intervention program was a 12-week program that used cognitive-behavioral methods in group treatment. The researchers were interested in developing correlational knowledge about the relationship between the treatment program and changes in the domestic violence inventory; they were also interested in determining whether there would be any cross-cultural differences in domestic violence variables as a function of race. The authors utilized literature from the United States that focused on domestic violence and on social differences.

They concluded that the program was effective in changing the male batterers' perceptions on these variables related to domestic violence: alcohol, drugs, violence, control, and stress. They pointed out that they did not have control of internal validity threats, since they did not employ a true experimental design; hence they could not say they achieved causal knowledge. However, they did achieve correlational knowledge for that particular sample of batterers. Moreover, they found no differences between African American and Caucasian batterers in the degree to which the program was effective. This study clearly was national and not international, since they did not use literature or make implications for other countries; in addition, it was cross-cultural, in that it focused on differences between Caucasians and African Americans and utilized the literature regarding Caucasian and African American batterers.

Supranational Research

In a study by Zeira, Astor, and Benbenishty (2003) conducted in Israel and published in the U.S. journal *Social Work*, the authors reviewed studies on violence in the schools in the United States, Israel, and other countries; and they, themselves, were from American and Israeli universities. From a theoretical perspective, from the literature they collected data from students in Israel from grades 4 through 11 regarding their perceptions of the degree of school violence and their fears of attending school. A nationally representative sample stratified on age-related school type and Arab or Jewish ethnicity was obtained, using a two-stage stratified cluster, probability sampling procedure. Research instruments were based on the California School Climate Survey and translated into Hebrew and Arabic. The authors reported preliminary findings that were quantitative-descriptive and correlational knowledge. They reported on the "Percentages of Israeli Students Who Perceived School Violence as a Big or Very Big Problem by Gender, Ethnicity, and School Setting," "Victimization of Israel Students by School Type," "Victimization of Israeli Students by Gender," and "Percentages of Israel Students Who Reported Missing School for at Least One Day in the Preceding Month because of Fear of Violence, by Gender, Ethnicity, and School Setting" (pp. 474–479).

They discussed cross-cultural differences between Arab and Jewish students, finding, for example, that Arab students were more likely to avoid school because of their fear of violence than Jewish students. The authors felt that social work should encourage a global perspective on violence and that policy and interventions could be informed as a result of their data. Their data were clearly useful for Israel and had direct implications for policy and future research that could be done there. In the authors' discussion of the implications of their data, they focused on Israel, and wisely did not generalize to other countries from their data set. However, they implied that other countries could be informed by their data. We believe their study is international and supranational for these reasons: they used a data collection instrument from another country and translated it for their use in Israel; the designers of the research were from two different countries; literature was used from two or more countries to frame the research problem; and, although the implications discussed focused predominantly on Israel, references from the literature were used to place their discussion of implications in an international context.

Intranational Research

An article by Gellis (2003), "Kin and Non Kin Social Supports in a Community Sample of Vietnamese Immigrants," is an example of intranational research. The author formulated the research study by placing it in a context of previous literature on social support and depression, cultural characteristics of Vietnamese, and previous research on immigrants in the United States.

The purpose of the study was to examine the relationship of social support and depression for 79 Vietnamese immigrants who received mental health services from a public psychiatric hospital in the United States. The author conceived social support as sources of support and satisfaction with the support received. In particular, social support was categorized and measured as kin social support (e.g., family) or nonkin social support (e.g. friends, coworkers). Depression was assessed by the Center for Epidemiologic Depression Scale. Questionnaire data were collected one month after the patients were released from the hospital and six months later.

The author found that demographic variables such as age, marital status, education, income, and number of years in the United States were not related to any changes in depression over time. However, it was discovered that "kin (ethnic) social support networks were associated with negative effects on individual psychological distress, whereas non kin (nonethnic) social supportnetworks from the broader community had a positive effect in reducing depressive symptoms" (Gellis, 2003, p. 254). The author was careful to conclude that generalizability was limited due to his use of a relatively small convenience sample. Implications were discussed for American mental health professionals who work with Vietnamese immigrants. This study is *intranational research* for the following reasons: literature about Vietnamese and American social support networks is utilized to develop the correlational hypotheses of the study; there is a translation of measuring instruments used in the United States in Vietnamese with cross-validation with other Vietnamese immigrant populations; implications are made for American mental health professionals, including the need to develop cultural competency in working with immigrant groups such as Vietnamese.

Transnational Research

"Assessment Processes in Social Work Practice When Children Are at Risk: A Comparative, Cross-National Vignette Study," by Jergeby and Soydan (2002), is an example of transnational research. The authors compared the responses of social workers in child, adolescent, and family services in Denmark, Germany, Sweden, and the United States to "vignettes about a family in which the four-year-old child is reported as being exposed to hardship or abuse" (p. 130). The vignettes were presented in three stages that represented varying and increasing amounts of information over three points of time. Social workers were asked to respond to the information as to whether or not there is a problem and whether or not action should be taken. The social workers were also asked what they considered to be the main problem, and what additional information they would need before accepting the case for investigation. The same vignette technique had previously been used by one of the authors in a transnational study comparing Swedish and English social workers' responses. In this study, samples of social workers were obtained by contacts with social agencies. These included 198 from Sweden, 156 from the United Kingdom, 151 from the United States, 201 from Germany, and 130 from Denmark. The authors were careful to point out that these convenience samples were not necessarily representative of the countries, but they believed it was useful to compare the responses of workers from those countries. Many of the questions were open-ended and produced qualitative information about social workers' assessments of problems and information needed to accept the case. The researchers also obtained information on respondents' actions in all three stages. Hence they were interested in obtaining quantitative and qualitative descriptive knowledge and comparing social workers' responses in their reactions to the case vignettes at three time periods. The researchers framed the research problem by using literature from several countries; they made implications for social workers working in child protection cases in different countries; they had researchers from several countries gather data; and they provided comparative data for social workers from five countries. Hence the study is a transnational study, which offered the following conclusions (p. 143).

- There are differences in how social workers in the countries of study assess information and develop strategies for action.

- The information gathering after a referral focuses on different sources: the family, the kin, and agencies, with each being given different priority depending upon context.
- The social workers show great concern about the child and/or the family but do not always reflect upon the family's need in the first place.
- There are differences between the social workers within the countries in assessing the information and the case. There seems to be a lack of a common set of concepts that is agreed upon by the social work profession.
- There is a lack of common understanding about when to use serious interventions, such as removing a child from the house.

SOURCES OF INTERNATIONAL SOCIAL WORK RESEARCH

Our typology serves as a framework for selecting international social work research studies and for providing a context for discussing methodological and substantive issues in conducting and utilizing international social work research. In subsequent chapters, we will provide a number of examples of international social work research for each of the types posited in our typology. Sources for identifying these studies are international and national social work journals, databases and the internet, national and international organizations, and conferences, governmental organizations, and nongovernmental organizations.

International Social Work Journals

There are numerous journals that focus on special substantive areas in the international arena such as child care, gerontology, substance abuse, and so forth. These can be found easily on the internet by looking up the substantive area and by specifying one's search to international journals. We present here several international journals that are relevant to and that contain articles that are reports on international social work research. From these journals, and from national journals of social work, we will select and present five studies of each of the three categories of international social work research in chapters 3, 5, and 7.

The journal *International Social Work* is an official journal of the IASSW, ICSW, and IFSW. It is published quarterly by Sage Publications, and it emphasizes cross-national research and comparative analysis, that is, transnational research. *International Social Work* aims to promote knowledge regarding service delivery, social work tasks and roles, trends and issues in social policy and practice, international developments in social work education, and so forth.

New Global Development: Journal of International and Comparative Social Welfare is published annually by *Dialogues*. Articles emphasize theoretical or empirical contributions that promote international discussion, especially in reference to international peace and social justice. "European Reactions to Global Challenges: The Cases of the Netherlands, the UK, Sweden, Spain, and Germany" (Koch, 2004) and "Canadian Fiscal Federalism, Regionalization, and the Development of Quebec's Health Care Delivery System" (Palley & Forest, 2004) are examples of recently published articles.

The *British Journal of Social Work* is an international social work journal that is published for the British Association of Social Workers by Oxford University Press. The journal is published eight times per year and publishes a variety of articles relevant to social work. It publishes articles from other countries as well as from the United Kingdom. The articles deal with, for the most part, social work practice, research, theory, and education.

The *Journal of Social Work Research and Evaluation: An International Publication* is published biannually by the Springer Publishing Company. Like the journals already mentioned, it is a refereed journal that aims to provide an international forum for the dissemination of research and evaluation on social work and social welfare. All articles provide international perspectives on a wide range of topics and represent quantitative and qualitative studies, methodological innovations, review essays, and discussions of contemporary issues in research. Special issues have dealt with such topics as research with immigrants and refugees, the empowerment of women, evaluation for practice, and human trafficking.

Finally, *Social Development Issues: Alternative Approaches to Global Human Needs* is published by the IUCISD in cooperation with the Center for Social Development at the George Warren Brown School of Social Work at Washington University in St. Louis. It is an internationally refereed journal that is focused on the development of knowledge pertaining to developing countries and social justice within a global context. An example of a recent article is "Gender, Bureaucracy, and Development in Ghana: An Examination of the Civil Service" (Gadzekpo, 2004).

National Journals

There are numerous journals that reflect social work interests in many countries. Some journals are multidisciplinary; others are more focused on particular disciplines, fields of inquiry, or areas of practice. In the United States, the journal *Social Work* has the widest circulation and covers a wide range of social work endeavors, including international social work and reports of research studies. It is published by the NASW. The main national research journals, that is, journals that publish quantitative and qualitative research, are *Social Work Research*, also published by NASW; *Journal of Social Service Research*, published by Haworth Press; *Social Service Review*, published by the University of Chicago Press; and *Research on Social Work Practice*, sponsored by the Society for Social Work and Research (SSWR) and published by Sage. In these journals one can locate national and international research studies.

Social work researchers also publish in interdisciplinary journals. An example is the journal *Evaluation and Program Planning*, which includes articles pertaining to program evaluation and evaluation research from disciplines such as economics, political science, sociology, planning, psychology, public administration, education, psychiatry, social work, and so on. The aim of the journal is to assist evaluators and social planners in developing their skills in evaluation. Articles are devoted to methodology, evaluation, and utilization of findings. An example of an article on evaluation is "A Case Study of Methodological Issues in Cross-Cultural Evaluation" (Jinkerson, Cummings, Neisendorf, & Schwandt, 1992).

Databases and the Internet

The Campbell Collaboration

The Campbell Collaboration builds on the work of the Cochrane Collaboration in health care and on advances in metaanalysis and synthetic data analytic techniques. It is "an international, nonprofit organization that sets standards for, and prepares, maintains, and disseminates, high quality systematic reviews of studies of interventions in social welfare, education, and crime and justice" (Littell, 2004, p. 10).

The Campbell Collaboration (C2) Library consists of these databases (Littell, 2004, pp. 10–11):

- The C2 Social, Psychological, Education, and Criminological Trials Registry (C2-SPECTR) contains over 11,700 entries on randomized and possibly randomized trials. C2-SPECTR is updated regularly, and its entries are potential ingredients for C2 systematic reviews.
- The C2 Reviews of Interventions and Policy Evaluations (C2-RIPE) database contains approved titles, protocols, reviews, and abstracts.

The Internet

Gibbs (2003) refers to 10 databases. Of special relevance to social work researchers are the Cochrane Library, Sociological Abstracts, and Social Work Abstracts databases. The Cochran Library provides metaanalyses of studies in psychiatry and health care. Sociological Abstracts "contains information from approximately 2,500 journals," and the "Social Work Abstracts database, produced by the National Association of Social Workers, Inc., contains over 35,000 abstracts to articles, dissertations, and other materials from social work and related journals" (p. 136).

Simply using Google as a search mechanism can produce valuable information in the search for articles pertaining to international social work research. For example, the website of Richard J. Estes (http://caster.ssw.upenn.edu/~restes/praxis.html) contains Resources for Social and Economic Development, which includes major reports of international and comparative social research. And Gibbs (2003) provides principles and guidelines for using the internet to search for practice articles that are based on evidence.

Social Work, Governmental, and Nongovernmental Organizations

National and international social work organizations can be the source of research studies presented at conferences and as reports of task forces on selected topics. In addition, governmental and nongovernmental organizations such as the United States Department of Health and Human Services, groups representing social welfare interests in the United Nations, and so on can serve as a source of research reports and of international social work research. Healy (2001) provides an excellent description of these potential sources.

THE FORMAT OF THE BOOK

This chapter is an introduction to international social work research, including our definition and typology of international social work research, and examples of research and sources that can be used to locate international social work studies. Chapter 2 focuses on supranational research. Distinguishing between the conduct of national research and supranational research, the chapter describes the research model and the evaluation model, social work problems amenable to research, barriers and incentives to research, and research issues involved in the conduct and utilization of supranational research. Chapter 3 describes five supranational research studies and discusses methodological and substantive issues pertinent to the studies. Chapter 4 defines and illustrates intranational research, and discusses social work problems and barriers and incentives to research and methodological and substantive issues, including cultural and international sensitivity, involved in conducting and utilizing such research. Chapter 5 presents five examples of intranational research, and research issues are discussed for each of the studies. Chapter 6 is focused on transnational research and discusses possible comparative models, social work problems across countries, barriers and incentives to research, and methodological issues related to conducting and utilizing research. Chapter 7 includes five examples of transnational research and discusses substantive and methodological issues in each study, as well as issues stimulated by the studies. Chapter 8 is a summary chapter and concludes with a discussion of prospects for future international social work research.

SUMMARY

This book is intended for professional social workers who are involved in international social work and are interested in evidence-based practice and the evaluation of practice; social work researchers and educators who are interested in international social work research; and social work students from around the world who have had a basic course in social research methods and statistics. In this chapter we specified the purpose of the book as presenting a perspective on international social work research, issues involved in the conduct and utilization of international research, and examples of international research studies. We indicated how definitions of international social work and social work research could be merged to form a definition of international social work research, which is considered to be social work research that is relevant to international social work. And social work research was defined as the use of social research methods for developing, producing, and disseminating knowledge (concepts, qualitative and quantitative descriptions, hypotheses, and correlational and causal knowledge) that is pertinent to policies and practices that affect and/or are implemented by social work organizations, practitioners, and educators. We indicated how social workers are involved in international activities and affected by globalization even if they practice only within their countries; and we presented a definition and typology of international social work research, indicating how such research can be distinguished from national research. National research is directed at native populations within a country and does not use literature from other countries to formulate the research problem, nor does it draw implications for two or more countries. In contrast, all three international research types use literature from other countries and make implications from the research for two or more countries. The three types of international social work research are: *supranational*, which deals with research within a country; *intranational*, which studies a population from another country that resides in a different country, such as immigrant and refugees; and *transnational*, which is comparative research between populations of two or more countries. We concluded with a discussion of sources of international social work research and the format of the book.

2

SUPRANATIONAL RESEARCH

In this chapter, we distinguish national from supranational research in social work by discussing a hypothetical example of what might be involved in conceptualizing the research process in studying differential usage of social services, and in chapter 3 we present five actual studies of supranational research, highlighting issues in the conduct and utilization of research. We delineate similarities and differences between national and supranational research, and we note that knowledge of the three types of international research is cumulative. Problems and prospects of research in supranational research also occur in intranational and transnational research; likewise, issues in the conduct and utilization of research in intranational research occur in transnational research. In other words, transnational research is more complex than intranational research, which in turn is more complex than supranational research in terms of the methodological issues encountered at each stage of the research process, and the barriers and incentives to the research.

To provide background information prior to discussing particular issues involved in supranational research, we review the notions of substantive and methodological knowledge, knowledge objectives and criteria for achieving those objectives, and notions of and criteria for generalizing knowledge. This is followed by a review of four interrelated models of the research process: quantitative research, qualitative research, program evaluation, and single subject design for evaluating social work practice.

This background information is then employed in discussing salient issues in the conduct and utilization of supranational research, focusing on key steps in the research process: problem formulation; instrument construction; research design; sampling and generalizability by population, time, and place; data collection and analysis; and conclusions and implications. In problem formulation we discuss narrative literature reviews, metaanalysis, and our scheme for appraising knowledge objectives and their generality. We focus on cross-validation of instruments for use in studying different subcultural groups, and we provide general guidelines for selecting research designs in relation to knowledge objectives. We also discuss the problem of generalizability with respect to sampling, ethics, and cross-cultural sensitivities, and we consider problems and strategies for deriving conclusions and social work implications from data gathered and analyzed in research. We conclude the chapter with a discussion of barriers and incentives to supranational research, including funding and costs, availability of and translations of literature, cross-cultural instrument usage, and the utilization of findings.

DISTINGUISHING SUPRANATIONAL FROM NATIONAL RESEARCH

Similarities and Differences

Both national (domestic) and supranational research follow steps in the research process as discussed by Rubin & Babbie (2005): the problem for research is formulated; a research design is constructed in relation to the problem and the sampling of the population relevant to the research; instruments are selected or constructed for gathering data; data are analyzed; and conclusions and implications are drawn from the data and compared to existing knowledge in the literature (table 2.1).

As indicated in chapter 1, national research can occur in any country. Suppose a researcher in the United States is interested in studying the extent to which people in a particular geographical area, say Boston, Massachusetts, use social services. The researcher would first review the literature in the United States pertaining to social service usage. The researcher would explore how social services are defined; whether there are studies showing differential usage; how usage is defined; there are avail-

Table 2.1 Conceptual Similarities and Differences Between Domestic and Supranational Research in Social Work

Feature	Domestic research	Supranational research
Follows steps in the research process from problem formulation, sampling, and research design to instrument construction, data gathering, analyses, and conclusions	Yes	Yes
Uses literature from two or more countries	No	Yes
Generalizes substantive knowledge beyond one country or specifies differences between countries in formulating research problem	No	Yes
May conceptualize generalizability of methodological knowledge beyond one country in formulating research problem	No	Yes
May generalize across subcultural groups within a native population	Yes	Yes
Seeks to apply research findings to population where study is conducted	Yes	Yes
Seeks to generalize implications beyond one country	No	Yes

able instruments, for example, questionnaires employed to study use of social services; whether factors such as eligibility, availability, waiting lists, hours of accessibility, and knowledge of services are important for specifying service usage. The researcher may conceptualize family and children counseling; referral to other services such as health, legal, and other professions; child protective investigations; employment services; determination of welfare eligibility; and so on as social services. She or he may decide to construct a questionnaire aimed at discerning whether people in Boston know what services are available, whether they have ever used any services, under what conditions they would use services, and their attitudes toward usage of services. The overall purpose of conducting a survey of the populace might be to determine whether potential clientele have needs for such services and whether there are sufficient resources available to meet those needs. A survey design is chosen whereby neighborhoods representing different income levels are specified and a combination of cluster and stratified sampling is employed to locate the elderly, working and nonworking adults, and children within public and private housing, as well as public and private institutions.

In reviewing the literature, the researcher may have found studies indicating that different ethnic groups have different attitudes about the extent to which they need social services and the extent to which they trust and would be willing to receive services such as counseling from social service providers. Thus, the researcher might believe there would be differential usage for such groups as African American, Irish Americans, and Italian Americans. Incorporating stratification on these characteristics in the survey would set the stage for cross-cultural research in which the researcher would seek to generalize across subcultural groups within the native-born American population in Boston (table 2.1). Cross-cultural research in this instance is still regarded as national research, since it deals with a native-born population, for example, second- and third-generation Italians and Irish who may have subcultural identities in differing neighborhoods in the Boston area. In contrast, if the researcher were studying recent immigrant groups from different countries, she or he would be involved in intranational research (see chapter 4). In cross-cultural research in national or international research, the researcher would search the literature for substantive knowledge regarding similarities and differences between subcultural groups, as well as methodological knowledge regarding procedures, such as questionnaires for producing knowledge about those subcultural groups. If there is very little knowledge available about the attitudes of current subcultural groups, the researcher may change or add to the research design qualitative features such as the use of focus groups and techniques of participant observation.

Finally, in this brief example of national research, the researcher gathers and analyzes the data; and she or he derives conclusions, attempting to apply the research findings to the population where the study is conducted. For example, it might be discovered that Italian Americans are more likely to use recreational and group work services than individual counseling, which is partially explained by data that indicate they are not aware of what individual counseling services are available. Hence the researcher may hypothesize that provision of knowledge about individual counseling services in groups at recreational centers may lead to more usage of individual counseling services for Italian Americans.

This research can be altered to become international research if literature is used from two or more countries and if implications are made for two or more countries. Supranational research would involve the following characteristics: generalizing substantive knowledge across countries or specifying differences between countries in formulating the research problem; conceptualizing generalizability of methodological knowledge in formulating the research problem; and seeking to generalize implications across countries (table 2.1).

Suppose the researcher is interested in using literature from another country as well as literature from the United States in posing the research problem. The researcher chooses a large city in Canada, say Toronto, for comparative purposes. She or he searches literature from Canadian social agencies, the Canadian government, and the University of Toronto with respect to the conceptualization of social services, usage, availability, accessibility, and so forth. It might be found that there appears to be a greater variety of services available at lower costs than in the United States and that the citizenry is more likely to use health services than social services. This may lead the researcher to also gather information about health services in the survey to be conducted in the Boston area. Moreover, it might have been hypothesized in the literature that Canadians were more likely to use counseling regarding family and marital relations than mental health counseling, due to the stigma attached to mental illness. In addition, it might have been ascertained that native-born, bilingual (French and English) Canadians were less likely to use any of the social services than native-born, English-speaking Canadians. This knowledge leads researchers to be sure to look at subcultural groups in their research, and to compare differential usage of social services in the United States and Canada. The researcher would be careful to determine whether similar definitions of social services and the use of social services were employed in both countries.

The researcher searches U.S. and Canadian literature for instruments that might have been employed in both countries for assessing attitudes toward the use of social services. Attitude instruments might have been used in cross-validational studies between U.S. and Canadian populations providing evidence of reliability and validity with the same questions and response categories for Canadians and for U.S. Americans. If there is cross-validating evidence, the researcher might employ instruments used in Canada for the research. In contrast, with no cross-validating evidence, the researcher might use the Canadian instrument with caution, seeking to provide some cross-validating evidence within the study and possibly providing other sets of questions that seem more appropriate to respondents in Boston. It is quite possible that different spellings of the same word could lead to different responses; for example, use of a "counseling centre" may elicit different responses from use of a "counseling center." Some respondents with low educational or literacy levels may not be familiar with such spelling variations; consequently, such respondents in the United States may be less likely to say they would use a "counseling centre." The important consideration here is that the researcher is careful to discern whether slight differences in spelling, vocabulary, and phraseology might lead to different responses. In order to shed some light on that possibility, the researcher might pretest (try out) the Canadian instrument with a sample of the population to be used in the study; and then in a focus group of respondents attempt to understand how and why the respondents answered the way they did. The purpose of this would be to determine the extent to which there appears to be content validity to the instrument.

Suppose in this supranational research, a survey is conducted in Boston neighborhoods with a questionnaire incorporating items from Canadian and U.S. questionnaires regarding attitudes and usage of social services. Further, suppose that these are some of the conclusions from the survey: there are no differences in attitudes toward and usage of social services among U.S. ethnic groups; those who say they would use mental health services are more likely to use services in evening hours than those during the day; there appears to be a greater need for parenting services than there are resources to meet that need. These implications might be drawn for the population involved in the study: since there are no apparent attitudes and differences in the use of social services, it may not be necessary to tailor services to specific ethnic groups; this may be determined in further research to explore this issue; there should be an effort to make more social services available in evening hours; more resources should be developed for the provision of parenting services.

These conclusions from research on the Boston population would not be generalizable as facts for the Toronto population. They could be considered as hypothetical. Hence, from the finding that there are no differences among ethnic groups, the researcher might hypothesize there are no differences among Italian Canadians, African Canadians, and Irish Canadians in their use of social services. Of course, a Canadian researcher would seek to determine the extent to whether those populations exist in Canada; and then test the hypothesis on research with Canadian ethnic groups, referring to the available literature. Canadian researchers might be interested in determining whether there are differences in second- and third-generation Chinese Canadians and Italian Canadians, for example. The purpose of such research would be to ascertain whether or not social services should be tailored to these groups. A Canadian researcher might also hypothesize that more services should be provided in evenings and that there should be more parenting services. However, prior to implementation of that idea, one would determine whether or not the provision of social services occurs in a context similar to that in Boston by referring to available literature and documents from social service agencies in Canada.

Social Work Problems

In table 2.1, the similarities and differences between national and supranational research are summarized with respect to different aspects of the research process. Our hypothetical example provides some idea of the type of social work problem that is considered in research. A natural question to consider is whether all types of social work problems are amenable to both national and supranational research. Theoretically, any social work problem can be considered for both types of research. However, in our opinion, those social work problems that clearly occur both within and between countries are considered to be global problems and should be studied internationally, referring to conceptions and research data from more than one country. For example, these social problems are global: trafficking of drugs, human trafficking, substance abuse, HIV/AIDS, physical health, domestic violence, child abuse, mental health, and so forth. National problems are those that are specific to a particular context within a country. Hence evaluations of social programs within U.S. welfare departments and other social agencies, for example, can be regarded as national. This is especially the case if the programs are unique and not evident in other countries. However, it should be pointed out that this is merely a relative distinction, and that it is quite possible to utilize literature and make implications for social work policies and practices in most other countries from research carried out in one country. Social workers from other countries can derive knowledge from U.S. research, and U.S. social workers can derive knowledge from research in other countries. Thus, most research that is currently domestic may be readily expanded to be international, through consideration of the global aspects of the problem addressed, and inclusion of the literature from and implications for other countries.

KNOWLEDGE FROM SOCIAL WORK RESEARCH AND ITS GENERALIZABILITY

Knowledge Objectives

Social work research, national or international, has the general purpose of producing knowledge that pertains to social work processes and problems. We employ the notions of knowledge objectives and criteria for determining whether knowledge objectives have been achieved as a basis for developing and choosing research strategies and for utilizing social work research knowledge. In addition, we believe it is fundamentally important to consider the extent to which social work knowledge can be generalized. As indicated in chapter 1, social work research studies can be conducted as well as assessed by referring to research aims in terms of knowledge objectives and the degree of generalizability of the knowledge (Nurius & Tripodi, 1985; Shadish et al., 2002; Tripodi, 1974, 1981, 1983; Tripodi, Fellin, & Meyer, 1983). These knowledge objectives and criteria for achieving them were discussed briefly in chapter 1 and are summarized here in table 2.2.

Table 2.2 Knowledge Objectives and Criteria for Achieving Them

Knowledge objectives	Criteria for achieving objectives
• Development and operationalization of concepts	• Concept translatability
• Qualitative and/or quantitative description of concepts	• Measurement accuracy (reliability and validity) • Existence of credible qualitative relationships
• Formation of hypotheses	• Hypothesis researchability
• Testing of correlational hypotheses	• Statistical evidence of correlations • Measurement accuracy
• Testing of cause-effect hypotheses	• Time order of independent and dependent variables • Control of extraneous variables • Evidence of a correlational relationship

Let us point out that a research study may have more than one knowledge objective. For example, an evaluative study of a social program may aim to produce quantitative and qualitative descriptions of program outcomes, as well as testing correlational relationships between program interventions and their outcomes. In that instance, the research strategy should aim to provide evidence of measurement accuracy (reliability and validity); the existence of credible, qualitative relationships; and statistical correlations and effect sizes. Measurement accuracy refers to the precise operational definitions of variables with evidence of reliability (e.g., test-retest, internal consistency, interobserver reliability), and validity (e.g., face validity, content validity, criterion-related validity, construct validity, and factorial validity; see Rubin & Babbie, 2005).

Measurement accuracy of variables is a precondition for producing knowledge about the statistical relationship of variables in quantitative research. For qualitative research in which there are statements of relationship among variables that are defined nominally and are coded by themes, Padgett (1988) and McRoy (1995) describe procedures for verification and trustworthiness such as negative case analysis, triangulation, and multiple data sources, as well as attempts to reduce reactivity, researcher bias, and respondent bias. Cause-effect hypotheses are most difficult to test; and as Shadish et al. (2002) illustrate, researchers infer causal relationships between variables with procedures aimed at establishing the occurrence of the presumed cause (independent variable) prior in time to the presumed effect (dependent variable); the statistical relationship of independent and dependent variables; and the control of threats to internal validity, construct validity, and any other variables that might be responsible for observed changes in the dependent variable.

Substantive and Methodological Knowledge

The research knowledge objectives that we referred to earlier are substantive knowledge, that is, knowledge about the social work problem under investigation. Another type of knowledge that can be produced from social work research is *methodological knowledge*, that is, knowledge about how to produce data that can lead to substantive knowledge. Hence there may be conceptual methodological knowledge about how to construct an instrument, guidelines to follow in selecting samples for study, when to employ different types of research designs, criteria for choosing research instruments, and so forth. Methodological knowledge may also be empirical. For example, data may be gathered and analyzed to show the extent to which instruments and test protocols are reliable and valid for studying social phenomena in various types of populations.

The Generalizability of Knowledge

Table 2.3 refers to four types of generalizability and procedures for inferring generalizability. The results of a research study may not be generalizable at all and may be specific to the particular context in which the study is carried out. For example, an evaluation of a social program in a particular community may not be generalizable to other programs or other communities. However, the goal of research

Table 2.3 Generalizability of Knowledge Objectives and Criteria
for Assessing Generalizability

Types of generalizability	Procedures for inferring generalizability
Conceptual generality	Qualitative judgment
Representativeness	Representativeness procedures
Replication	Replication criteria
External validity control	Experimental procedures

is often to generalize beyond the specific setting in which the research occurs. In research on social work interventions, there might be interest in generalizing across workers, recipients of social work services, time, and place. There are guidelines for generalizing the results of research, but there appears to be no agreed-upon calculus for doing so. Shadish et al. (2002), realizing that it is extremely difficult and usually not practical to combine representative sampling techniques with experimentation, combine qualitative methods of grounded theory with their notions of construct and external validity to offer a way of inferring the generalizability of causal relations. Their procedures appear to be cumbersome and difficult to operationalize; however, they do indicate the problem of generalizability in social research. For our purposes here, we provide some relatively simple guidelines for producing and assessing generalizability. These notions are adapted from conceptions of generalizability in evaluative research (Tripodi, 1983).

Conceptual generality is the extent to which concepts and hypotheses can be generalized for use in situations other than those in which the research takes place. The achievement of conceptual generality depends on *qualitative judgment*, which involves decisions about whether or not hypotheses can be generalized to other situations. If a hypothesis is researchable in situations or countries other than those in which the research occurred, the hypothesis is conceptually generalizable. For example, a program intervention for teaching principles of health care may have been successful in one country, say, China. If the program intervention can be replicated in another country and evaluated with respect to whether program recipients can learn and apply principles of health care, then it can be inferred that the hypothesis is generalizable and subject to research in another country. General guidelines for determining the extent of generalizability of a hypothesis are as follows (Tripodi, 1983, p. 92).

- Determine the extent to which the hypothesis is researchable.
- Specify situations (i.e., agencies, workers, etc.) to which one wishes to generalize.
- Decide whether the hypothesis is researchable in those situations. The extent of conceptual generality is proportional to the number of situations in which the hypothesis is applicable.

Representativeness is the extent to which the sample of persons participating in a research study is representative of the population from which the sample was drawn. Typically, a sample is regarded as representative of the population if the distributions of relevant variables in the sample are equivalent to those in the population. For example, a sample of social service recipients may have identical proportions of sex, age groupings, income, ethnic groups, and education to the population of eligible recipients. The concept of representativeness can be expanded to include settings, time periods, social service providers, and so forth. A social service program may have a representative sample of persons, but not of service providers, for instance. In that event, one could not generalize across service providers. There are three basic procedures for *determining representativeness* of a sample: (1) an enumeration or census of every element in the population to which one wishes to generalize; (2) comparison of sample characteristics to a finite population of known characteristics; and (3) nonprobability (purposive and snowball) and probability (simple random, systematic random, stratified random, and cluster) sampling (Tripodi, 1983; Rubin & Babbie, 2005). Probability sampling can produce representative sampling on most relevant variables, but purposive and snowball sampling may not (McCroy, 1995; Padgett, 1998; Rubin & Babbie, 2005). However, purposive and snowball sampling as employed in qualitative research may produce samples that are representative of possible themes about a given phenomenon.

Generalizability can be inferred by *replications*, that is, research studies on the same phenomenon that are repeated with consistent results. There are no universal criteria for determining whether the number and type of replications are sufficient to infer generalizability. Tripodi (1974, p. 167) suggested that "replications are obtained when the empirical correlations in a number of research samples result in approximately the same strength, direction, and level of statistical significance." To generalize correlational knowledge from single-subject designs, Henson and Barlow (1976, p. 334) suggest that "one successful experiment and three successful replications will usually be sufficient to generate systematic replication on topographically different behaviors in the same setting or the same behavior in different settings." It is plausible that generalizability is enhanced as the number of replications continue to produce consistent results. If the replications are independent of each other and if it can be assumed that the probability of success, that is, a consistent result, is 0.5, one could use a statistic such as the binomial to determine the probability of success, say at the .05 level of significance.

External validity control is a factor in considering the extent to which inferences can be made to populations other than the one from which the sample was drawn (Campbell & Stanley, 1966; Cook & Campbell, 1979; Shadish et al., 2002). Campbell and Stanley (1966) specified four factors that should be controlled to increase external validity: (1) interaction between initial measurement and the independent variable; (2) interaction between selection biases and the independent variable; (3) reactive effects of experimental treatment arrangements; and (4) multiple treatment interference. These threats can be controlled to some extent by the use of the following experimental procedures that are elaborated by Campbell and his colleagues (Campbell & Stanley, 1996; Cook & Campbell, 1979). (1) The interaction between initial measurement and the independent variable is controlled by using experiments with control groups that do not have initial measurements prior to the introduction of the independent variable. (2) Interactions between selection biases can be minimized by replicating the independent variables of intervention with different individuals and subpopulations. (3) Placebo effects or other reactive effects to the experimental procedures are reduced by using control groups that receive the attention of persons dispensing the intervention but not the contents of the intervention. And (4) multiple-treatment interference can be reduced by providing evidence of the amounts and types of relevant interventions, other than those on which the research is conducted; and by factoring that evidence into analyses of data.

THE RESEARCH PROCESS

In this section we briefly describe four interrelated models of research: quantitative research, qualitative research, program evaluation, and single-subject design. These models or approaches are used in the research literature and should be familiar to social work students who have taken a basic research course. Having reviewed these approaches, we then use aspects of the research process to focus on key issues in supranational research and, in subsequent chapters, intra- and transnational research.

Quantitative Research

Rubin and Babbie (2005) clearly describe elements of the research process that are quantitative or qualitative, depending on the research method selected for the research study. When the research methods involve single subject designs, experiments and quasi experiments, surveys and secondary data analyses, that is, methods that employ quantitative procedures and statistical data processing and analysis in relation to sampling procedures, the research process is that of quantitative research. Although qualitative research is incorporated in Rubin and Babbie's depiction of the research process, it has distinctive elements of its own, as discussed by qualitative researchers (Padgett, 1998), and will be treated here as a separate but interrelated approach. The elements of the research process presented by Rubin and Babbie are similar to those presented by Grinnell and Unrau (2005) and other writers of research in social work and other fields such as education, sociology, psychology, and so on.

Rubin and Babbie (2005) refer to seven phases of the research process that are interrelated: problem formulation, designing the study, data collection, data processing, data analysis, interpreting the findings, and writing the research report. In problem formulation, the problem for research is posed after considering the extent to which there is a need for the research, and whether there are theories and previous studies regarding the possible research. In posing the problem, hypotheses, variables, and their possible measurement are considered after a thorough review of the substantive and methodological literature. Moreover, the research is concerned with the degree to which the study can be carried out, that is, its feasibility, and whether there are possible barriers to the research with respect to ethical considerations, costs, and so forth. Most important, within the United States, social work researchers need to receive approval of their proposed research from institutional review boards who review the potential risks and benefits for research participants. In the second phase of designing the study, the researcher (or research team) considers the kinds of research design and sampling that are necessary to provide evidence in relation to the knowledge objectives of the study; for example, a survey for producing descriptive data, a quasi experiment for testing a correlational hypothesis, and so on. Decisions are made about sampling with respect to generalizability, and available instruments are employed or new ones are constructed to measure variables for answering questions and testing hypotheses. If the research objectives are to develop concepts and hypotheses, combinations of qualitative and quantitative procedures, for example, structured and unstructured questionnaires, observations, and/or interviews might be employed.

In the phase of data collection, the research design is implemented, including sampling procedures as well as the gathering of data. Modifications in the design might be made with respect to ethical and cultural considerations, particularly with respect to the degree to which people are willing to participate in the research. The data are then processed. The raw data are transformed into coded categories, summarized on measurement scales, and prepared for data analyses. Limitations of the data are also recorded; for example, response rates to survey questions and/or to other instruments. These limitations are factored into methods for analyzing the data and are considered in the formation of conclusions from the data. Data are analyzed in the fifth phase of the research process. Statistical procedures are employed to yield information regarding the distributions of variables and to test hypotheses about the relationships between the variables. Judgments might be made about the degree to which the sample of people included in the research is or is not representative of a larger population. If the research is testing the effectiveness of an intervention, judgments might also be made about the representativeness of the sample of those providing the intervention to a larger population of service providers. In phase 6, the findings are interpreted. Methodological limitations are considered, and the findings are interpreted with respect to the extent to which knowledge objectives are achieved and can be generalized beyond the confines of the study. In addition, implications for social work and social welfare are considered in relation to the interpretation of the data in the study.

Finally, the research report is written.

Typically the report begins with an *introduction* that provides a background to the research problem, informs the reader of the rationale and significance of the study, and reviews relevant theory and research. This introduction is followed by an explication of the conceptual elements of the study, including units of analysis, variables, hypotheses, assumptions, and operational definitions. A *methodology* section delineates in precise terms the design of the study, including the logical arrangements, sampling and data collection procedures and the measurement approach used. Next come the *results* of the data analysis, which identify the statistical procedures employed; display data in tables, graphs, or other visual devices; and provides a narrative that reports in a technical, factual sense what specific data mean . . . followed by a discussion section . . . [and] the major findings and conclusions. (Rubin & Babbie, 2005, p. 111)

Qualitative Research

Padgett (1998) distinguishes qualitative from quantitative research as follows: qualitative research is inductive, seeking to discover; it is naturalistic and holistic; it deals with open systems and dynamic reality; the qualitative researcher is an instrument of data collection; and categories result from data analysis. In contrast, quantitative research is deductive, based on the scientific method, employs controlled conditions, is particularistic, studies a stable reality, and uses standardized data collection instruments; and in quantitative research, categories precede data analysis. Padgett describes four general phases of qualitative research: *formulation of the problem*; *data collection*, which feeds back to problem formulation; *data analysis and interpretation*, which are interactive with data collection and problem formulation; and the *write-up*. The focus of qualitative research is on developing concepts and hypotheses from the research. Hence there is a great deal of interaction, recursiveness, and flexibility as the researcher engages in the phases of research. In essence, the approach is less formalized and standardized than quantitative research; however, some qualitative procedures, such as grounded theory, are relatively orderly, and qualitative researchers might use working hypotheses and questions to guide their research.

Sampling in qualitative research has the purpose of providing depth in the study of phenomena by employing nonprobability sampling methods such as purposive and snowball sampling. Particular attention is paid to the researcher as a participant in the research and how potential biases on the researcher's part might be reduced. Data are gathered from multiple sources and multiple perspectives to ensure the credibility of findings through triangulation. Data are gathered in these ways: "(a) *observation* (of the respondent, the settings and oneself), (b) *interviewing*, and (c) *review of documents or archival materials*" (Padgett, 1998, p. 55). Data are in the form of taped interviews, recorded observations, field notes, and documents. After they are gathered, they are transformed and coded into categories. The procedure is inductive. Categories are coded with the purpose of providing depth in understanding the phenomena being studied. Computer programs are used to efficiently categorize data; however, as pointed out by Padgett, it is the researcher who must create the connections among categories. Qualitative researchers test their theories by searching for negative instances, by returning to the data after hypotheses are made about the linkage of categories, and by affirming or disaffirming their notions within the data at their disposal.

Program Evaluation

According to Seidl (1995), social workers emphasize the formative aspect of social program evaluation, that is, the provision of information to further develop the program being evaluated. Tripodi, Fellin, and Epstein (1978, p. 10) indicated that

> social program evaluation is the systematic accumulation of facts for providing information about the achievement of program requisites and goals relative to efforts, effectiveness, and efficiency within any stage of program development. The facts of evaluation may be obtained through a variety of strategies, and they are

incorporated into some designated system of values for making decisions about social programs.

Methods other than social research can be employed, such as cost-benefit and cost-outcome analyses, as well as a variety of accounting and auditing procedures. With respect to the research process, both quantitative and qualitative methodologies can be employed.

Most of the evaluations conducted in social work are agency-based evaluations; therefore, we will describe the notions of Seidl (1995), who has described the process of agency-based program evaluation. The evaluator needs to decide on the stakeholders of the program, those who fund the evaluation, what information is desired, whether the program is sufficiently developed to be evaluated, what are the program objectives, and what is the purpose of the evaluation. This is decided in negotiations with the sponsors of the evaluation and the key stakeholders, that is, those interested in the program and its evaluation. Evaluation possibilities may be ascertained by interviews, small group meetings, and focus groups. Hence the problem formulation is focused on the program, types of similar programs, types of evaluation methods to be used, and the sociopolitical context in which the evaluation is to take place.

After the purpose of the evaluation is explicated, the research proceeds like the quantitative research process. Hypotheses about the program and its outcomes are specified. Outcome variables are operationally defined. Available reliable and valid instruments are used, or new ones are developed as a part of the process. Ethical issues concerning confidentiality, possible risks to program beneficiaries, and so on are considered. Sampling and research designs are selected to produce knowledge about the program and its relation to outcome variables and its generalizability to a population of potential program recipients. Data are gathered and analyzed in relation to the achievement of program objectives and the extent to which the program was actually implemented. Additional information might be obtained to describe the way the program was or was not implemented, and recommendations might be made with respect to possible program changes if the evaluation is to be useful.

Single-Subject Design for Social Workers

Single-subject designs involve a series of procedures that pertain to assessment, implementation of interventions, and evaluation of practice effectiveness and client follow-up (Tripodi, 1994). The process of single-subject design includes three successive phases that can be geared to clinical social work: baseline, intervention, and follow-up.

In each phase there are repeated measurements of one or more variables that are indicators of client problems or needs over specified periods of time. At baseline, repeated measurements are made of the nature, severity, and persistence of client problems. Analyses of these measurements by graphic or statistical means can provide the practitioner with information regarding assessment and the formulation of intervention or treatment plans. During intervention, when a specified plan is implemented to change client behaviors and/or attitudes, information is provided about changes in the nature and severity of the client's problem as measured by the same variables as were employed during baseline. The practitioner observes the extent to which the planned intervention is implemented and whether the measured variables are similar or different from the pattern of variables at baseline. Inferences can then be made regarding practice effectiveness in terms of attaining specified changes, such as significant increases or decreases in the severity of the problem. When and if the practice objectives are achieved and when there are no other practice issues to consider, the intervention is terminated. The practitioner can continue to take repeated measurements of the same variables to determine whether changes observed during intervention are maintained at follow-up. (Tripodi, 2002, p. 748)

Prior to the implementation of this model, there must be a conceptualization of the client's problem, the intervention to be used, what variables can be examined, and what instruments are available or need to be constructed to measure those variables. With repeated measurements, graphic and statistical procedures can be employed to measure change or stability. The research design presented in this model is one of many single-subject designs. A description of other designs is available in Tripodi (1994).

ISSUES IN THE CONDUCT AND UTILIZATION OF SUPRANATIONAL RESEARCH

Having reviewed the research process presented in the foregoing interrelated models, we decided to use these categories for discussing issues in international research: problem formulation; instrument construction; research designs; sampling and study populations; and data collection, data analysis, conclusions, and implications. Issues pertinent to national research as presented in research texts apply to all of our types of international social work research. Within each type, there may be more or less emphasis on the different categories involved in the research process. For example, issues regarding research designs between countries will be relatively more important for transnational research, while issues in problem formulation, conclusions, and implications are the most salient of the research categories for supranational research.

Problem Formulation

In the process of problem formulation, it is necessary for the researcher to review literature to determine what knowledge is available, whether it is generalizable, and whether it pertains to the ideas that are being developed to formulate the research problem. According to Rubin and Babbie (2005), the researcher reviews the literature not only to develop questions and hypotheses for research but also to ascertain information about the extent to which the research problem can be pursued in light of ethical considerations, the sociopolitical context of the proposed research, the projected costs, and the extent to which potential research participants are available and willing to participate. Obviously, reviewing the literature from more than one country is more complicated than simply reviewing the literature pertaining to the research problem in the country in which the research is to take place. In contrast, not reviewing the literature of other countries may be shortsighted, not taking account of substantive and methodological knowledge that may be essential. Questions like these might be considered: Has knowledge about the problem for research already been accumulated? Have research instruments been developed from other countries that could be employed? Under what conditions is it possible to use representative sampling procedures, randomization, and control groups? How relevant is the proposed research problem to social work policies and practices? Have nominal and operational definitions of key concepts been delineated?

Crisp (2004) has discussed several issues involved in reviewing the literature from other countries. First of all, she noted the tendency of U.S. researchers to limit literature reviews to their own country. Language may be a barrier; however, one might use a translator, particularly if the research problem is global, having been pursued in countries where English is not the dominant language. Crisp (p. 77) indicates that "the development of Web-based translation programs such as Babel Fish (http://babel.altavista.com) which provide almost instantaneous translation between English and a number of other languages, would seem to provide one answer to the problem of reading that is available in foreign languages." However, many documents for review may not be available on line, which is a requirement for their use in web-based programs. Crisp points out that studies in the literature may represent different time periods, with older times not necessarily representing current times. Moreover, methodological procedures may be viewed differently by other countries, with participatory and qualitative research, for example, considered as more favorable approaches to securing knowledge than field experimentation. Crisp (pp. 81–82) proposed guidelines for viewing evidence for social work practice; and, although she focused on practitioners, the guidelines can be useful for researchers in problem formulation:

- Why am I using this evidence?
- Am I only using this evidence because it is readily available to me or because I believe it to be credible?
- Is the basis of this evidence methodologically sound?
- Am I using this evidence without considering how apt it is for the context because it comes from an eminent source?
- To what extent do personal factors impinge on my evaluation of this evidence? If so, do I have the resources (including time) to search for other evidence?
- Are there reasons why this evidence cannot be applied?
- Is it possible that this evidence has been superseded?

It is important in problem formulation for supranational research to consider cultural and national differences. The researcher should learn about these differences by reviewing pertinent literature about subcultures within a country, as well as national and cultural differences between countries. Potocky and Rodgers-Farmer (1998) review and consider methodological issues and innovations with minority and oppressed populations in the United States. One of the articles included in their book focuses on the problem of cross-cultural validity in the measurement of depression; and the authors, Ortega and Richey (1998, pp. 60–61) provide some recommendations for researchers:

> *Methodological diversity* [is] . . . the utilization of multiple research methodologies simultaneously or in coordinated sequalae that subsequently link and integrate qualitative and quantitative procedures. . . . When selecting or developing measures for research with people who represent ethnic/cultural minority groups, social work scholars would likely benefit from reviewing relevant cross-cultural literature in other disciplines, and from ongoing consultation with bilingual and bicultural experts in the communities of interest . . . we would suggest greater attention to more creative forms of scaling in measures bound for multicultural use. For instance visual analogue scales. . . . In addition to attending to the content and equivalence of measurement tools, and expanding assessment to include consideration of environmental variables, it is also important to think about how information will be collected . . . it is important for social work researchers to assess their own levels of cultural competence as they embark on and sustain research activity with individuals and communities of color.

An important question in reviewing the literature is how it should be located, accessed, and reviewed. We describe three different procedures for analyzing research studies: narrative review, metaevaluation, and metaanalysis.

Narrative Review

Shadish et al. (2002, pp. 423–424) believe that narrative reviews are superior to the use of quantitative review methods for "hypothesis generation, for thick description of a literature, and for theory development with qualitative categories and relationships among variables." In narrative reviews, the researcher reads, examines, and organizes research studies; and then makes judgments about their quality, results, differences, and similarities (Videka-Sherman, 1995). Narrative descriptions are provided, and there is no attempt to synthesize quantitatively the results of research studies. Judgments are made about available knowledge and whether or not there is a need for research regarding the concepts and hypotheses that the reviewer creatively formulates from the available literature. In addition, the reviewer notes the potential barriers and facilitators to answering questions and testing hypotheses. Shadish et al. (p. 424) indicate that narrative reviews are especially problematic when one wishes to generalize the knowledge obtained in research studies:

> First, as the number of studies increases, it becomes increasingly difficult for reviewers to keep straight all the relationships between effects and potential moderators that might be important. . . . Second, narrative reviews traditionally rely on box score summaries of results generated from the significance tests of study outcomes. . . . Third, narrative reviews are not very precise in their description of study results. . . . Fourth, matters become even more complex when a narrative reviewer tries to examine relationships among outcomes and potential moderator variables.

Metaevaluation

Patel (2002) describes a procedure of metaevaluation that is a process of quality control for evaluating the quality of evaluation studies in Africa. Quality control guidelines were developed and endorsed by 11 evaluation associations or networks in Africa. These guidelines, the African Evaluation Guidelines, were a list of 30 standards that served as items to check to assure that the evaluations were performed well. They are adaptations of program evaluation standards used in the United States; for example, evaluation impact, valid information, stakeholder identification, report clarity, cost effectiveness, and so forth. Patel (2002) used twenty of these guidelines as standards for reviewing 14 evaluation studies completed in various parts of Africa. Each study was rated on all of the standards by the reviewer, who used a rating scale that ranged from 0, not at all, to 3, average, to 5, very good with respect to how the evaluation study met the standard. All 20 standards were given a rating, and then a median of the ratings was presented for each study. This procedure provides an estimate of whether the evaluations conformed to guidelines indicative of best practices. They are an indication of how the studies were implemented, but do not provide estimates of substantive knowledge about the relationship between the programs and their outcomes.

A related procedure for assessing the quality of treatment effectiveness research, assessment and risk studies, and descriptive and qualitative studies is described by Gibbs (2003). He employs the Quality of Study Rating Form for Rating Evidence Regarding Effectiveness (Individual Studies), the Client Assessment and Risk Evaluation form, and the Qualitative Study Quality form. In each of the forms, criteria for the quality of the study are presented, and points are assigned to each criterion. For example, in the Quality of Study Rating form for assessing treatment effectiveness, *subjects randomly assigned to treatment or control* is given 10 points, *treatment outcomes measure was checked for reliability,* 5 points, and so on. Ratings for the first 19 criteria on that form are made and summed. The total possible score is 80 points. The higher the score, the more confidence the reviewer has that the treatment caused a change. The assigning of points appears to be arbitrary, and the criteria emphasize internal validity control, with only one related to generalizability, *subjects randomly selected for inclusion in the study.* There were no criteria dealing with generalizability of service providers, results over time, generalizability across subcultural groups, interactions of initial measurement with treatment, generalization to populations beyond the confines of treatment, or other threats to validity in making causal inferences (Shadish et al., 2002). Nevertheless, Gibbs goes beyond Patel in making an estimate of the knowledge obtained in various studies, and attempting to use these forms to provide evidence that social workers can consider applying in their practice. Moreover, he indicates that two of the forms for assessing quantitative studies can be used as building blocks for a metaanalysis.

> These two forms were designed to rate a single effectiveness study. The unit of analysis for these two forms was data from individual subjects participating in each study, one form for each study. In a metaanalysis, the unit of analysis becomes the study; so, if the metaanalysis includes ten studies, the number for the metaanalysis is ten. Metaanalyses are studies of studies. (p. 185)

Metaanalysis

Metaanalysis is the use of quantitative techniques for cumulating effect sizes of studies obtained from the literature. Effect size is employed as a common metric across studies. "Metaanalysis converts each study's outcomes to a common effect size metric, so that different outcomes have the same means and standard deviations and can be more readily averaged across studies" (Shadish et al., 2002, p. 425). Involved in a metaanalysis are:

- The development of a research question
- The location of research studies that meet criteria of relevance; research-ability, availability, and accessibility; and ethical acceptability (Videka-Sherman, 1995)
- The specification of time periods for the literature review, and criteria for whether or not unpublished literature, if available, should be included
- Coding the studies regarding salient characteristics of each study such as sample size, the intervention, quality, and so on
- Computing effect sizes, such as the standardized mean difference statistic and the odds ratio (Shadish et al., 2002)
- Analyzing and interpreting the data

It should be noted that Shadish et al. (2002, p. 434) believe that "with few exceptions, metaanalytic data are correlational." That is, metaanalyses of data from field experiments typically produce correlational rather than causal knowledge.

The primary advantage of metaanalysis is that it can provide information that is used consistently across studies, and it focuses on relationships between independent and dependent variables. However, it is subject to the quality of the studies that are included in the metaanalysis. If the studies are flawed, so is the metaanalysis. Some of the potential problems are: unreliability of studies, restricted range of included studies, missing effect sizes, publication biases, possible lack of statistical independence when multiple effect sizes are obtained within studies, biased sampling, inappropriate weighting, and so forth.

One example of a problem of metaanalysis is what occurs when social workers attempt to apply the results of a metaanalysis to practice. Gibbs (2003), as previously mentioned, indicates that in his use of metaanalysis, the unit of analysis changes from the individual to the study. Applying those results to an individual would be inappropriate, due to the ecological fallacy (Twenge, Zhang, & Im, 2004, p. 313), which "occurs when the magnitude of change is calculated using the variation in mean scores rather than the variation within a population of individuals." In addition, as Rubin and Babbie (2005, p. 134), indicate, "the ecological fallacy means . . . making assertions about individuals as the unit of analysis based on the examination of groups or other aggregations."

Appraising Knowledge and Generalizability

One can easily become enamored of metaanalysis; for, despite its drawbacks, it is a means of synthesizing data from a variety of studies. However, it is possible that the user of those studies may ascribe a different level of knowledge (e.g., causal) and a greater degree of generalizability (e.g., to populations across countries and cultures, to service providers, across time, and to different sittings) than is warranted.

We propose a very simple scheme to summarize the knowledge and its generalizability generated from a research study:

- Read the study and classify it in relation to knowledge objectives. There may be more than one objective, for example, to yield a quantitative description and to test a correlational hypothesis.
- Decide, on the basis of the criteria for achieving objectives, what knowledge objectives have been achieved. For example, there may not have been reliable and valid measurements of the variables in a study; and no evidence of a correlation is presented in the research. Hence the criteria have not been satisfied to test a correlational hypothesis, or even to yield an accurate quantitative description. Hence the knowledge objective achieved is that of an untested hypothesis.
- Decide on the aspects of generalizability in which you are interested. For example, if one is reviewing intervention studies, one might be interested in these aspects: providers of the intervention, recipients of the intervention, time of the study, setting of the research, generalizations across subcultures, and generalizations across countries. No one study is likely to cover all of these populations. The critical issue is whether the results of the study are confined only to the sample in the study or there is some basis for generalizability; for example, use of representative sampling procedures, replications, comparing sample characteristics to known characteristics of a population, and so forth. If the study is qualitative and has the purpose of developing concepts and hypotheses, then the criteria of conceptual generalizability and hypothesis researchability are most relevant.
- If there are numerous studies, one can summarize the knowledge. One would indicate for each study: a description of the knowledge obtained; an indication of the knowledge objectives; a description of the degree of generalizability achieved and to which populations. Results of 10 studies might be summarized in this way. Of the 10 studies, 3 achieved correlational, 4 quantitative-descriptive, and 3 qualitative-descriptive knowledge. All three qualitative-descriptive studies produced researchable hypotheses. Three of the quantitative descriptive studies were not generalizable, beyond local communities; and one was a nationally representative survey generalizable to the population of adults in the United States. None of the correlational studies were generalizable beyond the settings in which the research occurred. These results would suggest the possible need for replicated studies for generalization, possibly across subcultures and nations.

Instrument Construction

Choosing and/or constructing research instruments for collecting data and measuring key variables is paramount for national and international research. Research texts in social work, psychology, sociology, and other disciplines inform us to use reliable, valid, and sensitive instruments in our research. A basic concern in cross-cultural research is whether the instrument (test, questionnaire, interview schedule, observation protocols, etc.) is meaningful in the same way across populations that represent different cultures or subcultures. In the United States, for example, there are a number of different cultures or subcultures, such as Native American, African American, Asian American, Hispanic/Latino American, European American, and further subdivisions of all these. When selecting research instruments for cross-cultural research, a prime consideration is that there is cross-validation of the instrument. This means that there is reliability and validity in the use of the instrument for the populations of a research study. If, for example, the researcher is studying populations of Hispanic/Latino Americans, African Americans, and Asian Americans, the instruments should have the same meaning and be valid and reliable for each of those populations. There may be differences in language, syntax, and idiomatic phraseology among those groups leading to noncomparable responses to test items. What may appear to be differences among the groups may be artifacts arising from the instrumentation that is not calibrated to those groups. Moreover, it is important to understand what the labels of subcultural groups signify. Are all those classified as Asian (e.g., Chinese, Japanese, Korean, etc.) similar to each other? Are those labeled Hispanic/Latino (e.g., Puerto Rican, Mexican, Argentinian, etc.) similar with respect to their responses to an instrument? If there are differences within the categories, then it may not be sufficient to say that an instrument is cross-validated, for example, because it produced similar results for non-Hispanic Whites and Hispanics/Latinos. Non-Hispanic Whites may have been similar to Mexican Americans on certain variables but not to Puerto Ricans. If the researcher uses an instrument cross-validated with Mexican Americans on a population of Puerto Ricans, the researcher would not, in effect, be using a cross-validated instrument. The lesson here is that we should not make assumptions about the subculture being studied.

Agbayani-Siewert (2004) studied the assumption of cultural similarity of Filipino and Chinese American college students. Employing a cross-sectional survey design, she studied responses to questions about spouse abuse and intimate violence on a sample of Chinese, Filipino, Hispanic, and non-Hispanic White undergraduate students from a large U.S. university in the 1996–97 academic year. She tested and found support for the hypothesis that "Filipino American students have more similarities in attitudes with Hispanic and White American students than with Chinese American students" (p. 46). The implication of her study is that the stereotypic use of four ethnic categories in the United States (Non-Hispanic White, African American, Asian American, Hispanic/Latino) should be discontinued, and more homogeneous subpopulations should be selected for study.

If there are no instruments that have been validated across subcultures, the researcher should cross-validate the instrument with the populations to be studied, that is, seek comparable indices of reliability and validity. Springer, Abell, and Nugent (2002) provide examples from their work on constructing rapid assessment instruments to measure client functioning. They show how they determined content and face validity by using a panel of experts to rate the items in the instrument;

and they indicated how they computed coefficient alpha and the standard error of measurement as indices of reliability. Although they were interested in using their instruments to measure client changes over time, they did not discuss whether or not their instruments would be stable over time. Changes over time could be due to actual changes or a lack of test-retest reliability.

Research Design

Research design involves a logical strategy for providing evidence related to the achievement of knowledge objectives. Research textbooks such as those by Rubin and Babbie (2005), Shadish et al. (2002), Grinnell and Unrau (2005), Padgett (1998), Blythe, Tripodi, and Briar (1994), and Tripodi (1983) present a variety of research designs that can be employed in national and international research. These research designs, in a sense, are ideal types that are subject to compromises and alterations when carried out in the field. Designs may shift due to events that the researcher is not able to control: unsuccessful attempts at randomization, refusal of potential research subjects to participate, the risk of harm to potential participants, participants dropping out of the research, failure to locate participants at follow-up in community studies, possible dishonest responses of research participants, the biases of the researcher, low response rates leading to nonrepresentative sampling, and so forth. The art of research design involves accommodating to problems that occur during the research and shifting aspects of the design to produce knowledge; it may involve a shift in the knowledge objective that can be obtained. For example, a researcher may use the classical experimental design to test the effectiveness of a social work intervention. Research participants are to be randomly assigned to an intervention group or a control group after being accepted for social work services at a social agency. The intervention is designed to change participants' attitudes about the use of health processes to increase their quality of life. The participants are measured on attitude scales before and after they receive the intervention; those in the control group are measured at the same time periods but receive no intervention. The experiment is devised to provide evidence for testing a causal hypothesis. Suppose that in the conduct of the experiment there is a high dropout rate in the control group, and those who remain are not comparable to the experimental group on variables such as gender, age, income, and education. This destruction of the randomization process changes the nature of the experimental design to that of nonequivalent comparison group, and the knowledge obtained would be correlational rather than causal.

The ideal design types are what researchers strive for in their use of procedures for conducting the research, collecting, and analyzing data. We list some of these designs in relation to knowledge objectives in table 2.4. The reader should also refer to table 2.2, in which we list the criteria for achieving knowledge objectives.

For developing and operationalizing concepts and formulating hypotheses, qualitative research, participatory research, and case studies are the ideal type. A cross-sectional survey is the design of choice for yielding quantitative descriptions. Cross-sectional surveys, interrupted time-series, and nonequivalent comparison group designs can be employed to test correlational hypotheses, and the

Table 2.4 Knowledge Objectives and Research Designs

Knowledge objectives	Research designs
• Development and operationalization of concepts	• Qualitative research
	• Participatory research
• Qualitative description	• Case study
• Formation of hypotheses	
• Quantitative description	• Cross-sectional survey
	• Replicated cross-sectional survey
• Testing correlational hypotheses	• Cross-sectional survey
	• One group pretest-posttest
	• Static group comparison
	• Interrupted time-series
	• Nonequivalent comparison group
• Testing causal hypotheses	• Classical experimental
	• Posttest-only control group

classical experimental design can be used to infer causal relationships. These are a sample of possible designs that can be employed. The logic of the designs is to provide arrangements so that data can be collected and analyzed to achieve the knowledge objectives of the research. Of course, this presentation oversimplifies the art of research design. There are often multiple knowledge objectives in a study, and there may be combinations of qualitative and quantitative procedures to provide evidence regarding these objectives. In addition, as we have indicated, practical events that occur during the conduct of research often alter the nature of the research with respect to its ability to produce evidence to test hypotheses.

Among the biggest problems in research design is the issue of denying intervention or treatment to members of the control group. The researcher may not receive permission to use a control group. If the intervention is of short duration, the researcher can assure the control group members that they will receive the intervention at a specified, later period of time. This would enable the researcher to employ a more powerful design, the crossover design:

$$R\ O_1\ X_1 O_2$$
$$R\ O_3\ X_0\ O_4\ X_2\ O_5$$

where R refers to randomization; O_1 and O_3 to observations before the intervention is introduced to the experimental group; X_1 to the intervention; X_0 to the absence of the intervention; O_2 and O_4 to observations after the intervention is completed with the experimental group; X_2 to the introduction of the intervention to the control group; and O_5 to the observations after the control group received the intervention.

The crossover design is an experimental design that uses a time-lagged control group that receives the social program after the experimental group has completed it. . . . Subjects are randomly assigned to an experimental or a control group, X_1 or X_0. Measurements on the dependent variables are obtained before the program (O_1 and

O_3) and after the Program (O_2 and O_4). After the control group is measured on O_4, it receives the program (intervention). When the program is completed, measurements are again obtained. Differences between O_2 and O_1 and O_4 and O_3 are compared for statistical significance by analysis of variance (and co-variance). In addition, $O_5 - O_4$ is tested for statistical significance by use of a statistic such as a t test for matched pairs. If both results are consistent, there is one successful experiment with one replication. (Tripodi, 1983, p. 144)

The reader is referred to Shadish et al. (2002) for a comprehensive treatment of dealing with problems that occur in the use of experimental and quasi-experimental designs.

Sampling

Sampling issues for supranational research are, for the most part, the same as for national research. The basic problem for the researcher is to secure samples of the study population that are representative of the knowledge objectives, at the same time adhering to ethical principles and being culturally sensitive to minority, ethnic groups in cross-cultural research. Gillespie (1995), Padgett (1988), and Rubin and Babbie (2005) have indicated ethical principles involved in social work research and procedures for adhering to them when selecting samples. Participants in research should be protected from potential harm. Risks for participants might involve such factors as physical abuse or injury, psychological harm, discrimination, and social, economic, and legal sanctions (Gillespie, 1995). These risks can be reduced by (1) securing informed consent, apprising the potential participants of the purpose of the research, and indicating that their participation is voluntary and confidential, with no sanctions introduced and with the understanding they can withdraw from the study at any time; (2) having the proposed research reviewed by outside panels, as well as, in the United States, the customary review by institutional review boards for studies conducted by governmental agencies and university personnel; (3) adhering to professional ethics promulgated by international and national social work organizations so that regulations are not violated, confidentiality is maintained, and investigators do not plagiarize and falsify data.

Subscribing to these notions and being particularly sensitive to communicating them to those from the dominant culture, as well as minority subcultures, will have an effect on obtaining and retaining participants in the sample. Padgett (1988) indicates that qualitative researchers need to establish rapport with participants and provide them with some incentive to participate in the research with small gifts or cash. In many federal grants in the United States, provisions are made to provide some incentives for participants. While provision of incentives may enhance participation, it does raise the question as to whether the results of a study from a sample of participants who receive incentives would be the same as from a sample of those who do not.

Since sampling of study populations may have different purposes, it is worthwhile to consider different sampling strategies as a function of different research objectives for securing knowledge.

Sampling for Developing Concepts and Forming Hypotheses

In exploratory research or qualitative research (Padgett, 1998; Rubin & Babbie, 2005) several nonprobability sampling methods are employed: convenience, purposive, and snowball. The objective of sampling here is not to be representative of a population of persons, but rather to represent a population of themes that can be generated by persons. Convenience sampling involves research with those who are available, who are nearby, and whom the costs of sampling are minimal. Purposive sampling is more focused than convenience sampling and may be selected because it is the judgment of the researcher that it would provide a variety and a range of opinions about the research problem, for example, a group of community leaders and citizens who are knowledgeable about the phenomena being investigated. As Rubin and Babbie (2005, pp. 247–248) indicate,

> sometimes purposive sampling is used not to select typical cases, but atypical ones. This is commonly done when we seek to compare opposite extremes of a phenomenon in order to generate hypotheses about it. . . . Researchers conducting qualitative studies are often particularly interested in studying deviant cases—cases that don't fit into fairly regular patterns of attitudes and behavior—in order to improve their understanding of the more regular pattern.

Snowball sampling is a technique that is employed to locate populations that are difficult to reach, for example, those with HIV/AIDS, undocumented immigrants, and so on. One locates a few members of the population in question, and then asks them to name other persons who belong to that population. The researcher continues the process until a sufficient number is obtained. Rubin and Babbie (2005) indicate that this procedure, although not necessarily representative of the population, is useful for locating ethnic minority persons. Minorities in the United States who are poor or in the poor working class are often suspicious of the intentions of middle-class researchers. It is important for the researcher to show respect to each participant, to indicate how the participant can be helpful, and to be sure to communicate the purpose of the research and to what extent the participant will receive any benefits from the research. The reader is referred to Potocky and Rodgers-Farmer (1998), who discuss a number of methodological issues and innovations in their book on social work research with minority and oppressed populations.

Yielding Quantitative Descriptions

The basic format for yielding quantitative descriptions is to employ survey research techniques with probability sampling methods. Obviously, one possibility is to survey the entire population itself. Therefore, when one is interested in representing a small population—say, all of the clients receiving services at a social agency—one can enumerate all of the elements in the population, thereby conducting a census. When the population is relatively large—say, all of the people receiving social services at one point in time in a geographic area, state, province, country, and so on—the researchers should use probability sampling procedures such as simple random sampling, systematic random sampling, stratified random sampling, cluster sampling, or combinations of those procedures. Even though probabilistic procedures are employed, it is possible that the sample obtained will not be representative on key variables such as age, income, education, primary language spoken in the home, ethnicity, social class, and so forth. Therefore, the careful researcher will check the results of sampling against any information available about the characteristics of the population being studied. It is important to point out that the "population" is defined differently in different studies. It may be the population of all those who have received social services from a particular agency at one point in time, or over a certain period of time; it may be the population of all those who have received social services from all agencies in a particular geographic area; and so on. The point is that a population needs to be delimited and that the sample is considered to be representative only of that population from which the sample is drawn.

Another point to consider is that there is also a population of time. In a cross-sectional survey, only one point of time (or a small range of time, say three months) is considered. If the survey is about opinions and attitudes, it is quite possible that those opinions and attitudes change over time as a result of societal and global influences. Hence replicated cross-sectional surveys attempt to correct for that problem by conducting representative surveys at different points in time.

To include ethnic groups in samples for research, researchers often build proportions of those groups to be included in the sample. This is done by stratified random sampling procedures, stratifying on different ethnic or minority groups. It is also recommended to stratify by income levels as well. In this way, one can describe results of a study as a result of ethnic status, economic status, or their interactions.

Testing Correlational Hypotheses and Causal Hypotheses

Researchers can use the same probability sampling procedures as for surveys, but it is less likely when experiments and quasi experiments such as nonequivalent comparison groups and interrupted time-series are employed. In fact, the sampling is often accidental or by convenience, restricting the generalizability to the confines of the study itself. One procedure that may be employed to increase the generalizability is to repeat the study simultaneously at different sites. The sites may be selected in a purposive manner, for example, conducting the research in large, medium-sized, and small cities in different geographical locations. If the results are consistent across sites, the generalizability can be enhanced.

A noteworthy procedure to use in securing difficult populations is presented by Roffman, Picciano, Wickizer, Bolan, and Ryan (1998) in their article "Anonymous Enrollment in AIDS Prevention Telephone Group Counseling: Facilitating the Participation of Gay and Bisexual Men in Intervention and Research."

With funding from the National Institute of Mental Health, the authors designed and assessed the effectiveness of a 14-session cognitive-behavioral group intervention, delivered entirely by telephone, and tailored for gay and bisexual males who sought support in becoming sexually safer. In addition to its delivery via the phone, toll-free access and the option to enroll anonymously were other key components designed to reduce barriers to enrollment. . . .

The project's publicity strategies, implemented during a recruitment period that lasted from April 1992 through December 1993, included advertising in the gay press, news coverage in the mainstream press, distributing materials to HIV testing centers and gay/lesbian/bisexual health and social service agencies, and mailing posters to gay bars and baths. . . . The materials emphasized that individuals could choose to remain anonymous. . . . After being given assurances of confidentiality of client information, potential participants were asked whether they would like to enroll confidentially or anonymously. Those who chose the confidential option were asked to provide an address to which written materials and incentive payments could be mailed. They were also asked for a phone number and instructions as to the type of message that could be left so the staff could contact them. . . . Clients who chose to enroll anonymously were asked to rent a postal box in a nearby post office. The anonymous enrollee was advised that he would need to provide documentation of his identity to the postal service, but could request that the project use a pseudonym when mailing materials to him at that address. He was asked to rent the postal box for an initial six-month period, and a money order for $17.50 was then mailed to him, with no name written on the payee line, to cover this cost. (pp. 8–10)

Shadish et al. (2002) indicate that generalizing causal inference from experiments regarding treatment effectiveness involves populations of these entities: treatments, outcomes, persons, and settings. They then point out the difficulties and impracticalities of using representative sampling methods for these populations during any one experiment, and suggest alternative approaches for generalization based on replications and purposive sampling strategies. They discuss purposive sampling of typical instances and purposive sampling of heterogeneous instances to be used in replication of experiments, and they consider the utility of metaanalysis in summarizing the results of those studies. The reader is referred to their lengthy discussions regarding the deficiencies of representative sampling procedures and the promise of combining replicated experiments and purposive sampling for testing causal hypotheses.

Data Collection, Data Analysis, Conclusions, and Implications

The issues involved in data collection, data analysis, and conclusions are essentially the same for national and for supranational research. Differences arise, for the most part, when dealing with implications for two or more countries. However, prior to discussing implications, it is important for the researcher or for one who utilizes research to pay particular attention to the following.

- Instruments employed in cross-cultural research should be validated for each of the subcultures being studied, that is, the instrument should evoke similar degrees of reliability and validity as well as factorial structures in the response systems. Moreover, it is paramount that the researcher's biases regarding the subcultures should be exposed so that checks and balances can be employed to reduce their impact in collecting, analyzing, and interpreting data.

- To minimize the possible error due to the researcher's biases, arrange to have the data available so others can review them.

- Be cautious in reporting "acceptable" degrees of reliability, validity, and response rates. For example, some disciplines, such as public health, demand higher acceptable response rates than other disciplines. Nevertheless, if the response rate is, for example, less than 90%, it does reflect on the representativeness and possible generalizability of the sample in quantitative research. The investigator should consider low response rates with caution, indicating why it is believed the response rates are low, preferably with empirical data to support the researcher's assertions.

- Compute effect sizes in addition to statistical significance tests. Effect sizes are more direct measures of the relationship between variables, and they can be used in metaanalyses when combining the results of studies.

- Be careful to indicate whether any assumptions in the use of statistical methods are violated; and, if so, indicate the reasons for employing the statistical methods.

- In interpreting data, be sure the conclusions are based on the data in the study rather than on preconceived notions or hunches from the literature.

- For each substantive knowledge objective of the study, assess the degree to which you have confidence in the knowledge achieved and generalizability of the knowledge with respect to populations of service providers, potential recipients, outcomes, social agencies, time, and so on.

- In attempting to apply the results of a metaanalysis to social work practice, be mindful of Gibbs's (2003, p. 187) admonition: "Always examine the study to see whether its subjects resemble your client(s) closely enough to warrant generalizing the metaanalysis findings to your clients. If their subjects are dissimilar to your clients, use caution when generalizing to your clients." The same consideration should also take place when considering the results of a single study. Recognize that in essence you are hypothesizing that the same relationships noted in a study will also occur in social work practice in settings different from the one in which the research occurred.

- Examine the research to determine whether there is any methodological knowledge that might be useful for other investigators.

Drawing Implications for Two or More Countries from Supranational Research

We have devised recommendations for deriving implications for two or more countries from a supranational research study. Just as developing hypotheses from the literature is a creative act, so is the derivation of implications from a study. Typically, the implications are in the form of hypotheses and must undergo further testing in practice and research to be considered valid. The facts generated from tested hypotheses are most likely to be relevant in the contexts where the studies were carried out, for example, evaluations, needs assessments, surveys, and intervention studies of localized social programs. Of course, those hypotheses that are empirically supported in one setting can be generalized conceptually as hypotheses to test in other situations and in other countries.

RECOMMENDATIONS

- Analyze the results of research, and determine the substantive knowledge objectives that are achieved and the generalizability of that knowledge. If instruments are employed, one should determine the extent to which they are reliable and valid for each of the countries for which one wishes to use the instruments. Determine whether there are any methodological procedures that can be conceptualized for use in other countries, for example, sampling procedures, recruitment of people for research, and so on.
- Be sure that conclusions are derived from the data, not from the researcher's biases or from preconceived notions from the literature about the countries in question. However, the conclusions should be discussed in the context of knowledge about other countries.
- Very carefully indicate the limitations of the study with respect to substantive and methodological knowledge, indicating how that affects the study's implications.
- If the researcher uses the literature to support the results of the study, the use of the literature should be comprehensive, not selecting only a few (i.e., if more are available) studies that appear to be supportive. Limitations of those studies should be reported, and consistencies and inconsistencies with the results of the researcher's study should also be indicated.
- If the results of studies attempting to yield descriptions or test correlational hypotheses indicate there is no basis for generalizing the descriptions or correlations, the findings from those studies should be considered hypothetical when extrapolating the results to other countries.
- When drawing implications from the conclusions, be clear about as to what populations and to what countries one can generalize: populations of interventions, service providers, programs, recipients, and social agencies.
- Understand from the literature and ideally from discussions with social workers from another country the nature of social services and social work in that country, and the cultural and sociopolitical conditions that might influence the implementation of research in that country.
- Be clear as to whether the research to be applied is relevant to the countries, and note whether it pertains to policies and practices that affect recipients, providers, agencies, or other systems.
- If the research is about interventions that can be employed in social work practice, decide to what extent it can be applied in the countries, considering whether it is culturally and ethically suitable and whether the intervention can be implemented at an affordable cost.

INCENTIVES AND BARRIERS TO SUPRANATIONAL RESEARCH

Incentives and barriers to supranational research involve the same issues as does national research; and they include additional problems and prospects that are unique to supranational research. In national research, some of the main barriers are costs of time and labor, environmental constraints, access to research participants, and the lack of participation. Costs include the price and labor involved in all aspects of the research: instrumentation; sampling; recruiting; participants; implementing and managing research designs; statistical and data processing, including consultation; and the preparation, printing, and dissemination of research reports. Environmental constraints refer to the lack of permission to carry out the research from institutional review boards due to the possibility of harming research participants; from organizations and people who have responsibility for potential research participants, such as social agencies, parents, guardians, and so on; and from sociopolitical influences affecting research institutions, social agencies, and communities. Potential research participants—such as migrant workers, illegal aliens, the homeless, and so forth—may be difficult to track due to their mobility and lack of a permanent residence. People in poverty and minority groups may be distrustful of social work research, and access might be difficult. There may be refusals to participate once potential participants are contacted. When participants give their informed consent and agree to engage in the research, there may be reluctance to continue. There may be dropouts in control and experimental groups, dropouts at follow-up, and falsification of answers to questionnaires and other research protocols.

Incentives in research are intended to counteract barriers such as these. Costs can be defrayed through research grants and through the willingness of social agencies to be involved in research. They can be minimized by researchers from academia and social agencies who contribute time and other resources involved in the conduct of research. The task of the researchers and research teams is to gain environmental support by indicating its value to communities and society. Research involving the assessment of community needs and the evaluation of social programs provides necessary information for social planners and social developers. As the expressed need for social work research continues to grow, as is evident today, environmental influences will be less of a barrier and will be regarded as research incentives. Social work researchers have the incentive of contributing knowledge to the social work profession about social work clients, practices, and policies. Moreover, they receive personal gratification through publications, research reports, and research grants; and this may lead to professional advancement and prestige. Ultimate gratification may come from having helped members of the population in need as a result of the research. These attitudes lead to creativity in developing techniques for engaging participants from populations that are difficult to access; hence researchers have developed participatory research that includes participants in the planning of research, key informants involved, techniques used, such as snowball sampling, and so forth. In addition, techniques for engaging and retaining people in the research process have been developed that involve incentives for the participants: gifts, money, access to recreational activities, and the contribution of knowledge to others similar to themselves with respect to social, economic, and/or psychological problems.

Barriers to supranational research include those cited for national research, as well as lack of availability and accessibility of literature, translations, and time to thoroughly review the literature and the costs involved in reviewing the literature and discussing the results and their meaning with social workers from a country other than the one in which the research was conducted. Literature for the research problem may not be available, particularly if it is unpublished or regarded as confidential by social agencies and organizations. The literature may be in another language, and it may need to be translated. This may lead to the researcher's own reluctance to pursue the knowledge in foreign publications. Finally, it takes time to analyze research carefully, and even more time to conduct metaanalyses or other data synthetic techniques to summarize the literature.

The incentives to social work researchers for engaging in this extra work should be reviewed within the spirit of internationalism and the context of globalization, which affects all of social work today. The international social work researcher is able to contribute knowledge to two or more countries; and she or he receives personal gratification and prestige by being regarded as a contributor to international social work. This incentive makes the extra time involved in international social work research worthwhile. At the same time, it is noted that more literature from around the world is immediately available through the internet, and there are movements in social work to systematically compile research that deals with interventions that are potentially useful for social work, such as the Cochrane Collaboration and other collaborations. In addition, social work researchers are becoming increasingly exposed to data retrieval techniques, computer assisted literature searches, and metaanalysis. In addition, bilingual persons might be engaged in the research, reducing costs of translation. Also, the researcher might find the funds through organizations or research grants to defray costs of translation. Obviously, costs of translation are insignificant if the publications from the countries involved in the research are in the same language, for example, English for Canada, the United Kingdom, Australia, and the United States. However, even in the same language, it is important for the researcher to be aware of differences in idiomatic expressions; collaboration with social workers from other countries could be helpful in this regard.

SUMMARY

In this chapter, we distinguished supranational from national research by indicating that both types of research

- Follow steps in the research process from problem formulation, sampling, and research design to instrument construction, data gathering, analyses, and conclusions
- May generalize across subcultural groups within a native population
- Seek to apply research findings to the population where the research is conducted

Supranational research also

- Uses literature from two or more countries
- Generalizes substantive knowledge across countries or specifies differences between countries in formulating the research problem
- May conceptualize generalizability of methodological knowledge across countries in formulation of the research problem
- Seeks to generalize implications across countries

We gave brief hypothetical examples of national and supranational research with respect to the same research problem, and we illustrated how both types of research could include cross-cultural investigations.

We presented our conception of knowledge objectives and the criteria for achieving them, and we noted that these objectives and criteria for achieving them are relevant to both national and supranational research: development and operationalization of concepts/concept translatability; formation of hypotheses/hypothesis researchability; qualitative and quantitative description/measurement accuracy (reliability and validity), as well as existence of credible qualitative relationships; testing of correlational hypotheses/statistical evidence of correlations and measurement accuracy; and testing of causal hypotheses/time order of independent and dependent variables, control of extraneous variables, and evidence of a correlational relationship.

The difference between substantive and methodological knowledge was discussed, and we presented types of generalizability and criteria for assessing generalizability; conceptual generality/qualitative judgment; representativeness/representativeness procedures such as probability sampling; replication/replication criteria of consistency; and external validity control/experimental procedures. Four interrelated but different research models were then presented: quantitative research, qualitative research, program evaluation, and single-subject design. We abstracted these aspects of the research process from those models: problem formulation; instrument construction; research design; sampling and study populations; and data collection, data analysis, conclusions, and implications. These categories were then used to discuss issues in the conduct and utilization of supranational research. We presented a series of guideline questions for summarizing knowledge and its generalizability in reviewing research studies, indicating how research designs are related to knowledge objectives; discussed sampling issues in cross-cultural research; presented caveats in analyzing data and forming conclusions; and provided recommendations for deriving implications for two or more countries from a supranational research study. We concluded with a discussion of barriers and incentives to conducting supranational research, noting that in this time of increasing internationalism and globalization in social work, the extra effort involved in supranational research is worthwhile, providing contributions to more than one country.

3

ISSUES AND EXAMPLES
OF SUPRANATIONAL RESEARCH

In this chapter, we discuss the criteria we employed for selecting five supranational studies. We then present the studies; within the discussion of each study, we describe it in terms of the research process, indicate why it is classified as supranational, present issues that are discussed or alluded to in the research, and discuss research and utilization issues that are derived from the study. We conclude with a summary of the issues considered in the five studies.

Criteria for Selecting Articles

We used six interrelated criteria for selecting the research studies:

- Excellence of study
- Study classifiable as supranational
- A variety of research methods are presented
- Studies are from several social work journals
- Studies are conducted in different countries
- Studies evoke and discuss issues pertinent to the conduct and utilization of research

The selected studies are intended to serve as illustrative examples, and of course do not represent the entire population of available studies that meet these criteria.

Excellence of the study is indicated by its publication in a peer-reviewed journal and by the thoughtfulness of the authors in implementing research methodologies, in view of the costs and the sociopolitical contexts of the studies. We do recognize that it is virtually impossible to answer all relevant questions that impinge on research during a study, particularly in relation to the provision of evidence pertaining to substantive knowledge and its generalizability. As a result, many of the issues presented are regarded not as criticisms of the research, but rather as considerations for future research and knowledge development.

All of the five studies are classifiable as supranational. Recalling our discussions in the two previous chapters, supranational research takes place in one country; literature from two or more countries is used to frame the research problem; and implications are considered for two or more countries. In describing each study, we indicate why we classify it as supranational.

To illustrate the pervasiveness of supranational research, we selected studies that represented different research approaches, were conducted in different countries, and were published in journals that are of interest to an international audience. We are limited in our presentation, however, by the fact that we chose journals that are in English. Although English may be considered a lingua franca, we recognize that in some parts of the world it may be less familiar to social work researchers than it is in England, the United States, Canada, Australia, Hong Kong, Israel, and India.

We also chose studies that discuss and evoke issues in the conduct of international research. Many of these issues, such as occur in sampling, research design, are pertinent to national research as well as to international research; other issues, such as are involved in translation, back translation, and so on, are more relevant to intercultural and international research. Issues, in our usage herein, refer to potential problems that affect the generation of substantive and methodological knowledge and its generalizability. For example, researchers in one country may use a research instrument that was validated in another country but not validated in the country where the researchers conduct their study. The issue is whether or not the instrument would have the same psychometric properties of reliability and validity in both countries. The remedy for that issue is crossvalidation. This same issue may occur when studying different cultures within a country; for example, Roma (gypsies) in the Czech Republic; African Americans and Hispanic/Latino Americans in the United States; Chinese Canadians in Canada; and so forth. Another example of an issue might result from an evaluation of an educational program about birth control in one country. The program may have been regarded as effective; however, the sampling might have been accidental or by convenience and, thus, not generalizable to the country in which the research took place, let alone to other countries. Generalizability would be enhanced with more representative sampling methods within studies, as well as replicated studies within and between countries.

The five studies were selected from these journals: *International Social Work*; the *British Journal of Social Work: An International Social Work Journal*; *Research on Social Work Practice (Special Edition on Research in China)*; and the *Journal of Social Work Research and Evaluation: An International Publication*. The research studies occurred in Israel, Hong Kong, India, Cyprus, and England. They involved convenience sampling and questionnaires; psychometrics and cross-validation of instruments; the researcher as an instrument in conducting semistructured interviews at two points in time; a randomly selected cross-sectional, telephone interview study; and a randomly selected survey employing questionnaires at two points in time. Issues occurred in all phases of the research process, from problem formulation, instrumentation, sampling and research design to data collection and analysis, conclusions, and implications. Issues range from understanding the cultural and political context of a study to the study's conclusions and generalizability.

Format for Presenting the Studies

For each study, we (1) describe it, (2) classify it, (3) discuss issues addressed within the study, and (4) discuss issues arising from the study, that is, those evoked from the study but not described therein. Each study is described in relation to the problem formulation leading to its substantive or methodological knowledge objectives; instrumentation and the process of data collection; relevant populations and research design; and data analyses, conclusions, and implications. The study is then classified as supranational, with the reasons for doing so. Issues suggested or discussed by the authors are presented. Finally, issues arising from the study are presented, those that are pertinent to the studies but not discussed in detail by the authors.

STUDY 1: "SOURCES OF SOCIAL SUPPORT AND ATTACHMENT STYLES AMONG ISRAELI ARAB STUDENTS," BY ADITAL BEN-ARI (2004)

Study Description

Problem Formulation and Knowledge Objectives

The author reviews Arab, Israeli, and American literature to frame the research problem. The literature pertains to Arab-Israeli relations, stress, social support, and personal characteristics based on attachment theory:

> Recent studies exploring sources of stress among Jewish and Arab Israeli students showed that the latter cultural group was the most salient background predictor of student stress. . . . The present study attempts to identify patterns of utilization of social support in stressful situations among Arab students living in Israel. It also explores the relationships between the identified patterns and personal characteristics, such as attachment styles. . . . These factors may have a significant bearing on the broader question of what any minority students face in a culturally dominant environment markedly different from their own. (Ben-Ari, 2004, p. 87)

The literature review also led the author to believe that the notion of social support is multifaceted and may not always be helpful in stressful situations:

> Scholars have distinguished between two related though independent components of support provided in specific situations: emotional support and instrumental support. . . . Emotional support refers to the expression of caring and the opportunity to share feelings with others, whereas instrumental support refers to the provision of services and resources, tangible aid and the means for solving problems . . . Emotional support is more beneficial in situations where events are uncontrollable and cannot be changed instrumentally, while instrumental support is more beneficial in situations where problem-solving responses can be implemented. (p. 188)

The author also reviews the literature on personal characteristics, which focus on the extent to which people will use their sources for support. Three types of attachment were identified: secured, anxious-ambivalent, and avoidant; and it was suggested that social support is used differentially as a function of attachment; for example, a secure individual would be more likely to use social support than one who is anxious-ambivalent or avoidant.

Noting the importance of the cultural and political context of Arab students in Israel, the author says:

> The Arabs in Israel are a socio-political minority, with a population numbering one million and comprising 18 percent of the total population of the state . . . the continuing Arab-Israeli conflict creates conditions in which a wide range of social and psychological problems can develop . . . the Arab sector is significantly disadvantaged as compared with the Jewish sector in terms of the quality and quantity of educational and social services as well as industrialization. (Ben-Ari, 2004 p. 189)

The author indicates that Arabs in Israel underutilize professional services due to the political tensions between Arabs and Jews. This is due to the notion that cultural differences are not taken into account by social agencies and to the possibility that ethnic minorities are more likely to seek help from culturally accepted sources.

As a result of the literature review, the author formulates the problem for research as follows.

> This article attempts to explore the relationship between the nature of the support provided in stressful situations and the personal characteristics of recipients among Arab students living in Israel . . . it considers . . . two main underlying questions. . . . What are the sources of social support that Arab students utilize when faced with stressful situations? What is the relationship between attachment style and utilization of sources of support among Arab students living in Israel? (Ben-Ari, 2004, p. 191)

The knowledge objectives of this research are to provide quantitative-descriptive information about sources of support and about attachment styles, and to provide correlational knowledge about the relationship between attachment styles and social support. The intended population to which the results are to be generalized is the population of Arab students in Israel.

Instrumentation and the Process of Data Collection

The instrument for data collection was made up of three parts. (1) Students were asked to choose (first choice) which source of social support she or he would use (no one, partner, mother, father, siblings, best friend, professional, relative, bank) under these conditions of stressful situations: relationships, depression, life changes, financial. (2) Each student responded to three questions about attachment styles, using a 7-point rating scale from 1, not at all, to 7, very much, to rate the extent to which the attachment style was like that of the student. (3) Students responded to questions about gender, religion, family status, level of religiosity, and form of residence.

All Arab students were asked to fill out the questionnaire during class visits in required courses in a school of social work at a major university in Israel.

Sampling, Relevant Populations, and Research Design

The sample, accidental or convenience, consisted of 64 Arab social work students taken from a population of 76 Arab students who participated in undergraduate and graduate programs in one social work school. The intended populations might have been the population of Arab students in that university or even all the Arab students in Israel. The response rate for the population of Arab social work students was 64/76; 84%. The research design was that of a cross-sectional survey; the students were queried at one point in time.

Data Analysis, Conclusions, and Implications

The background characteristics of the sample of Arab students was reported as follows: gender (male, 34.4%; female, 65.6%), religion (Muslim, 46.9%; Christian, 34.7%; Druze, 18.4%), family status (married, 20.6%; single, 79.4%), level of religiosity (secular, 47.3%; traditional, 49.1%; religious, 3.6%), form of residence (mixed town, 7.8%, Arab town, 29.7%; village, 62.5%); mean age, 23.9; number of years of education, 14.8; and mean number of years of marriage, 8.4 (Ben-Ari, 2004, p. 192).

Most frequently mentioned first choices of social support among the Arab students for the following stressful situations were: relationships (partner, 41.0%; best friend, 29.0%), depression (partner 35.9%; best friend, 32.8%), life changes (partner, 32.8%; father 17.2%); financial (father, 29.0%; bank, 17.7%; partner, 14.5%).

In describing attachment styles, the author conducted an analysis to determine what category (secured, anxious-ambivalent, avoidant) received the highest score for each student. Fifty of the 64 students were categorized into three types (secured, 29; anxious-ambivalent, 5; avoidant, 16). Others were not included in further analyses, since they gave their highest scores to two categories.

The relationship between attachment styles and social support was analyzed with respect to the stressful problem areas (relationships, depression, major life changes, financial problems). Due to the small numbers used, no statistically significant relationships were discernible; however, the authors noted some patterns in the data:

> Both the "secured" and "avoidant" type respondents quite consistently turn to members of their social support network more than to members of their family of origin in the three emotional problem areas; relationships, depression and major life changes. This pattern is not followed when instrumental support is needed, such as in the case of a financial problem, for which all three types turn mostly to members of the family of origin. The "anxious" type, while in very small numbers, marks an exception by turning to members of the family of origin in problems related to major life changes. (Ben-Ari, 2004, p. 195)

The author reported that the findings revealed that the Arab students' first choices for support in clearly defined emotional situations were partner, followed by best friend, rather than the family of origin. Referring to previous research with Israeli students, the author reported similar patterns of utilization.

The knowledge produced from the study is quantitative-descriptive knowledge that is focused on the particular sample that was studied. Although relationships among social support and attachment styles were posited and discussed, there was not sufficient evidence to support or reject the correlational hypotheses. Therefore, the knowledge remains at the level of correlational hypothesis formulation.

The author concluded that the findings suggest practical implications for social workers. In particular, it is suggested that provision of services to ethnic minorities can be increased by investing in resources to reduce the cultural differences between service providers and ethnic minorities. This suggestion is a hypothesis derived from the author's predilections, the data reported in the study, and literature from Israel, the United States, and Arab countries.

Classification of the Study

The study is classified as supranational research for these reasons:

- Literature from more than one country is utilized to frame the research problem.
- Literature from more than one country is employed along with the findings of research to derive implications for more than one country.
- The study deals with Arab students as ethnic minorities who have lived in Israel all their lives; they are not recent immigrants. Moreover, the study is not focused on implications for Arab countries and for Israel, as it would be if it were an intranational study.

Issues Addressed in the Study

The Cultural Context of the Research

The author demonstrates in the problem formulation and discussion of the findings a high degree of cultural competence, in that the author is aware of and responds to cultural factors and differences among the Arab students. According to Rubin and Babbie (2005), it is important for social researchers to be well read in the literature of the culture represented by the minority group in question. The issue in this study pertains to the necessity of understanding the political and cultural context of the study to interpret findings and to suggest further hypotheses for research:

> Significant barriers exist between the Arab population and governmental systems of service delivery. The Arab minority differs from the Jewish majority in a wide array of sociocultural parameters: language, religion, cultural orientation, family structure, social status, political orientation and nationality. . . . Understanding the cultural context within which Arabs in Israel currently live is significant . . . in so far as it reflects the cultural tension that they experience. The prevailing values of Arab culture determine individual self-orientation, interpersonal relations and relations with various formal and informal systems in the community. Arab society is still dominated by strong family systems. . . . Great emphasis is placed on family integrity, security, obedience and conformity. . . . Due to the strong sense of group affiliation with the family, the neighborhood and the community, problems in Arab society

are not generally brought before formal institutions, unless all other informal alternatives have been exhausted.... Such use of professional help or disclosure of problems to strangers is not an accepted norm of behavior and is typically seen as a sign of weakness, failure, or dependence ... the notion of predestination and the belief that God controls individual destiny is widely accepted in Arab culture.... There is an essential contradiction between a full acceptance of fate and a conscious investment in seeking external help. (Ben-Ari, 2004, p. 190)

Moreover, the author notes that Arabs in Israel have been undergoing a major process of modernization, in that "their constant exposure to Israeli mass media and continuous contact with the Jewish majority have resulted in their adoption of more modern standards of living, values and family patterns" (Ben-Ari, 2004, p. 191). The author further indicates:

Over 75 percent of the Arabs living in Israel were born after the establishment of the state and received their education in the Israeli educational system, which has an essentially Western orientation. Consequently, they have been raised with a fundamental conflict between two very different systems of values and perspectives. (p. 191)

The author uses the literature and an understanding of Arab culture to explain this finding:

Not only did the departure from using traditional family support in stressful situations surface as a common pattern among Arab respondents, but such a pattern also distinguished between the respondents according to their identified types of attachment. Partner and best friend emerged as the most prevalent pattern among the respondents with a "secured" attachment style when emotional support was needed, that is, in problems pertaining to relationships, depression and major life changes. (Ben Ari, 2004, p. 197)

Ben-Ari asserts:

These findings can be explained in the context of two distinct though related frameworks: modernization processes and help-seeking behavior in Arab culture. The process of modernization and exposure to a Western higher education system, particularly social work education, brings out values that are not normatively accepted in Arab culture, such as expression of feelings and disclosure of emotions ... the willingness to stay open to untraditional behavior, such as the disclosure of emotional matters to others outside the family, would be more typical of the secured type.... Therefore, it seems that turning to one's partner and best friend as the primary sources of social support represents a compromise made by Arab social work students between Traditional and Western influence. Although emotional problems are not traditionally discussed outside the family, students become cognizant in their professional social work training of the importance of airing such matters. (p. 198)

The Loss of Data in the Research

During the conduct of research, decisions are made and events can occur that are beyond the control of the researcher; this can affect evidence pertaining to the testing of hypotheses and the generalizability of research findings. In this study, there are two places where loss of data occur: the response to the questionnaire; and the researcher's manipulation of data in typologizing respondents into secured, anxious, and avoidant attachment styles. The issues for the researcher are to consider what can be done, if anything, to preserve lost information. In contrast, the issue for one who is to utilize the information is to interpret loss of data with respect to the achievement of knowledge objectives.

In this study, the response rate was reported as 64 out of 76 possible respondents, or 84%. If the researcher maintains that the same results would have been obtained with 64 as with 76 persons, some evidence can be provided in this regard. Although it was not reported by the author, one might be able to demonstrate that the sample of 64 is similar to the population of 76 if there is available information on demographic and other background characteristics for all 76 persons. For example, there might be available information on gender, age, and so on. If so, one could compare the distributions of the sample to the population on those characteristics. Similar distributions would indicate that the loss of data is not significant. Dissimilar (e.g., statistically different) distributions would indicate that one could not generalize from the sample of 64 to the population of 76, particularly if the background variables, for example, gender and age, are related to the research subjects' perceptions of social support. During the research, another alternative, as is common in the use of survey methods, is to distribute second and even third questionnaires for those who might not have been present when the questionnaire was first presented. Of course, there may be those who simply do not wish to participate. Even some of those might participate if some incentive is offered for research participation.

The second place where data is lost is in the author's use of the typology on attachment styles: "In order to identify the three types of attachment styles among the respondents, an analysis was conducted to determine which category received the highest score from each respondent. . . . Eleven people were not identified since they gave the highest score to two categories (Ben-Ari, 2004, p. 194). Recalling that the research participants were asked to rate, on 7-point scales, the extent to which the three categories of attachment were like them, it is possible that the highest score can be given to two or more categories. The 11 research participants might not have been lost if different rating procedures or different scales had been used. For example, expanding the 7-point scales to 10-point rating scales might have increased the variance in ratings, thereby reducing the likelihood of ties among the three categories. A different procedure would have been to have the research participants rank order the three categories into those that are most like the participant; hence, with forced rankings, there would not have been a loss of subjects.

It is important to note that the user of this information (11 participants lost by the research procedures) must factor this into an understanding of the research sample. Originally, 64 out of 76 responded for an 84% response rate. With 11 more lost, the completion rate is 53 out of 76, or 70%. The principle of analysis here is that the response rate as originally reported can change in the analyses of data. With respect to representativeness of the sample, the user of the information must then consider to what extent the distribution of 53 respondents is similar to the 64 respondents, as well as to the 76 elements of the population. Comparisons can be made between the 53 respondents and the 64 respondents, since information on them was collected on these characteristics: gender, religion, family status, level of religiosity, from of residence, age, and number of years of education.

Issues Arising from the Study

The following issues arise from the study but are not discussed in detail within the study. As noted earlier, the intent here is not to criticize the researcher but to illustrate issues that may arise in other supranational social work research.

Specification of Populations and Samples

An important consideration in survey research is the extent to which the results of a study are generalizable to a population. In this study, an apparent convenience sample of Arab students was obtained in a school of social work within a large Israeli university. No distinction was made between the sample and the population to which the results could be generalized. Consider these possible populations: all Arab students in Israel, all Arab students in Israeli universities, all Arab students in one university, all Arab social work students in Israel, and so on. It is quite possible that perceptions of social support could differ as a function of age and levels in school or with respect to students in other disciplines such as economics, biology, and so on. Hence it is important for the researcher as well as the user of such information to decide on the population. In this study, the population can only be considered to be the Arab social work students at that particular university, precluding generalization to other populations, for example, all students in that university, all social work students in Israel, and so forth.

As indicated in standard textbooks on research, such as Rubin and Babbie (2005), a convenience sample is a nonprobability sampling procedure; the researcher chooses persons conveniently, and there is no basis for being able to generalize to populations beyond the sample. Convenience sampling is useful when the knowledge objective is to develop concepts and hypotheses. The cost is much less than with other sampling procedures; so if the researcher is planning to test out some procedures and ideas, prior to engaging in a large-scale survey, for example, the sample may be sufficient.

The simplest procedure for generalizing to larger populations is to employ probability sampling methods. If the population were all Arab students enrolled at an Israeli university, stratified random sampling might have been employed. The population of students could be stratified on variables relevant to perceptions of social support such as gender, age, type of school, and educational level within the university; then students would be randomly drawn from within each stratum. A second procedure is to compare characteristics of the obtained sample with whatever characteristics are known about the population to which one wishes to generalize. For example, characteristics of gender, age, religion, and so on in the obtained sample for social work students would be compared with those characteristics in the population of all students within the university. This procedure obviously depends upon having available knowledge of population characteristics; the sample could be considered to be representative of the population on those characteristics, but only on those characteristics. Still a third procedure is to replicate the study with different samples of the population. To the extent that the results are similar, the generalizability is enhanced. For example, the study might be repeated with other types of students in the university. Consistent results would constitute some evidence for generalizability.

Pilot Testing

Including pilot testing in research is a procedure that invariably enhances the quality of research. Often researchers might proceed without pilot testing because it is believed the survey results must be obtained as quickly as possible. The issue is whether or not pilot testing should be employed. To the extent possible, in our opinion, pilot testing is a procedure that researchers should follow when planning to conduct a survey based on questionnaire responses. Basically, pilot testing involves trying out the questionnaire and obtaining responses from a sample that is relatively representative of the population to be studied. If pilot testing is done, it enables the researcher to detect possible problems in the collection and analyses of data. For the study in consideration by Ben-Ari, pilot testing was not reported. Nevertheless, we believe there are some functions of pilot testing that might have been helpful. First of all, a procedure like this could be followed. Construct a questionnaire with instructions for respondents to follow. Gather data from a group administration to respondents who are similar to those to be queried. If there is a large population of respondents, the researcher can draw a random sample of about 20 persons from the population. If there is not a large population—say, of Arab social work students at an Israeli university—and one does not want to risk losing data for an actual study, one could take a sample of students from other disciplines within the same university. After the questionnaire is administered, the researcher meets with the respondents in a focus group. The researcher might ask questions such as these:

- To what extent is the language clear, with easy-to-follow instructions?
- To what degree are cultural biases about Arabs and/or Jews reflected in the wording of the questions?
- What preferences do the participants have for formats that include ranking and/or rating instructions?
- What suggestions do the participants have for better questions?

In addition to questions such as those, the researcher can get information regarding sampling and data analyses. Potential participants would be informed that they must give consent to participate in the research and that it is voluntary; hence it would be expected that some would not participate, and an expected response rate could be calculated.

Within the questionnaire, different procedures might be tried. For example, in this study, participants were asked to give their first choice as to what forms of social support (e.g. best friend, father, mother, etc.) they would choose for potentially stressful situations. In a pilot test, the researcher could ask participants to give first, second, and third choices. Data would be scored for first choices only and for combinations of first, second, and third choices; they would then be analyzed and compared. It is possible that the data about choices of support might look different with different scoring systems. Ideally, the data would be similar under both systems, indicating the findings are not due to method variance.

In addition, the pilot test might be used to compare the relative advantages and disadvantages of different rating and ranking systems. In addition, it might be discerned as to whether a loss of data might occur due to the rating procedures themselves, as was previously indicated when discussing the issue of data loss.

STUDY 2: "ASSESSMENT OF FAMILY FUNCTIONING IN CHINESE ADOLESCENTS: THE CHINESE VERSION OF THE FAMILY ASSESSMENT DEVICE," BY DANIEL T. L. SHEK (2002A)

Study Description

Problem Formulation and Knowledge Objectives

As indicated by the author, "the purpose of this article is to report empirical evidence concerning the reliability and validity of the Chinese version of the Family Assessment Device (FAD). The FAD was developed to measure family problem areas based on the McMaster Model of Family Functioning" (Shek, 2002a, p. 502). The six dimensions of family functioning in the McMaster Model are problem solving, communication, roles, affective responsiveness, affective involvement and behavior control. Problem solving

> refers to the family's ability to solve problems. . . . Communication . . . refers to the effectiveness and content of information exchange among family members. . . . Roles . . . addresses the issue of whether the family has recurrent patterns of behavior to handle family functions. . . . Affective Responsiveness . . . refers to family members' ability to respond with appropriate affect to environmental stimuli. . . . Affective involvement refers to the amount of affection family members place on each other. . . . Behavioral Control . . . assesses whether the family has norms or standards governing individual behavior and responses to emergency situations. (p. 503)

The author reviewed literature on methodological knowledge regarding the reliability, validity, and factorial structure of these scales in Holland, Italy, Hong Kong, Canada, and the United States. His rationale for conducting a series of studies regarding psychometric properties of the FAD scales in Chinese adolescents is as follows.

- Reliabilities of some scales were not high, for example, alpha coefficients in one study ranged from .36 for behavioral control to .76 for problem solving.
- Researchers in the studies reviewed did not consistently report correlations between individual items and the total score, and there were few studies that provided information on test-retest reliability (temporal stability).
- Few studies included multiple measures of family functioning for providing evidence of convergent and construct validity.
- There was not sufficient evidence for the discriminant validity of the FAD scales in non-English-speaking countries.

- There was inconclusive evidence regarding the factor structure of the scales.
- Few studies provided information on the stability of derived factors.
- There are few studies of early adolescence with respect to the psychometric properties of FAD scales.
- There is very little information on the FAD scales in the context of Chinese culture.

Multiple measures of family functioning and psychosocial functioning were included along with FAD scales in three studies:

> In Study 1, the test-retest reliability, internal consistency, concurrent validity, and construct validity were studied. In Study 2, the reliability and validity of the FAD were examined in a clinical group and a nonclinical group. In Study 3, the reliability and validity of the FAD in a community sample were investigated. (Shek, 2002a, p. 506)

We note that these terms on reliability and validity are discussed in basic research courses. We refer the reader to Rubin and Babbie (2005) for clear and concise discussions of reliability and validity.

The knowledge objectives of this research are to produce methodological knowledge regarding the reliability, validity, and factor structures of the FAD scales employed on samples of Chinese adolescents, that is, to yield quantitative descriptions and test correlational hypotheses regarding scalar attributes of the FAD and other measures of family functioning. The intent is to generalize the results to Chinese adolescents.

Instrumentation and the Process of Data Collection

These instruments were used in the three research studies the author conducted: Measures of Family Functioning—the Chinese FAD, which is a translation of the 60-item measure based on the McMaster model into Chinese; the Chinese Self-Report Family Inventory; the Chinese Family Awareness Scale; and the Chinese Assessment Instrument. Measures of Psychological Well-Being—the Trait Anxiety Scale of the Chinese State-Trait Anxiety Inventory; the Existential Well-Being Scale; the Life Satisfaction Scale; and the Mastery Scale. Information on the reliability and validity of all of the instruments was reported.

All of the participants in the three studies "responded en masse to all the instrument scales in the questionnaire in a self administration format. Adequate time was provided for the participants to complete the questionnaire. A trained research assistant was present throughout the test administration session" (Shek, 2002a, p. 506). In Study 1, the participants responded to the questionnaires (which included the scales) at two time points two weeks apart, whereas in Studies 2 and 3, the questionnaire, containing the scales, was administered at one point in time.

Sampling, Relevant Populations, and Research Design

Study 1 was based on a sample of 240 boys and 121 girls from a school that is in the lowest range of academic performance in Hong Kong. It appears to have been a convenience sample with no clear purpose for its selection. The research design was a replicated cross-sectional survey, administered at two points in time.

Study 2, designed to test for the known-groups validity of the FAD, was administered to purposive samples of a clinical group of 160 boys and 121 girls and a nonclinical group of 269 boys and 182 girls. According to Shek (2002a, pp. 510, 512),

> Four different samples of clinical participants were included. . . . The first sample consisted of 114 participants (98 boys and 16 girls) attending schools admitting adolescents with behavioral and emotional problems. The second sample consisted of 123 participants (51 boys and 72 girls) whose families were currently receiving family counseling from family service centers because of family problems. . . . The third sample consisted of 22 female students who were receiving counseling services from school social workers because of family problems. The final sample consisted of 22 female adolescents who were out-patient, psychiatric patients suffering from nonpsychotic disturbances. The combination of participants in these four samples forms the clinical group.

The nonclinical group was based on 451 students from two schools. In contrast to the clinical group, these participants and their families never sought professional help due to family problems, nor had they received family counseling. The research design was comparative. One group with family problems was to be compared with another group that did not have family problems; and it was hypothesized that they would differ significantly in their responses to the FAD scales.

Study 3 included 3,649 adolescents in Hong Kong selected from 26 secondary schools by stratified random sampling, stratified on the ability of students. The research design was a cross-sectional survey at one point in time. The participants were from different geographic areas and socioeconomic classes in Hong Kong, with a mean age of 14 years.

For all of the studies, the relevant population was Chinese adolescents in Hong Kong. Study 3 included a representative sample. Study 2 served the purpose of demonstrating that the FAD could be used to discriminate clinical from nonclinical samples within the Hong Kong population. In addition, Study 1 provided descriptive information for a nonrepresentative sample of adolescents.

Data Analyses, Conclusions, and Implications

From Study 1, the FAD scales were regarded as reliable, being internally consistent at times 1 and 2 and temporally stable from time 1 to time 2. However, measures of internal consistency (alphas) for behavioral control (alpha at times 1 and 2 was .55) and affective responsiveness (alpha at time 1 was .57 and at time 2 was .61) were low. The FAD scale scores were substantially correlated with other measures of family functioning. The FAD scales were also significantly correlated with measures of trait anxiety, existential well-being, life satisfaction, and sense of mastery at times 1 and 2.

The results from Study 2 indicated there were significant differences between the clinical group and the nonclinical group, which provided evidence of known-groups validity. Results showed a consistency with Study 1, in that the FAD scale scores were significantly correlated with measures of family functioning and individual well-being, providing evidence for convergent validity.

Results of Study 3 on reliability and validity were consistent with those of Study 1. In addition, the author conducted a principal components factor analysis and derived three factors to represent the dimensionality of the FAD scales: emotion and communication, family pathology, and problem solving and family expectations. Moreover, it was shown that the factor structure was relatively stable across two random samples and for samples of male and female counterparts.

The author concludes that "these studies clearly demonstrate that the original and factor-derived scales of the Chinese FAD possess acceptable psychometric properties, although the structure of the Chinese FAD may be different from that based on the original English version" (Shek, 2002a, p. 520). Three implications are basically conceptual, methodological generalizations:

> First, the development of the Chinese FAD and the accumulation of research findings on the psychometric properties of the Chinese FAD enable social workers and family practitioners to assess family functioning in the Chinese culture. . . . The second implication of the present studies is that they reinforce the argument that it is necessary to validate Western family assessment measures when they are translated into other languages and used in a non-Western context. . . . The final implication is that social workers and clinical practitioners should be cautious in employing the related scales when the Chinese FAD is used. (pp. 520–521)

With respect to the knowledge objectives of the author, quantitative descriptions were provided and correlational hypotheses were supported for the local accidental and purposive samples in Study 1 but could not be generalized beyond these samples. Quantitative descriptions were provided and correlational hypotheses were supported for the community survey in Study 3 and were generalizable to the population of secondary school students in Hong Kong. The procedures of the tests are conceptually generalizable for use by social work researchers and, with caution, social work practitioners.

Classification of the Study

This study is classified as supranational for the following reasons.

- Literature is used from several countries regarding the methodology of the derivation, use, reliability, validity, and factor structures of the FAD scales.
- The Chinese scale is adapted from an English version of the FAD scales.
- The results of the studies are compared with those of studies from other countries with respect to consistencies and areas for further research.
- The literature from several countries is employed to explain the results obtained.
- The studies are conducted on samples of natives of Hong Kong, and the results are conceptually generalized to other countries when making comparisons to similar studies in those countries.

Issues Addressed in the Study

Ethics and Informed Consent

Prior to engaging people in research in the United States, it is necessary to provide them with knowledge about their rights to volunteer or not to participate in research. Potential participants must be informed of what risks, if any, are involved in the research, their rights to confidentiality, and that participation or nonparticipation in research does not have any consequences regarding treatment, the receipt of services from social agencies, and so on. Persons participating in research must give their informed consent, which means that they understand what the objectives of the research are and what they are required to do as research participants. Following these ethical notions, the researcher is faced with the possibility of losing people as research participants. This is evident in the research by Shek. In Study 1,

> the purpose of the study was presented, and confidentiality of the data collected was repeatedly emphasized, to all students in attendance on the day of testing. The students were asked to indicate their wish if they did not wish to participate in the study (i.e., "passive" informed consent was obtained from the students). They had to sign a consent form before completing the questionnaire. Because school participants normally treat participation in research studies as an educational activity, this method of obtaining consent from the participants is regarded as an acceptable and legitimate practice in the context of Hong Kong. A total of 15 students refused to participate in the study. (Shek, 2002a, p. 506)

Since 361 students responded in Study 1, the percentage of students lost is $15/361 + 15 = 15/376 = 4\%$. For this study, the loss of 4% would not necessarily alter the findings. However, a procedure that a researcher can follow, if any background data are available, is to compare the distributions of those participating with the distributions of those not participating. The more similar the distributions, the more likely it is that the results of the study are not significantly affected by the loss of subjects.

Shek employed the same procedures for obtaining informed consent for testing students in the schools for Studies 1, 2, and 3. For Study 2, in which a clinical sample was obtained, written consent was obtained for all clinical participants and their parents. There was no report of lost data in Study 2. In Study 3, there was only a 3% loss of potential participants.

Response Set

Another potential problem is the extent to which the research participants are honestly responding to the questionnaires. Just as there is "passive" informed consent, there can also be "passive" participation. For example, to the extent possible, participants would use noncommittal responses, such as the middle items of scales, "I don't know" responses, and so on, that is, what is termed "response set." One way to deal with this is to pilot test the questionnaire with a focus group that is representative of potential respondents, querying them about the questions and their responses, and then modifying the questionnaire accordingly.

Temporal Stability and Internal Consistency

Temporal stability refers to test-retest reliability, and internal consistency refers to the intercorrelation of test items at one point in time. Shek correctly points out that internal consistency computed by alpha coefficients is not sufficient if one is interested in assessing the effects of change over time. This can be seen by comparing test-retest reliabilities and alpha coefficients on 13 FAD scales, where one can see that 10 out of 13 test-retest reliabilities are lower than the alpha coefficients. For example, alpha for FAD is .91, while its test-retest reliability is .81. Hence researchers should use both forms of reliability in assessing changes over time.

It is common practice for researchers to quote one or more sources as to what should be considered as reliable. Obviously, based on a system of correlations ranging from 0 to 1, the higher the correlation, the higher the degree of reliability. Shek (2002a, p. 508) indicated that

> a scale must have an alpha level of .6 before it can be regarded as reliable. Based on this threshold standard, results showed that the FAD scales were basically internally consistent at Time 1 and Time 2, except that the alpha values for the Affective Responsiveness and Behavioral Control Subscales were not high. . . . The FAD scales were also found to be temporally stable.

Other investigators might have pointed to .7 or .8 as being acceptable. Rather than basing decisions of reliability on an arbitrary standard, the researcher should look into the meaning of the reliability for the particular research in which she or he is engaged. If the researcher, for example, is planning to use FAD as a measure of change for a family receiving social work intervention, the reliabilities should be as high as possible. Squaring the correlation coefficients gives some indication of the variance explained over time; hence a test-retest reliability of .6 explains 36% of the variance in scores over time, and a reliability of .8 explains 64% if the variance. The more unreliability, that is, variance not explained, the greater the likelihood that changes in the scores over time are due to measurement error.

Comparability of Groups in Known-Groups Analysis

In Study 2, Shek compared a clinical sample with a nonclinical sample on the FAD scales as a test of known-groups validity. Since the clinical sample is identified as having family problems and the nonclinical sample is considered as having no apparent family problems, it was reasoned that the two samples would score significantly differently on the FAD scales. As indicated, the clinical group showed a greater degree of pathology than the nonclinical group; the differences were statistically significant ($p < .001$), and the effect size was reported as .37. When comparing groups such as this, it is possible that other variables might be responsible for the observed changes in FAD. The task of the researcher is to show equivalence of the groups on other variables that are potentially related to the FAD scales. Shek (2002a, p. 512) followed this procedure and indicated that

> the findings further showed that the two groups did not differ in the background demographic and socioeconomic characteristics, including age (mean age = 15, SD =

1.5 for the clinical group and mean age = 15, SD = 1.6 for the nonclinical group), educational attainment (percentage of respondents studying Secondary 2 and below = 46% and 55% in the clinical group and nonclinical group, respectively), sex ratio (percentage of male respondents in the clinical group and nonclinical group = 57% and 60%, respectively), mean family monthly income (H.K. $20,429, SD = 14.407 for the clinical group and H.K. $18,680, SD = 9,880 for the nonclincial group), and number of persons in a household (4.4 persons, SD = 1.3 for the clinical group and 4.5 persons, S.D. = 1.2 for the nonclinical group).

For utilizers of research, the issue is to what extent the presumed known-groups validity of the FAD can be explained by other variables. If the FAD is to be used as an assessment device, social work practitioners would want to have confidence that the FAD is actually measuring what it is supposed to measure. One's confidence in the measuring device is increased when the researcher can demonstrate that the differences in test scores are not due to other variables.

Cultural Awareness

Data obtained on different cultural groups may be interpreted in different ways. It is important for social work researchers involved in international research to understand the culture of the research respondents. Shek demonstrates how his cultural awareness is used in an attempt to explain research findings within the context of Chinese culture:

> The alpha values with the Behavioral Control Scale in different samples were found not to be high. This finding is not consistent with the common observation that control is high in Chinese families. One possible explanation for this observation is in terms of the content of the items. When we examine the items in the Behavioral Control Scale, it was found that some of the items are related to reactions to emergencies. Because Chinese people do not place much emphasis on how to deal with emergencies, a situation in which family members do not know how to respond in emergencies does not mean that the family is not functioning well under the Chinese culture. (2002a, p. 518)

Shek also demonstrates cultural awareness in discussing why the Western FAD scale is highly correlated with an indigenous Chinese measure:

> One interesting point that should be discussed is that the magnitude of the correlation between the Chinese FAD scales and the indigenously developed measure (FAD) was quite high. This observation is contrary to the common expectation that Western measures may not be applicable to Chinese people because they are unique. There are two nonmutually exclusive explanations for this observation. First it is possible that the dimensions assessed by the FAD are important qualities of family functioning that are universally applicable. This explanation is plausible because qualities related to Roles, Behavioral Control and Problem Solving as assessed by the FAD are also emphasized by Chinese people as attributes of a happy family. . . . Second, because the participants in these studies are adolescents who are very much under the influence of Western culture and values, it can be conjectured that the FAD items, although originated in the West, are applicable to them. (2002a, pp. 518–519)

It is to be understood that these notions regarding Chinese culture and the cultural response to items in the FAD scales are essentially hypotheses. They are not findings based on the results of the study, but rather possible explanations that should be subjected to further research.

Issues Arising from the Study

Representativeness of Chinese Communities

Shek indicates that a limitation of his research is that it is based on adolescents in Hong Kong, and that it is not necessarily generalizable to other adolescents in Chinese communities, such as Chinese Americans. The issue of generalizability could be extended for other Chinese; those in Hong Kong are not necessarily representative of either adults or adolescents in different areas in Mainland China. People in rural areas may also have different customs and attitudes from those in urban areas. Moreover, different Chinese communities—for example, Chinese American, Chinese Canadian, and so on—may differ from each other with regard to their perceptions of family problems. Hence, to enhance generalizability, research should be conducted with different Chinese populations in different geographic areas.

It is unlikely that one could use probability sampling techniques to study all of the potential Chinese populations simultaneously, due to the costs involved, as well as the varying social political contexts of the Chinese communities. Hence one would resort to replicated studies with different aspects of Chinese communities selected in a purposive fashion (Shadish et al., 2002). To the extent that consistent results are obtained, the generalizability is increased.

It is also to be noted that the word "Western" is used ambiguously to refer to non-Chinese communities in the "Western" part of the world and/or to English-speaking research communities that are not Chinese speaking. Shek indicates there are differences in the results of factor analyses, in that his research produced three factors, while other researchers in other countries explained their factor structure with six or seven dimensions. Results from Canadian, American, and Dutch research were similar to each other, but different from Shek's results; however, results from Italian researchers were similar to those of Shek. Hence it appears that the generalization of non-Chinese cultures to Western cultures is unwarranted; especially since there appear to be differences among countries that might be considered to belong to Western culture. Is Italian culture Western? Or is it Chinese? Are Italian and American cultures similar or different? Are English, Canadian, and American cultures similar or different? Obviously, cultures are similar or different as a function of which particular characteristic or attribute—for example, language, attitudes, and so on—is considered.

Translation and Back-translation

A typical procedure that is employed when researchers adapt a research instrument from the language of another country to their own country is that of translation and back-translation. Shek used this procedure in creating a Chinese version of the FAD:

The Chinese version of the FAD was translated and back-translated into plain Chinese language by a research team with one social worker and two psychologists who are fluent in English and Chinese. Every effort was made to ensure that the translated version conveys both a literal and a comprehensive meaning in Chinese. With the exception of item 58 (not having reasonable means of transport), there was no substantial change in the content of the items. Consensus among the team members was required before any translated item was to be included in the final scale. (2002a, pp. 506–507)

The purpose of back-translation is to show that the process of translation does not depart from the original text (scales, items) that was translated. It is to reduce translation variance, that is, errors due to inappropriate translations. However, there is an assumption that language, its syntax, and its meaning are universal—equally understood among all genders, ethnic groups, ages, and so forth. In this particular research, the translators were educated adults. Since the population being addressed in the study is Hong Kong adolescents, the question arises as to whether they understood the item in the same way as the educated adults. This can be dealt with in two ways. (1) When the process of translation and back-translation is taking place, include one or two adolescents in the team of translators. There may be a common argot among adolescents that is unfamiliar to the adult translators, and this could be observed in the translation process. (2) After the scales are translated and ready to use, pilot test them on a representative sample of adolescents included in the research, for example, those who are designated as having lesser scholastic ability, as in Shek's study, those who have family problems, and those who do not have family problems. The researcher would be attentive to whether or not the intended meaning of the items is clear and understandable to those varying groups.

These observations indicate that it may be worthwhile and instructive for international researchers to conduct methodological studies of translation and back-translation. One could compare the possible distortion of using translations versus translations and back-translations. In addition, different groups of translators might be compared to determine whether there are differences that result from the literal meanings of words themselves and/or from different idiomatic expressions.

Factor Analysis

Shek used a principal components analysis to analyze the adolescents' responses to the FAD scales; and "eight factors with eigen values exceeding unity" accounted for 41% of the variance (2002a, pp. 514–515). He further used a scree test to reduce the eight factors to three factors.

Afifi and Clark (1990) say that principal components analysis "can be summarized as a method of transforming the original variables into new correlated variables. The new variables are called principal components." Kim and Mueller (1978, p. 11), in their discussion of factor analysis, distinguish between a common factor model and a principal components model, noting that "the principal components are certain mathematical functions of the observed variables while common factors are not expressible by the combination of the observed variables." In addition, Harmon (1960) has pointed out that there are different types of procedures for producing factor solutions, illustrating eight different types.

The issue here is whether or not different factor extraction models produce different factor structures. If so, then in comparing the results of factor analyses from one study to another, it is important to know whether the same procedure was employed. Shek indicated that he could not compare the results of many studies from the literature because the methods employed were not specified.

Method variance also occurs when different methods of rotating factors are employed to find "simpler and more easily interpretable factors" (Kim & Mueller, 1978, p. 28). As pointed out by Harman, there are a large number of methods that can be used for rotation. The method employed by Shek, varimax, is widely used, but there are others.

Apart from the methods of factor extraction and rotation, the interpretation of the factor structure is another issue. For example, Shek produced three factors, compared to six to eight in other studies. An obvious question for utilizers of research is whether the other researchers used the scree test, which reduced Shek's eight obtained factors to three. If they did not, then their results appear to be comparable to those obtained by Shek. The reader is referred to Norusis (1985), who describes the step-by-step procedure for conducting a factor analysis with Statistical Package for the Social Sciences (SPSS) programs. The point made here is that different factor solutions are produced by different extraction, rotation, and interpretation procedures, and one cannot compare different studies unless they employ the same procedures. Furthermore, differences in results of studies may be due to method variance.

Shek suggested that one could obtain an indication of stability of factor structures by taking two random samples of participants, discovering the factor structure for each sample, and then comparing them. To the extent that they produce similar structures, the factor structure for the population can be regarded as stable. However, this is not the same as temporal stability in the sense of stability over time. To further substantiate the consistency of factor structures, one could determine the factor structures of the same respondents over two time intervals. Temporal stability would be provided with consistent factor structures produced by the same methods of factor extraction, rotation, and interpretation.

Shek made the excellent suggestion that future factor analytic studies should be confirmatory rather than exploratory. In confirmatory factor analyses, the researcher uses a theoretical model and tests the model in the analysis of factors. Long (1983, p. 12) succinctly indicates the relative advantages of confirmatory factor analysis:

In the confirmatory factor model, the researcher imposes *substantively motivated* constraints. These constraints determine (1) which pairs of common factors are correlated, (2) which observed variables are affected by which common factors, (3) which observed variables are affected by a unique factor, and (4) which pairs of unique factors are correlated. Statistical tests can be performed to determine if the sample data are consistent with the imposed constraint or, in other words, whether the data *confirm* the substantively generated model. It is in this sense that the model is thought of as confirmatory.

STUDY 3: "MICROCREDIT AND EMPOWERMENT OF WOMEN," BY DEEPALI BAGATI (2003)

Study Description

Problem Formulation and Knowledge Objectives

The author reviewed the literature on microcredit programs, their evaluations, and empowerment of women, with particular reference to India, Bangladesh, and the United States. Providing the background for her study, she observed:

> With microcredit programs occupying center stage presently, the microcredit en- thusiasts across the world vow to provide such small loans to 100 million poorest families of the world by the year 2005, requiring at least $21 billion from govern- ments, aid organizations, commercial lenders, and other sources. . . . Such enthusi- asm toward spearheading the microcredit movement is based on numerous studies that have documented the positive impact of such programs. . . . However, not much is known about the empowerment experiences of the loan recipients, at the intimate level of the family. In addition, the increasing literature on female entrepreneurship and the informal sector casts an element of doubt on some of the explicit or implicit assumptions underlying the microcredit programs for women. (2003, p. 19)

Bagati examines assumptions underlying microcredit programs such as that the productive role of women can be used "as a strategy to instill changes in other tra- ditionally defined roles for women" (2003, p. 19) and that microcredit programs can provide women with experiences that will increase their bargaining power within their families.

The knowledge objective of her study is to develop ideas and hypotheses about ways microcredit programs can enhance the role and status of women within fami- lies. In particular, Bagati focused her exploratory case study on this question: "How do microcredit programs lead to empowerment of women at the household level?" (2003, p. 20). The rationale for her study is as follows.

- Most of the studies on microcredit programs have used income as an indi- cator of empowerment, ignoring other possible indicators.
- There have not been systematically conducted cross-cultural studies docu- menting different ways microcredit programs can result in empowerment for women.
- It is important to have a greater understanding of the extent to which women actually control and use the monies obtained from loans from microcredit programs.

- Many evaluations of microcredit programs have not investigated in depth the extent to which repayment of loans is an indication of program success.
- Evaluations of microcredit programs typically focus on economic indicators, ignoring "important concepts such as intrahousehold decision making, resource allocation, and control over the loan and subsequent income" (p. 21).

Instrumentation and the Process of Data Collection

The author conducted semistructured interviews, the contents of which were focused on gender roles (household, production, and reproduction) and bargaining power (decision-making and relative power) within the household. Bagati was interested in the meaning the female loan recipients and other adult members in the households attributed to their microcredit experience in this way:

> I conducted interviews twice—in a period of one year—with 33 respondents from the 18 sample households. The first phase of data collection spanned a period of 3 months, January 2000 to March 2000, with follow-up interviews being conducted after an interval of 6 to 9 months from August 2000 to October 2000. Considering the focus of this study was on the relative changes and renegotiations, if any, in women's bargaining power at the household level—with "change" being the key word—two rounds of interviewing allowed me to capture some element of flux in the sample households. (Bagati, 2001, p. 23)

> 6 to 9 months was the most feasible and useful gap between the two rounds of interviewing. I found that most loan recipients repaid their loans within a period of 6 to 9 months. It was during this period after the first loan, supposedly, that most loan recipients initiated or experienced various processes of adjustments related to their roles and bargaining power in their households. . . . What I aimed for was to bracket the assumed "high impact" period with early interviews, followed by re-interviews toward the end of the first loan cycle so as to understand the possible changes in the interpersonal dynamics within the household, specifically related to the gender role perceptions of these women and other adult household members. (p. 23)

> Data were collected in my native language of Hindi, and later transcribed into English. There were no more than three interviews in a week. Logistical issues related to the time and place for conducting these interviews were worked out according to the convenience of the respondents. I conducted all the interviews at the home of the respondent, interviewing all the adult members of each household separately to maintain confidentiality among them. (p. 23)

Sampling, Relevant Populations, and Research Design

The study site was a nongovernmental organization's microcredit program in the Inderpuri community in New Delhi, India. The program included five self-help groups, each consisting of 12–16 women. Each of the women was required to make a monthly savings of less than $1 to contribute to the group's saving pool. The members had access to the loans taken from the group's saving pool or to a loan from the microcredit program itself, designed to initiate an income-generating activity. The population was comprised of self-help groups created by microcredit programs in India; and for this study it consisted of adult women who participated in five self-help groups and their adult family members. The sample consisted of 18 loan recipients and 15 other adults in 18 households from two of the five self-help groups. The sample was a purposive sample that included different family types (nuclear, extended, and single-woman households) and loan recipients with two types of loan (from the group-savings pool, for an income-generating activity).

The research design was that of a longitudinal case study with semistructured interviews conducted over two points of time within an approximate period of one year. The sample households, for the most part, were of low income, "struggling to make ends meet"; and the loan recipients were semiliterate and "were engaged in contract work for export houses, worked as manual labor on daily wages, or had ironing stands in the neighborhood" (Bagati, 2003, p. 26).

Data Analyses, Conclusions, and Implications

Bagati developed code themes from the interview data from the first interviews to provide a conceptual framework for using NUD.IST 4.0 software to analyze the themes that appeared in her interviews. Qualitative software such as NUD.IST 4.0 can assist the researcher in managing and organizing text data. The researcher can browse data documents to create thematic codes and link them to the text. The codes (termed "nodes" in NUD.IST 4.0) may be organized in tree structures consisting of successive layers of themes and subthemes. The software can search the text for key words or phrases identified with each code. The software may be helpful in identifying patterns and refining analysis, as it allows the researcher to more quickly review codes and their associated text. Padgett (1998) provides a list of other software programs for analyzing qualitative research data, and she also indicates a number of additional readings on the topic of computer software in qualitative research.

The main nodes of the index tree that Bagati created in her use of the NUD.IST 4.0 software were:

- Factual information on the study sample
- Information on the microcredit program
- Data pertaining to household chores, role perceptions, and role satisfaction
- Attitudes related to gender roles
- Data related to household decision making

The findings of the study were grouped into three interrelated categories: using the microcredit loan for an economic activity; using the microcredit loan as a safety net; and taking proxy microcredit loans (i.e., loans that supported activities for other adult members of households). Of the 18 households studied, 7 used loans as a safety net, 2 started a home-based economic activity, and 6 took proxy loans. Bagati provided in-depth descriptions of the loan recipients and adult members of their households, indicating their struggles, uses of loans, and changing relationships. Bagati asserted that the empowerment experiences of the loan recipients differed but could be understood by referring to their starting points:

> The starting point of loan recipients is based on the cultural context and the social situation of each woman. According to the interview data of the present study, this starting point, in the journey to empowerment, was found to be a function of four interrelated factors: (a) the gender role perceptions in the loan recipients' families; (b) the familial support offered to them; © the need for additional income in their household; and (d) their skill set for starting an economic activity. These four factors interacted in a variety of combinations to explain how INDCARE's microcredit program took the form it did, and how despite being on the threshold of poverty, not many loan recipients started an economic activity with their microcredit loan. (2003, p. 30)

The author concluded with hypotheses regarding the relationship of microcredit and the empowerment of women being moderated by the starting points of women in the process of empowerment. In addition, it was hypothesized that microcredit programs can enhance the empowerment of women who are loan recipients by employing appropriate support mechanisms such as literacy classes, gender awareness classes for men, and so forth. These hypotheses obviously would need testing in subsequent research.

Classification of the Study

This study is classified as supranational for the following reasons.

- Literature from India, Bangladesh, and the United States is employed to form the research problem, exploring the relationship between microcredit programs and the empowerment of women.
- Literature from several countries is used to support and qualify observations made in the exploratory case study.
- Implications are drawn as to how microcredit programs could enhance the empowerment of women.
- Implications for evaluating microcredit programs are drawn; in particular, the author indicates that multiple outcome variables should be employed. This is corroborated by the literature from several countries.
- The study takes place with one native population within one country.

Issues Addressed in the Study

Conceptualization of Empowerment

Empowerment is a multifaceted concept, as is illustrated in Bagati's review of the literature. Different scholars have defined empowerment differently:

> Some scholars ... highlight the power relations at the household level as being central to the process of empowering women.... To make any sustainable change in the role and status of women it is necessary to understand the ideology involved in the power relations between men and women.... Any attempts at empowering

women to reduce gender inequities, at any level, include a component of conscious-
ness-raising. . . . Other scholars . . . define empowerment of women in the context of
women and development such that empowerment is related to opportunities available and choices made by women. . . . Empowerment of women is also related to the
ability of women to make these choices. . . . Empowerment of women is the ability
of women to exercise power in their concrete everyday experiences. . . . Since the
ability of women to make choices and exercise power is grounded in social, political, and cultural institutions, women have varying degrees of ability to make choices.
. . . Empowerment is also synonymous with self-reliance. (Bagati, 2003, pp. 21–22)

To further illustrate the complexity of the concept of empowerment, Andrews,
Guadalupe, and Bolden (2003) generated empowerment perspectives from a qualitative study of poor rural women in the United States, and as a result of their study,
they developed this definition of empowerment:

Empowerment is a personal and/or collective capacity that grows from personal
attributes, supportive connections among people, faith in the spiritual realm, and
access to resources for human needs. The empowered person has personal attributes
of optimism, persistence, will to surrender past burdens and relationships, trust in
others, and faith in a power beyond oneself. The empowerment process can begin
with contact between a person who seeks personal change and at least one other who
is willing to share part of the journey toward change. The person's attributes are
brought out by this connectedness; relationships are key to the emergence of personal capabilities. These dimensions of power are not linear, but transactional and
interdependent. Losses of power can stem from nonsupportive relationships in which
resources or entitlements are withheld or restricted. Obstacles to power can be overcome through mutual support that elicits the personal attributes. (2003, p. 16)

The issue for researchers is how does one operationalize a multidimensional
concept for which there is not a consensus as to how it should be defined. Bagati
indicated that income is one indicator of the concept, but there are also other indicators, such as the extent to which women are involved in decisions in the management of a household. Researchers can deal with the issue of complex concepts by
continuing to conduct exploratory studies to further develop the concept, locating
other indicators; they might conduct different studies in which different indicators
are employed; and they might conduct studies in which multiple indicators of empowerment are used simultaneously. The implication for utilization of research is
that one needs to be very careful to note what indicators are used and to accumulate the results of studies in reference to the same indicators of empowerment.
Moreover, if the concept is too complex to operationalize, the researcher may sub-
divide the concept into subconcepts and then develop indicators for the subconcepts of empowerment.

The Use of Purposive Sampling

Rubin and Babbie (2005) indicate that purposive sampling is based on the researcher's
knowledge of the population, the purpose of the research, and judgment as to what
is the best way to generate hypotheses. Typical contrasting and deviant cases of a

phenomenon might be employed to enrich one's understanding. Bagati selected her study sample not to be representative of all those who received loans, but rather to select them in such a way that she could discover processes that occur in obtaining and repaying loans:

> The study sample was purposely selected to include loan recipients who had taken the savings loan as well as others who had taken the employment based loan. Only those women were selected in the sample that were married and took their first loan within a 3-month period prior to their first interview. For the loan recipients se-lected in the employment-based loan category, there was an additional criterion of having no prior history of being engaged in any economic activity. In addition, the final sampling criterion was that all the adult members from the short-listed house-holds agreed to participate in the study. (2003, p. 20)

Since Bagati's study has the purpose of developing ideas about the relationship of microcredit programs to the enhancement of the role and identity of women who participate, the sample is not expected to be representative of all of those involved in loan programs. The issue for utilizers of research is to realize this is this is the case and not to generalize the results from a series of exploratory studies to all loan recipients, unless the generalizations are at the level of hypothesis formulation.

Credibility in Qualitative Research

A qualitative research study should overcome, to the extent possible, three threats to credibility: reactivity, researcher bias, and respondent bias. According to Padgett (1998, p. 92),

> reactivity refers to the potentially distorting effects of the qualitative researcher's pres-ence in the field. . . . A second source of distortion comes from the researcher's biases. The temptation to filter one's observations and interpretations through a lens clouded by preconceptions and opinions can plague even the most meticulously designed and well-intentioned qualitative study. . . . Finally, we have the threat that comes from respondents' biases. Respondents may withhold information and even lie to protect their privacy or to avoid revealing some unpleasant truths. At the other extreme, they may try to be "helpful" and offer answers that they believe we want to hear.

Bagati nicely illustrates how she employed the strategies of prolonged engage-ment and triangulation in an attempt to deal with the issue of credibility of her study:

> By the time actual data collection started, I was a familiar face in the community almost expected to be there. In addition, by successfully communicating the nature of the study and the need to tape-record interviews, I was able to minimize defen-siveness on the part of the respondents. . . . My presence in the field may have raised some subtle kinds of reactivity, such as encouragement to express more "modern" sentiments to a researcher from the United States. . . . I minimized researcher bias by following simple procedures such as using a predetermined sample selection cri-terion. This ensured that the respondents were not deliberately chosen, as the ones who would say what I wanted to hear. Also, I guarded against my own emotional pitfalls by spacing interviews in time, taking breaks from the field when the going

got intense or physically tiring, and by adhering to the interview agenda.... In terms of preventing respondent bias from regarding me as a friend or helper rather than a researcher, I was up-front about my role in the community—identifying myself as a researcher who was there for data collection.... Data were collected only after a trusting relationship had evolved with the respondents making them less likely to withhold information or lie. Triangulation—combining the interview data with corroborating information collected from the cluster leaders and the INDCARE staff—further reduced respondent bias. (2003, p. 24)

Issues Arising from the Study

The Use of Computerized Programs to Develop Categories

Bagati discussed how she first developed categories from the data obtained from the first interviews, and then used the NUD.IST 4.0 software for further developing categories from both the first and second interviews. The issue raised here is what are the relative advantages and disadvantages of using or not using computerized software. Obviously, if there are an extremely large number of categories, the computerized software can be more efficient. But it is the investigator who must discover and ascertain the relationship between categories, leading to the generation of hypotheses. To provide possible solutions to this issue, we suggest that methodological studies should be conducted to determine the kinds of hypotheses that can be generated from computerized and noncomputerized analyses of categories from data from semistructured interviews. One could employ criteria such as the number and range of hypotheses, the relevancy of hypotheses, the researchability of hypotheses, and the amount of time taken to generate hypotheses. Moreover, different researchers can be compared within both types of analyses, computer-aided or not, to determine the extent to which there is variability among the researchers with respect to either of the procedures.

A Priori versus a Posteriori Evaluation

A priori evaluation is based on the development of criteria for evaluating the program in relation to its objectives and then gathering data in relation to those criteria. For example, in microcredit studies that have the objective of increasing the income potential of loan recipients, data are gathered about the extent to which loan recipients used the microcredit loan amount to start an economic activity. As a result of Bagati's study, she says,

> if one were to consider only the economic form of empowerment using income as an indicator, then in the context of the present study only those loan recipients were "empowered" who were engaged in an income-generation activity. In the entire sample of loan recipients, only four women constitute the "empowered" lot. (2003, p. 32)

A posteriori evaluation is based on the development of criteria for evaluating a program after it has been completed. This is illustrated in Bagati's analysis of the 14 loan recipients who would have been considered disempowered in the a priori evaluation:

I am putting forth the argument that besides "income" and "economic independence" as indicators of empowerment, there are other equally important criteria for identifying empowerment. More important, earlier on in the journey to empowerment, "empowerment" is defined in the context of efforts or instances where the loan recipients attempted to alter their attitudes, status, self perceptions, or gender roles. ... These "noneconomic" forms of empowerment are based on the starting point of the loan recipient. ... Using the concept of different starting points, I argue that whether it was the patriarchal set up preventing the woman from stepping out of the house (Meenu), or it was the need for additional income to feed the children since the man of the house was a drunkard (Rukmini Devid), or it was a matter of feeling useful and important in the family so as to enhance one's status (Kamlesh, Maina Devi and Harrawat), all the loan recipients questioned their own specific structures, and put in motion mechanisms to change it in nonthreatening ways. Therefore, most loan recipients in the sample were empowered in the context of their "starting point." (2003, p. 32)

The issue highlighted here is that different results can be obtained as a function of different indicators of the concept of empowerment (see the earlier section "The Conceptualization of Empowerment") and when those indicators are identified, before or after a program is implemented. Obviously, if criteria are not specified beforehand, the evaluator may be in the position of searching for indicators of success; the more inventive the evaluator, the greater are the chances that the program may be considered successful. To avoid this problem, the exploratory research here should be thought of as pointing out other criteria that should be applied in subsequent a priori evaluations of microcredit programs. The more criteria that are used in an evaluation, the more comprehensive it is. It should be pointed out that most evaluations are not completely comprehensive and the delineation of criteria are a result of agreements among the stakeholders such as program sponsors, providers, and recipients, as to which criteria should be employed in an evaluation.

Translation from Hindi to English

In this study, Bagati indicated that her native language is Hindi but that she is fluent in English, working in the United States. She conducted semistructured interviews in Hindi, and then translated the interviews into English. There is no apparent problem with respect to language translation because the purpose of the study is to generate insights and ideas. Although complete accuracy is desirable, the lack of it would not necessarily detract from hypothesis development. In contrast, if the study were intending to provide quantitative descriptions and test correlational hypotheses, language translation might be an issue. The methodological issue that arises is whether the actual translated transcripts would be similar or different in comparisons of translations by a single investigator purportedly fluent in the language with a team of data collectors, translators, and back-translators. The approaches could be compared on costs and efficiency as well as accuracy. Those who were interviewed would be the judges as to whether or not the translations are accurate; this could be determined in either a focus group or in interviews with the individual participants. Questions might arise as to whether interviewers fluent in the language came from the same area of the country as the respondents and were versed in the idiomatic expressions and syntax of the respondents. In other words, linguistic studies may indicate whether bilingual interviewers are, indeed, more accurate and less costly than the employment of translators to translate ✎nd back-translate interview data (which is the apparent "common-sense" assumption that is often made). Our point of view is that issues such as this should be resolved methodologically so that researchers receive the best advice possible for conducting studies.

Respondents' Perceptions

In this study the researcher was female and her native language, Hindi, was apparently similar to that of the respondents. She interviewed all respondents, female and male, separately in their households to preserve the confidentiality of the interviews. The procedure was straightforward and sufficient for the researcher to collect and analyze data with respect to uncovering new concepts and relationships, such as the notion of a starting point and the extent to which it moderates relationships between activities. However, it is possible that the perceptions of the respondents can be affected by characteristics of the interviewer, instructional sets of the interview, characteristics of the respondent, where the interview takes place, and so on. Responses may vary as a function of the gender, ethnicity, nationality, religion, age, and status of the interviewer. Or they may vary with respect to respondents' age, marital status, gender, religion, relative income level, and so on. The purpose of the interview may be explained to the respondent as research; however, if respondents believe the researcher is a representative of the program being evaluated, they may fear that the status of their loans may be in jeopardy. Moreover, interviewing respondents in their homes may produce different responses from interviewing them in other places.

The issue presented here is that the decisions of researchers in collecting data are often arbitrary and not necessarily based on sound methodological knowledge. Seasoned researchers may make their decisions on the basis of their experience as to what practices help them to achieve their research goals. Methodological studies of the decisions that researchers make and comparative studies of the effectiveness of different alternatives can assist us in developing research strategies and methods that are based on evidence. Just as one would argue that social work practice should be based on evidence, one could assert that social work research should also be based on evidence, that is, evidence-based research.

STUDY 4: "PUBLIC PERCEPTIONS OF SOCIAL WELFARE SERVICES IN CYPRUS," BY SAVVAS GEORGIADES AND MIRIAM POTOCKY-TRIPODI (2000)

Study Description

Problem Formulation and Knowledge Objectives

This study took place in Cyprus, which is the third largest island in the Mediterranean and has a population of approximately 725,000. The authors indicate that by 1973, every Cypriot was eligible for financial assistance for the maintenance of a minimum standard of living and the satisfaction of basic needs, and was provided access to social services for dealing with personal problems and for improving living conditions. . . . The Department of Social Welfare Services, under the Ministry of Labour and Social Insurance (MLSI), is the designated body accountable for the provision and promotion of social welfare services. (Georgiades & Potocky-Tripodi, 2000, pp. 139–140)

Four service divisions of the Department of Social Welfare Services provide social services: Family Welfare and Social Services, Public Assistance and Services for the Elderly, Community Development, and Training and Research. In addition, nongovernmental programs such as day care centers, health clinics, family and individual counseling services, nursing homes, and so on also provide social services.

According to the authors, the objectives of their research were to answer these questions: "What are the public perceptions about social welfare services in Cyprus? . . . Which social welfare services in Cyprus are perceived by the public to need most improvement? . . . What solutions for improving social welfare services in Cyprus are offered by the public? (Georgiades & Potocky-Tripodi, 2000, p. 141). These three objectives are essentially to yield quantitative descriptions. Two further objectives were to "identify the effects of gender, age, educational attainment, and level of personal experience with the services upon public perceptions" and to explore "whether the relationships between personal characteristics and public opinion that have been found in the United States also extend to another country" (p. 141). The researchers were interested in testing correlational hypotheses and in providing possible evidence of generalizability.

These objectives for research were formulated after the authors reviewed literature pertaining to social welfare services in the United States, Cyprus, Zaire, Guinea, Kenya, and the Philippines. Their rationale for the study is as follows.

- Since there were few efforts to evaluate social services in Cyprus, this study was envisioned as a starting point for evaluating social services.
- The research focused on public perceptions of social welfare services for these reasons: "First, social services cannot exist and be deemed viable in the absence of community sanction. . . . Second, the public has electoral power that could influence the government's decision to continue, increase or decrease funding for these services. . . . Third, research from a variety of countries . . . suggests that public use of social services can be predicted on the basis of public perceptions about the services and providers. . . . And lastly, in the limited geographic context of a small country like Cyprus, the public is highly likely to know individuals who have received social welfare services, and therefore can give relatively detailed accounts of the latter's experiences and perceptions" (Georgiades & Potocky-Tripodi, 2000, p. 141).
- Research in the United States has shown relationships of gender, age, education, and personal experiences of social welfare services with public and consumer opinion.
- The substantive and methodological knowledge produced from this study may be useful in other countries.

Instrumentation and the Process of Data Collection

The data were collected by telephone interviews conducted by Savvas Georgiades, a Cypriot native. Respondents were randomly chosen from the Nicosia telephone directory, were guaranteed confidentiality, and were told that their participation was voluntary. Interviews were conducted in the evenings from 6:00 to 9:00 p.m. with persons 18 years or older. Interviewees were told that the objective of the interview was to obtain public perceptions about social welfare services in Cyprus. The interview schedule was divided into three sections. The first section consisted of 10 questions about social welfare services, and the respondents were asked to rate the extent to which they rated their perceptions of each question as favorable on a random scale of 1, least favorable, to 10, most favorable. Examples of the 10 questions are:

> How would you rate: 1. The social welfare services in Cyprus in terms of their organization? . . . 4. The effectiveness of social welfare services in Cyprus? . . . 10. The need for the government to assist the social welfare department with additional funding for the improvement of social welfare services in Cyprus? (Georgiades & Potocky-Tripodi, 2000, p. 143)

The second section of the instrument included three open-ended questions:

> 1. What do you think are the positive characteristics of social welfare services in Cyprus today? 2. Which services do you think are not delivered sufficiently by the Social Welfare Department in Cyprus and for what reasons do you think so? 3. Overall, what needs to be done to improve the social welfare services in Cyprus? (p. 144)

The third section contained questions on demographics and the respondents' experiences with social welfare services. The duration of each interview was approximately from 10 to 20 minutes.

Sampling, Relevant Populations, and Research Design

The sample of 168 Greek Cypriots was randomly drawn from the Nicosia telephone directory, with 56 refusing to participate in the research, for a response rate of 67%. The population from which the sample was drawn consists of Greek Cypriots who are residents of Nicosia, the capital of Cyprus, have listed phone numbers in the Nicosia telephone directory, who themselves were available or had a family member available to answer the telephone between the hours of 6:00 to 9:00 p.m., and are 18 years of age or older. Other relevant populations include the census population of Nicosia and the population of Cyprus.

The research design was that of a cross-sectional survey. It was conducted at one point in time with no questions repeated over time, as in replicated cross-sectional or longitudinal studies. The basic intent of the study was to be able to generalize findings of quantitative descriptions and correlations from the sample to residents of Nicosia, and to generalize the methodological procedures and substantive findings as hypotheses to Cyprus and to other nations.

Data Analyses, Conclusions, and Implications

Mean ratings of the extent to which the respondents favored questions about social welfare services ranged from 3.6, need to educate the public, to 8.7, need for more governmental funding for social welfare services (1 is least favorable and 10 is most favorable); all of the other items received average ratings, from 5.1 to 6.4. The responses to open-ended questions were categorized into four main areas: services' strengths, services that need major improvements, service improvement recommendations, and more humanistic services. Seventy percent or more of the respondents indicated the following: there should be more/better information about services (81%); the delivery of services should be based on merit (79%); a strength of social welfare services is the focus on alleviating human suffering and improving living conditions (74%), and another strength is that there is provision of significant assistance to some people (72%).

Regression analyses with age, gender, education, and service experience as predictor variables were conducted with each of the favorableness ratings for the 10 service attributes. The regression model predicted statistically significant amounts of variance for all 10 items, ranging from 12% of the variance in favorableness about social workers' qualifications to 30% for service quality and 31% for service objectiveness. Service experience was significantly inversely related to 9 out of 10 favorableness ratings; education was significantly directly related to 7 out of 10 favorableness ratings; females were more likely to be favorable than males in 9 out of 10 ratings; and age was not significantly related to any of the 10 items.

The authors essentially achieved their objectives of providing quantitative descriptions and testing correlational hypotheses in the context of Nicosia and of describing the methods of their study so that they can be conceptually generalized.

The findings of this study, particularly the respondents' own recommendations, suggest that to improve public perceptions the social welfare department in Cyprus should:

- Disseminate more and better quality information about its services;
- Enhance humanistic and meritocratic treatment of clients; re-evaluate its services, especially those targeting elderly and children;
- Generate more governmental funding that will allow for the appointment of more and better qualified direct service staff;
- Maintain ongoing staff training and development; and
- Encourage and support research efforts that aim to inform direct services practice through such initiatives as needs assessments, quality assurance studies, and outcome evaluations.

(Georgiades & Potocky-Tripodi, 2000, pp. 148–149)

The authors also utilized research from other countries as well as their own findings to provide international implications:

Although the findings of the study bear implications primarily for Cyprus, the methodology used herein can be adopted in other countries that have a similar dearth of research on social services. This study has demonstrated the feasibility of the random telephone survey as a starting point for evaluation of social welfare systems in settings where research efforts may be constrained by limited resources. Further, this study provided evidence of limited generalizability of relationships between personal characteristics and public perceptions of social services. Some of these relationships which had previously been established in the United States were confirmed in this study, whereas, others were not. Thus, similar research in other countries would be useful to further establish the cross-national validity of these findings. (Georgiades & Potocky-Tripodi, 2000, p. 149)

Classification of the Study

This is a supranational research study because:

- The authors used literature from several countries to formulate the problem for research and to develop the methodology for the study.
- The research studied a native, Greek Cypriot population.
- One of the authors was a native Greek Cypriot, and he conducted telephone interviews in Cyprus.
- The authors compared their correlation and regression analyses of predictors of ratings of social welfare services with those of other countries.
- The literature of several countries was utilized in forming international implications.

Issues Addressed in the Study

The Importance of Conducting a Pilot Study

It is recommended in research textbooks that a pilot study be conducted before employing questionnaires or interview schedules in a survey (Rubin & Babbie, 2005). However, many investigators in the press of time—that is, to obtain results as soon as possible—ignore this procedure. Georgiades and Potocky-Tripodi in their research clearly indicate the advantages of a pilot study.

First, the pilot test was employed to test the procedure for selecting the sample:

initially, 30 individuals were randomly selected for a pilot study. From these, 9 individuals (3 men, 6 women) refused participation while the remaining 21 individuals (6 men, 15 women) provided feedback upon which the study procedure was finalized. The age range of the pilot study respondents was 21–63 and their mean age was 40 years. (Georgiades & Potocky-Tripodi, 2000, p. 142)

The response rate for the pilot study, 21 out of 30 (70%), gives an indication of what the response rate might be in the actual study. The response rate in the complete study was 112 out of 168 (67%). In addition, some information regarding characteristics of the sample is provided. In the pilot study, 15 out of 21 of the respondents who remained in the sample were women (71%), compared to 64% women obtained in the sample for study. The mean age in the pilot test was 40, with a range of 21–63, compared to a mean age of 41 with an age range of 18 to 70 in the sample.

Second, the pilot test provided information on the clarity of the rating scales in the interview schedule:

> As a result of the pilot study, it was determined that the study procedure was clearer to participants when they were asked to rate the research items on a 10-point scale as opposed to a 5-point scale. This is probably because use of the 10-point scale is more widely reinforced by Cyprus's educational system and culture. (Georgiades & Potocky-Tripodi, 2000, p. 143)

Third, information was provided on the length of the interview:

> The second stage of the interview involved open-ended items. These items were field-tested in the pilot study and were determined to be unambiguous and captivating of respondents' interest. The pilot study initially utilized 5 questions. However, it was observed that the length of the interview was overwhelming to participants when 5 open-ended questions were used, and therefore 2 open-ended questions were excluded from the final interviews. (Georgiades & Potocky-Tripodi, 2000, pp. 143–144)

Checking for the Representativeness of the Sample

It is recommended that characteristics of a sample be compared with characteristics of the population from which a sample is drawn. This is due to the fact that some samples will not be representative of the population, even when the samples are randomly selected. For example, 5 out of 100 random samples will not be representative of the population (i.e., not within the + 2 standard deviation margin of error) when the confidence level is 95%. However, in order to check the representativeness of the sample, the characteristics of the population must be known, that is, the characteristics of all of those listed in the Nicosian telephone directory. Since that information was not available, a proxy was employed, that is, data from the 1992 census of Nicosia:

> According to the most recent (1992) census, Nicosia had a population of 177,451 residents, of whom 89,889 (50.7%) were females and 87,562 (49.3%) were males. Therefore the present study sample is overrepresented by females (63.4%). In addition, the sample underrepresents the elderly, as only 8.1% of participants were over age 60, compared to 14.0% in the Nicosia population. Finally, the study sample seems to be more highly educated, compared to the Nicosia population. . . . The disproportionate figures for educational level could be explained by the fact that the comparable population figures included only university and college graduates whereas the sample figures involve both partial and full completion of these two levels of higher education. Another complication involved in these comparisons is that the educational figures provided by the Nicosia census are pertinent for individuals 15 years old and older, whereas the study did not include individuals younger than 18. . . . Lastly, no individuals without any schooling responded to the study, despite their presence in the Nicosia population. It may be speculated that such individuals were working during the study hours (6:00 P.M.–9:00 P.M.) or that they were more disinclined to provide consent for study participation. (Georgiades & Potocky-Tripodi, 2000, pp. 142–143)

Generalizability

The researchers also point out additional problems related to the generalizability of the study sample. These problems are critical for utilizers of research who might assume complete representativeness simply because a random sample is drawn. Checking for representativeness and analyzing relevant populations provide information that has a direct bearing on conclusions and implications of a study:

> Caution is warranted when generalizing the findings of this study to the entire Cypriot population. This study was conducted in an urban milieu. Research from the United States shows that individuals in rural contexts have less favorable attitudes toward social welfare services and providers. . . . Therefore, it may be illegitimate to assume that the information generated by this study applies identically to the rural population of Cyprus.
>
> Another attribute of the study that limits its external validity is that only individuals with telephone numbers listed in the directory were interviewed. This strategy leaves out individuals who opt not to have their telephone numbers listed in the directory (1% of Nicosia residents) as well as individuals who lack personal telephones. . . .
>
> These excluded individuals may differ in important ways from the participants. For example, individuals without personal phones may live in more impoverished conditions and/or may be more socially isolated than the rest of the population. (Georgiades and Potocky-Tripodi, 2000, p. 148)

Issues Arising from the Study

Evaluation of Social Welfare Services and Providers

Part of the rationale for this study was based on the inference from research studies in several countries that "public use of social services can be predicted on the basis of public perceptions about the services and providers" (Georgiades & Potocky-Tripodi, 2000, p. 141). An evaluation of public perceptions provides useful information for Nicosia social welfare agencies; however, in future research, evaluations directed at different populations might provide data that could be used to increase the comprehensiveness of evaluations. A survey, for example, could be directed at those who actually were in contact with social welfare services, that is, more disadvantaged populations, who received social welfare services. One issue concerns the extent to which public perceptions of welfare services actually are predictive of the users of those services. Results of a survey of users can be compared with a survey of public perceptions to validate the extent to which public perceptions of social welfare services in Nicosia are actually predictive of use of the services.

Studies of the users of social services can provide information on the extent to which social welfare programs meet the needs of Greek Cypriots in Nicosia. Still another target of evaluation is that of the service providers. Are the perceptions of social welfare providers congruent with those who use social services? If the results of public perception of social welfare providers and social welfare recipients are consistent, the confidence in the results of the evaluation could be increased. If the results are not consistent, the issue for social welfare managers is how to reconcile different perspectives of different stakeholders. Questions like these might be important considerations for future social welfare planning and research: Are Cypriots who are eligible to receive services receiving them; if not, why not? To what extent are the services that are provided actually meeting the social welfare needs of recipients? Would an increase of public awareness about social welfare service result in an increased use of social welfare services?

Use of Other Sampling Methods

The authors indicate that there are relative advantages for the use of random sampling from a telephone directory. It provides an indication of the general public's perceptions of social welfare services at minimal costs and serves as a basis for raising questions about future research and planning. In discussing the limitations of the study the researchers say:

> in the Greek culture expression of feelings about personal matters, especially dissatisfaction and needs, to strangers is not encouraged. . . . It may be that the chosen study procedure did not generate as much information as could have been produced by more personal approaches, such as rapport-building strategies followed by face-to-face interviews. (Georgiades & Potocky-Tripodi, 2000, p. 148)

More personal approaches might also have been used in selecting the sample, particularly those who are disadvantaged and may not have the use of telephones. However, other techniques like snowball sampling and purposive sampling (Rubin & Babbie, 2005) are less likely to produce representative samples. One suggestion is to combine sampling strategies. Random sampling from a telephone directory would be supplemented by random sampling from the records of social welfare agencies; in addition, snowball sampling might be employed to obtain information from those who are hard to reach. Methodological studies comparing the results and the costs of different methods would be useful for the Training and Research Division of the Department of Social Welfare Services in Cyprus.

The Reliability and Validity of Content Analysis

The researchers indicated that the content analysis of qualitative data, that is, analyzing the responses of open-ended questions, was conducted by one person; hence the reliability and validity of the analysis is unknown. Recall that, in the analysis, responses to open-ended questions were categorized into services' strengths, services that needed major improvements, service improvement recommendations, and more humanistic services. In addition, within each category the frequency of participants' responses was tabulated. Therefore, there are two domains where reliability of the categories needs to be established. First, would different investigators derive the same categories? Second, would different observers agree with the content analysis on the count of frequencies of items within each category? An indication of reliability would be the extent to which different investigators who independently analyze the data agree (percentage agreement) in their categories and frequency counts. The information from the content analysis can be partially validated by comparing the responses on open-ended questions (e.g., service providers try hard to help) to responses to similar questions that would be asked of service providers and service recipients.

It is obvious that the reliability and validity of the content analysis is extremely important; for it is in this analysis that recommendations were made for improving social welfare services. The purpose of reliable and valid information is to ensure that the conclusions are not simply due to possible biases of the researchers.

STUDY 5: "INTEGRATION AND TARGETING OF COMMUNITY CARE FOR PEOPLE WITH SEVERE AND ENDURING MENTAL HEALTH PROBLEMS: USERS' EXPERIENCES OF THE CARE PROGRAMME APPROACH AND CARE MANAGEMENT," BY JOHN CARPENTER, JUSTINE SCHNEIDER, FAYE MCNIVEN, TOBY BRANDON, RICHARDS STEVENS, AND DAVID WOOFF (2004)

Study Description

Problem Formulation and Knowledge Objectives

Mental illness is a world health problem, and Carpenter and colleagues (2004) set their study within that context, noting that countries such as Australia, Sweden, the United States, and the United Kingdom are interested in improving the coordination of mental health services. In England, two methods of coordination of community mental health services were introduced in the early 1990s: the care program approach (CPA) in health services and care management in social services. The authors point out that

> the English Department of Health . . . has consistently urged the integration of health and social care in policy and practice, emphasizing that the two systems are based on a common approach: systematic assessment, and agreed plan of care and treatment, the allocation of a case worker/case manager and regular reviews. The key principles include multidisciplinary teamworking, involving carers, and . . . the involvement of users in their own care and treatment. (Carpenter et al., 2004, p. 315)

The objectives of this study were to provide generalizable information from the perspectives of users with severe mental problems, such as schizophrenia, bipolar disorder, and severe depression, about the achievement of CPA and care management functions and the implementation of their key operative principles. The researchers were also interested in studying the relationship of different patterns of service organization and the users' perceptions of service implementation. The patterns of service organization were based on the integration of CPA and case management versus discrete services; and targeting, a service strategy focused on users with severe and enduring mental health problems, versus inclusive services for all users. In addition, the researchers believed that the models of coordination could be conceptually generalized to other countries. In essence, the researchers aimed to provide quantitative descriptions and correlational hypotheses that could be generalized within an English context and that could be generalized as hypotheses for other countries.

The rationale for this study is as follows.

- The researchers believe the perceptions of users of mental health services are important for designing and evaluating those services.
- There "have been few large-scale studies, nationally or internationally of users' views of community mental health services" (Carpenter et al., 2004, p. 314).
- Data from available larger studies have involved nonrandom samples and are, therefore, nongeneralizable.
- Previous studies of users did not provide any information "about the users' experiences of care planning and the extent to which 'involvement' included, for example, their own views being listened to and acted on, whether they had any choice, or whether the agreed plans were realized and successful" (p. 316).
- "In England, there have been few published studies of users' views of the CPA and care management, although some unpublished local audits have been completed" (p. 316). Those local audits were based on convenience samples and were not generalizable.

Instrumentation and the Process of Data Collection

Services users were interviewed by independent research workers at two points in time, six months apart. Users were asked 35 questions that dealt with their experiences of care planning and choices they were able to make regarding their services, relationships with key workers and knowledge of their medication, dissatisfaction and complaints, their views of care programs, and their views of family involvement. The authors reported: "Questions included factual ones (e.g., Were you given a copy of your care programme?') as well as five-point Likert-type rating scales with comment boxes (e.g. 'Do you feel that you have been encouraged by professionals to say what your problems and needs are?')" (Carpenter et al., 2004, p. 318).

Sampling, Relevant Populations, and Research Design

The researchers used stratified random sampling. First they chose four districts in northern England where they judged the local CPA and care management as "in place for at least three years" and "having assessment forms and substantial local policy and practice guidance" (Carpenter et al., 2004, p. 318). In addition, the four districts were chosen on the basis of scores on the dimensions of integrated, discrete, targeted, and inclusive that were used to classify the districts with these patterns of service organizations: District A (discrete/targeted), District B (discrete/inclusive), District C (integrated/targeted), and District D (integrated/inclusive).

Within each of the four districts, users with severe and enduring mental health problems

> were randomly selected from the computerized data bases of the caseloads of community mental health workers. In accordance with the requirements of the Local Research Ethics Committee, permission to approach the users had first to be obtained from the user's consultant psychiatrist and general practitioner, who could exclude patients in crisis, at risk of hospital admission, or whom they believed were potentially dangerous to researcher interviewers. Participating users were seen at home or in a service setting as they chose, and were offered an honorarium of 10 pounds per interview. (p. 318)

The population of users was, therefore, comprised of users in northern England districts chosen by the researchers as well established and who were given permission by local psychiatrists to participate in the research. Other relevant populations would be users of community mental health services in northern England, without restrictions named above. The population of users throughout England is a larger relevant population; but, as the researchers indicate, the sample is not representative of that population because it does not include inner-city residents in large metropolitan areas. According to the researchers, "samples of users in metropolitan areas such as London and Manchester contain a much higher proportion (37–48 percent) of black and Asian users" (Carpenter et al., 2004, p. 238).

The research design was a panel survey, conducted at two points in time. At time 1, there were 260 users, and at time 2, there were 230. Those who dropped out refused continued participation, had personal crises such as hospital admission, or moved away from the district. The researchers reported that characteristics of mental health, gender, ethnicity, and diagnosis were similar for the samples at both points in time.

Data Analysis, Conclusions, and Implications

Questionnaire items were scored and analyzed for multinomial responses, and differences between the four districts were explored at times 1 and 2. Statistical tests such as paired t-tests and nonparametric Wilcoxon sign tests were employed to analyze changes from time 1 to time 2.

The majority of findings were comparisons of districts A, B, C, and D on bar graphs indicating percentages of users' responses to 29 questions. These are among the many important findings that were presented (Carpenter et al., 2004, pp. 319–327):

- Analysis of the ratings showed that around three-quarters of service users with severe and enduring mental health problems considered that they had choice in their care and treatment when living in the community.
- Over 80% of users in District D (Integrated health care program approach and care management in social services with inclusive services) felt they were able to participate in care planning and felt encouraged to express their needs. There were statistical differences between District D and District A (discrete services targeted to the severely mentally ill) with

respect to the extent to which users felt they had a say in planning their own mental health care (more than 80% for District D; less than 40% for District A).

- Over 80 per cent of users felt that they would be able to say if they were dissatisfied with an aspect of their care. . . . Three-quarters thought that they would be able to complain if they needed to.
- Fewer than 40% of users knew that both health and social services have official complaints procedures, except in District D, where 54% said that they did know.
- Users in integrated districts . . . felt in comparison to those in discrete districts . . . more encouraged to state their aims for care and treatment; less limited about their desire of care; better informed about their medication; less negative about their family's involvement in their care; and more positive about being helped to become independent.

The researchers derived several implications for programs in the districts they studied in northern England:

- Since more than half of the users did not take advantage of their entitlement to care programs, the researchers believed social workers and health practitioners should put in extra efforts to apprise users of care programs.
- More efforts should be made by professional staff to inform users about their prescribed medication.
- Social workers and health professionals should make sure that they provide information to all users about how to express dissatisfaction and how to file complaints.
- Social workers should take a more active role in seeking to involve the families of users as carers.

The researchers also believed that their findings are supportive of integrated care in the health systems of other countries.

Classification of the Study

This is classified as a supranational social work research study for these reasons:

- The research is pertinent to the practice of social work in community mental health in northern England.
- The authors employed the literature and knowledge of mental health systems in other countries to formulate the problem of coordination of mental health services in England.
- The authors carefully reviewed studies of care systems similar to the one they were evaluating from the users' perspectives.
- Studying perceptions of users of mental health service is considered to be of global interest.
- Literature was used to discuss approaches of different countries.
- The authors attempted to generalize their concepts to other countries.

Issues Addressed in the Study

Minimizing Socially Desirable Responses

The researchers were aware of the potential problem that users might have made positive responses about mental health services because they may have feared that negative responses might affect the care they receive from mental health professionals. These socially desirable responses, according to the researchers, were reduced by guaranteeing confidentiality and by stressing the independence of the researchers from the mental health practitioners. The researchers might also have assured the participants more directly that their responses would not affect their care and that they could withdraw from the study at any time, which is a customary procedure promulgated by ethics committees.

Apparently overlooked by the researchers is the fact that each of the participants was offered a payment of 10 pounds for interview. This may have affected the participants' inclination to say what they believe the researchers wanted to hear. In this respect, both positive and negative responses could be regarded as socially desirable. This could be possibly further minimized by procedures such as the following.

- Be more explicit about the researchers not expecting the participants to respond as they think the researchers want them to; this would be included in the instructional set given prior to asking questions.
- In the instructions indicate that payment of 10 pounds is for their participation, not for what they think the researchers want them to say.
- Pretest the procedures with a focus group of potential participants. After giving them instructions and asking them questions, discuss with them as to what they think the researchers wanted to discover; then make corrections on the protocols based on those data.
- To the extent possible, seek from the literature social desirability tests, for example, those that might be available in personality inventories such as the Minnesota Multiphasic Personality Inventory.

Assessing the Generalizability of Studies in Problem Formulation

The authors reviewed studies on mental health care critically. They did not simply look at the verbal findings of studies; they reviewed the sampling critically, and considered whether those samples were representative of the populations studied. For example, they reviewed reports of home-based crisis intervention teams that indicated higher levels of satisfaction for those who received the intervention in comparison to standard services; however, in those controlled studies, the samples were accidental or convenience samples, and not generalizable. The researchers reviewed studies that involved mailed questionnaires, and they indicated that their samples were nonrandom, and not generalizable.

As we indicated previously, the extent of generalizability is a critical issue in all research. The review of studies should focus not only on conclusions but also on the generalizability of those conclusions. Analysis of the sampling procedures and their implementation is paramount. Not only should investigators be critical of sampling and generalizability in studies they review, they should also critically analyze their own implementation of sampling procedures. In this study, random sampling was employed within districts; however, psychiatrists in each district decided whether the potential respondents should be involved in the research, that is, they were not included due to crisis, being at risk of hospital admission, or posing a danger to the research interviewers. Whether or not these judgments affected the randomization procedures was not clear, since it was not discussed in the study. However, depending upon how many were actually excluded, the population to which generalizations could be made would be different, that is, only those users in the community who are not at risk for hospitalization or rehospitalization.

Issues Arising from the Study

Reliability of Clinical Judgments

Since there appear to be different psychiatrists at each of the four districts, it is important that they use the same criteria for accepting and rejecting users as participants in the research. With unreliability in the system, the confidence one would have in comparing results from users in the four districts would not be great. Reliability can be enhanced in ways such as this. First, the psychiatrists would meet, discuss the criteria, and try them out on either a sample of users or on vignettes or cases about users. Percentage agreement or correlational statistics could be employed to test the degree of reliability among the psychiatrists. Second, there should be a reliability check, say on five cases randomly chosen from each of the four districts. Reliability can then be determined regarding decisions of inclusion or exclusion. Obviously, this would not be a serious issue if the actual number of excluded users were small. If one still was interested in the reliability of psychiatric judgments, one could test for the reliability in diagnosing schizophrenia, bipolar disorder, or severe depression. This becomes more important if the researchers wish to claim similarities on diagnoses across the four districts.

Ethical Considerations

The researchers indicated that the local ethics committees in the four districts required permission from the user's consultant psychiatrists and general practitioners to be included in the study. Other requirements were not made explicit in the study. However, common practices such as the following should take place; and if they occur, characteristics of the samples in the districts could be altered:

- The users should be apprised of the study and told what it entails, whether there is any possible risk of harm, and given the choice of participation or not. The user and/or his/her legal guardian should give informed consent.
- The user should know she or he has the right to refuse participation at any time during the research process. This appears to have been the case. The researchers noted a reduction of users who participated in the second in-

terview at time 2, and it was indicated that some users refused to continue with the process.

- If the information from the researchers is independent of the services provided in community mental health as indicated by the researchers, then the users should be guaranteed confidentiality of the research results. For example, they would not be identified as those patients who complained about the services.

- Recalling the discussion of the issue on social desirability, it is important to indicate that the money (10 pounds) offered to the users for their efforts in participation should not be construed as an attempt to have the users say what the researchers want to hear, whether it be positive or negative perceptions about the community mental health services. Moreover, the users should be informed that the researchers are only interested in the users' genuine opinions.

Exploratory Data Analyses

In studies such as this, it is possible to generate new hypotheses for subsequent research from exploratory data analyses, that is, analyses that were not planned for but arise from data produced in the research. Three examples can be provided from this research. First, the researchers reported that

> Three-quarters of the sample had been given a diagnosis of schizophrenia (53 percent) or bipolar disorder (22 percent), and 2 percent had a diagnosis of severe depression. A quarter of users were considered to have concurrent substance abuse problems. Half the sample had been admitted to the hospital compulsorily at least once and 30 per cent had been in the hospital for six months on at least one occasion. (Carpenter et al., 2004, p. 319)

This information indicates that several variables could be introduced into the analyses of user perceptions: diagnosis, concurrent substance abuse, and previous hospital admissions. Researchers could investigate the extent to which the perceptions of users are similar or different as a function of any of these variables.

Second, the researchers presented a table showing whether or not users from each of the four districts believed they had a written care program. The researchers were very interested in combining the districts that had integrated programs, C and D, and comparing them with those with discrete programs, A and B. This was in line with their notion that integrated or coordinated programs would lead to greater knowledge on the part of the users. The percentages of users who agreed with the statement from the integrated districts were 51.7 and 46.4, as compared to, in discrete districts (less coordinated), 60.3 and 37.1. In contrast, one could compare the districts with targeted services A and C with percentages in agreement of 60.3 and 51.7 compared with districts with inclusive services, districts B and D, with percentages in agreement of 37.1 and 46.4. The differences between districts with targeted and inclusive services were obviously more discrepant than the differences between districts with integrated and discrete services. From this one might infer that users are more likely to be aware of their programs if greater efforts are made by the staff to impart information to them. This hypothesis can be investigated in further study.

Third, the researchers state that

> users in inclusive districts generally gave more positive responses than those where services were targeting people with severe mental health problems. There is some evidence from measures of users' mental health that, on average, the samples in the targeted districts experienced somewhat more severe problems compared to those in inclusive districts. Thus, they were rated as having a lower life skills profile and had poorer scores on a composite measure of psychiatric and social problems. (Carpenter et al., 2004, pp. 329–330)

This suggests that views of users may differ as a function of the severity of their illness. Therefore, additional exploratory analyses, such as regression analyses with districts, previous hospital admissions, severity of illness, and diagnosis, for example, could be employed as predictors of users' opinions. It is theoretically possible that the variables of severity of illness, diagnosis, and previous hospitalizations might explain more of the variation in opinions than the organizational patterns of the districts.

These examples are meant to illustrate the point that hypotheses for future research can be developed with additional exploratory analyses that might not have been previously planned by researchers. They also illustrate the difficulty of controlling all possible variables in field surveys. Obviously, additional analyses are only possible if there are large enough samples to pursue the simultaneous effects of several variables.

SUMMARY

In this chapter we presented five studies that originated in different countries and were illustrative of a variety of research methods and strategies. They were excellent studies classified as supranational research. All of the studies were described in relation to the research process: problem formulation and knowledge objectives; instrumentation and the process of data collection; sampling, relevant populations, and research design; and data analysis, conclusions, and implications. In addition, reasons for classifying the research as supranational were provided.

Issues pertinent to the conduct and utilization of supranational research were presented and discussed. Issues that were considered by the authors were presented, as were issues that we derived from a critical analysis of each study. The issues considered by the authors were: the cultural context of the research, the loss of data, ethics and informed consent, temporal stability and internal consistency, comparability of groups in known-groups analysis, cultural awareness, conceptualization of empowerment, the use of purposive sampling, credibility in qualitative research, the importance of conducting a pilot study, checking for the representativeness of the sample, generalizability, minimizing socially desirable responses, and assessing the generalizability of studies in problem formulation. Issues that we derived from a critical analysis of the research studies were: specification of populations and samples, pilot testing, representativeness of Chinese communities, translation and back-translation, factor analysis, the use of computerized programs to develop categories, a priori versus a posteriori evaluation, translation from Hindi to English, respondents' perceptions, evaluation of social welfare services and providers, sampling methods, the reliability and validity of content analysis, the reliability of clinical judgments, ethical considerations, and exploratory data analyses. Issues were discussed in reference to the contexts of each of the five studies.

4

INTRANATIONAL RESEARCH

This chapter builds on basic concepts about international social work research that were presented in chapters 1 and 2: definitions of international social work research and concepts pertinent to the research process. Notions about knowledge objectives, criteria for achieving them, and their generalizability are essential for discussing intranational as well as supranational research. We discuss salient issues in the conduct of intranational research, focusing, as in chapter 2, on aspects of the research process: problem formulation; instrument construction; research design; sampling and generalizability; data collection and analyses; and conclusions and implications. First, we define intranational research (essentially, research with international migrants), provide a hypothetical example, and distinguish similarities and differences between intranational research and supranational research. We then discuss social work problems that are dealt with in intranational research. We define various populations of international migrants, and briefly refer to causes, stages, and policies that affect them.

We briefly refer to the research process that was discussed in detail in chapter 2, delimiting aspects of the research process to serve as a context for discussing issues in the conduct and utilization of intranational research. Under *problem formulation*, we discuss notions of cultural competence and its meaning for research. In particular, we discuss cultural competence when doing research that involves populations from more than one country, that is, cultures of native and migrant populations. Within the rubric of *instrument construction*, we present models for constructing instruments, and we include materials on cultural competence as well as ideas about measurement. Under *research design*, we focus on longitudinal research and difficulties involved in retaining participants, and on participatory research, an important method for engaging international migrant populations. In the section on *sampling*, we discuss the context of relevant populations of the host country and other countries in considering sampling modalities, as well as combinations of sampling modalities. Regarding *data collection and analysis*, we discuss notions of language and its translation in collecting data, as well as issues of cultural competence that impinge on data collection. Also, we discuss differences within migrant populations. In addition, under *conclusions and implications*, we discuss the notion of information that is static versus that which is continually evolving. Acculturation and the degree of acculturation in parents and children of immigrants is considered, as well as changes in ethnic identity with respect to the country of origin and to the host country. Moreover, we discuss changes in attitudes and perceptions of the host country that change as a function of international events and policies. We conclude the chapter by discussing incentives and barriers to intranational research: costs, collaboration, time, recruitment and retention, availability of cross-cultural instruments, and resources.

DEFINING INTRANATIONAL RESEARCH

Intranational research is international research that studies a population from one country residing within another country; that is, international migrants. Literature from both countries is used to formulate the research problem and to interpret data and derive implications for both countries. A variety of social research methods are used for producing knowledge that pertains to social work practices and policies in working with these populations.

As in supranational research, intranational research has the following characteristics.

- It follows steps in the research process from problem formulation, sampling, and research design to instrument construction, data gathering, analyses, and conclusions.
- It uses literature from two or more countries.
- It generalizes substantive knowledge across countries or specifies differences between countries in formulating research problems.
- It may conceputalize generalizabilitiy of methodological knowledge across countries in formulating research problems.
- It may generalize across subcultural groups within a population.
- It seeks to apply research findings to the population where the study is conducted.
- It seeks to generalize implications across countries.

In addition, intranational rsearch has these characteristics:

- It studies populations from two or more countries, for example, the migrant population or populations, as well as the population of the host country.
- It may study populations within the country of origin in addition to those who migrated from the country of origin to live in another country.
- Migration may be studied over time, including postmigration patterns such as repatriation in the country of origin.
- Whereas supranational research may involve the use of more than one language when there are cross-cultural studies within a native population, intranational research often involves more than one language. For example, studies in the United States may focus on populations from around the world: Iraqi refugees, immigrants from Europe, asylum-seekers from Africa, and so forth.

A Hypothetical Example

Suppose that a research team is interested in studying the extent to which Russian migrants use mental health and families services in the United States The researchers refer to the available literature regarding migration patterns to the United States and the geographical location of Russian migrants. It may be discerned that there are relatively large concentrations of Russian migrants in New York City, Chicago, and other large cities. However, there is no single list of Russian migrants and their characteristics, so the researchers decide to narrow their search and seek populations of Russian migrants who are receiving or have received mental health and/or family services from social agencies. The researchers decide they need to obtain information in an exploratory study before embarking on a large-scale survey. They need to know where the migrants are located, what services they received, and more specific information about their experiences in America. The research team focuses its research even further by locating family service and mental health agencies in New York City. They then have to seek permission from the agencies to obtain lists of Russian migrants who have received services. The researchers would need to gain approval from institutional review panels regarding the ethical permissibility of their research: confidentiality, assurance of no intended harm in their interview questions, assurance that their participation is voluntary and will not affect their immigration status or the services they might receive, and so forth.

The researchers are interested in questions such as these:

- How proficient are the migrants in English?
- What sources of income do they have?
- What is their occupation?
- How long have they been in the United States?
- What is their marital status?
- What is their gender, age, and level of education?
- What are their perceptions of those with whom they came in contact at the mental health or family service agencies?
- What services have they received; what services are they receiving?
- Do they have social, psychological, economic, and health needs that are not being met?
- Do they have children?
- How many people do they live with?
- In what type of domicile do they live?
- Do they know of other Russian migrants who might be in need of services? How would they be located?

These questions are tentative and would need further refinement. To begin their research, the research team selects a focus group of 10 possible participants who have received services from two agencies in New York City and who are willing to participate in the research. The research team includes bilingual interviewers proficient in Russian and English. The researchers develop a semistructured interview schedule with the objective of learning whether the questions are understandable in Russian and English, and the extent to which the respondents understand what services are available and what the eligibility requirements are for receiving those services. For their participation, the research team plans to give each participant $100, in the hope that this will also give them insight into locating other Russian migrants, particularly undocumented immigrants, as well as others who have not made contact with social agencies. The researchers conduct the interviews separately with each participant; then the group is queried about their reactions to the questions, the necessity for better translations, the possible location of other migrants, and so on.

The researchers observed that Russian migrants who were in the United States for longer periods of time appeared to be more knowledgeable about services provided by the agencies. This coupled with notions from the literature suggested to the researchers that those who are more assimilated into the U.S. culture are more likely to use mental health and family services than those who are not. More specifically, those who have a high degree of identity with the new culture and a low degree of identity with the native culture (assimilation) are more likely to receive services than those who maintain a high degree of identity with the native culture and a low degree of identity with the new culture (separation; Potocky-Tripodi, 2002). Hence it was decided in subsequent research to ask questions related to cultural identity.

The research team analyzed the data, refined the questions, and then wondered whether they could reduce the $100 amount given to participants to a more affordable amount if they were to seek large numbers of participants. They learned that they could develop a list of participants who were not receiving services by snowball sampling, and those who were receiving services were willing to participate. Therefore, their subsequent sampling procedure was two pronged. Stratified sampling would be employed, as well as snowball sampling. Mental health and family services agencies would be listed and stratified by geographic area and the type of services. Within agencies with lists of Russian clients, assuming lists are available, random samples would be obtained. Second, within samples, participants would be asked to indicate where other Russian migrants might be located. The researchers would gather information regarding the types of services that were used and what the correlates of service usage might be. The hypothesis regarding assimilation would be tested, and information regarding why services are used or not used would be produced. Implications for service provision and cultural compatibility of services and the service recipients would be explored. Moreover, the research team would thoroughly examine the extent to which their procedures reflected cultural competence on the part of the research team.

BASIC CONCEPTS IN INTERNATIONAL MIGRATION

Definitions of International Migrants

There are many differing categories of international migrants. Table 4.1 shows some common conceptual (not legal) categories. The table categorizes international migrants as either voluntary or forced, and either permanent or temporary. These

Table 4.1 Conceptual Categories of International Migrants

Length of residence	Impetus for migration	
	Voluntary	**Forced**
Permanent	• Immigrants • Repatriates • International adoptees	• Victims of atrocities: • Refugees • Human trafficking victims
Temporary	• International students • Tourists • Professionals on assignment • Guest workers • Seasonal workers	• Victims of atrocities: • Asylum-seekers • Victims of disasters: • Natural disasters • Manmade disasters

Note. Persons in any of these categories may have *legal* or *illegal* status. This is a guiding framework only. Categorical distinctions are not always clear-cut in reality. Persons may move from one cell to another over time.

categories are intended to provide a guiding framework; in reality, such distinctions are not always clear-cut. For example, many international migrants experience a mixture of both voluntary and forced reasons for migration.

Voluntary, permanent international migrants include immigrants, repatriates, and international adoptees. Immigrants are persons who leave their countries of their own will, usually in search of better economic opportunities. Repatriates are people who have lived abroad for an extended period of time and have returned to their homelands. International adoptees whose birth parents and home governments have consented to their adoption abroad would also be considered voluntary permanent migrants (as minors, they themselves are not considered capable of giving consent; thus their parents'/guardians' consent makes this a voluntary situation).

Forced migrants are those who have left their homelands because they had no other choice. In the permanent category, these include victims of atrocities, such as refugees and human trafficking victims. Refugees are victims of war and other human rights violations who cannot return to their countries because of fear of persecution. Human trafficking victims include persons who have been brought across national borders for purposes of enslavement in labor markets such as agriculture, domestic work, or the sex trade. They also include infants and children sold into adoption on the black market.

Temporary voluntary migrants include students, tourists, and so on who intend to stay in the country for a limited period of time and then return to their homelands. Temporary forced migrants include asylum-seekers; these are persons making a claim for refugee status, for whom a decision is pending. This status is temporary because ultimately they are either granted refugee status or are returned to their homeland. Victims of natural and manmade disasters are also usually temporary migrants, as they typically return to their homelands after the disaster has abated.

As noted earlier, these are conceptual, not legal, categories. Thus, persons in any of these categories may have legal or illegal status. Persons may also move from one cell to another. For example, students or tourists who stay in the country after their visas have expired become illegal, permanent immigrants (of course, permanency itself is relative).

The main point here for intranational researchers is that it is a crucial task to understand such definitions as they pertain to their particular populations of interest. Researchers must clearly define the group they are studying, specify whether their definition is conceptual or legal, and identify who is included in and excluded from the defined group. This is critical in order to be able to appropriately generalize a study's findings to the relevant population.

Causes of International Migration

Closely related to the preceding definitions are the causes of international migration. The classical theory that attempts to explain these causes is the *push-pull theory*:

> It posits that people migrate in response to "push" factors in the country of origin and/or "pull" factors in the country of destination. "Push" factors are generally negative, such as better economic opportunity, political, freedom, and favorable reception toward immigrants. Often, refugees are viewed as being "pushed" out of their countries by oppression and war, whereas immigrants are viewed as being "pulled" into the destination country by the prospect of economic improvement. (Potocky-Tripodi, 2002, p. 13)

However, this theory is now generally regarded as simplistic:

> More comprehensive theories recognize that international migration is a result of factors operating at three levels: the *macro* or *structural level*, which entails political, economic, cultural, and geographic forces in the international arena, the country of origin, and the country of destination; the *meso* or *relational level*, which entails the relationships between potential movers and stayers in both the country of origin and the country of destination; and the *micro* or *individual level*, which entails personal characteristics and the individual's freedom to make autonomous decisions about moving or staying. . . . The macro level forces are those which are addressed by the push-pull theory. . . . The meso level concerns an individual's family and social network, including ties to kinship groups, friends, neighbors, coworkers, acquaintances, and ethnic, religious, and political associations in both the sending and receiving countries. . . . The micro forces include personal characteristics such as age, ethnicity, religion, education, and financial assets. . . . People who are contemplating moving to another country take into consideration all of these macro, meso, and micro factors in making their decisions. Within each level there are advantages and disadvantages. The individual must weigh these out both within and across the levels. Often the factors within one level predominate over another level. In the case of refugees, the macro factors usually predominate. In this case, the necessity of escaping war or political oppression outweighs such considerations as disrupting family ties and losing all assets. This is why refugees are forced migrants, because in the absence of these negative macro-level factors, they probably would not have chosen to leave their countries. For economic migrants, the macro and micro levels may outweigh the meso level. That is, the prospect of improvement in living conditions

combined with personal risk-taking initiatives may outweigh the force of family ties. On the other hand, for the vast majority of people who choose not to leave their countries despite poor economic conditions, family and individual factors are probably the overriding consideration. (pp. 14–16)

Stages of Migration

The process of migration is generally considered to consist of three major stages: *premigration and departure, transit,* and *resettlement* (Drachman, 1992).

> In the premigration and departure stage decisions are made about the circumstances of when and why there is to be a migration. For immigrants, the planning is made in advance under relatively calm conditions, whereas refugees often leave their countries of origin under traumatic conditions such as war and political oppression. The transit stage entails the actual physical move from one country to another. The transit stage is generally more traumatic for refugees and illegal aliens than it is for legal immigrants. The last stage of the migration process is resettlement. This stage lasts as long as the people stay in the host country, which may be for the rest of their lives. It is typically the stage where social workers in the host country work with immigrants and refugees. (Potocky-Tripodi, 2002, pp. 17–18)

The resettlement is also the most typical stage in which intranational research takes place. Finally, for a relatively small but growing number of international migrants, there is a fourth stage, *repatriation,* in which the migrants return to reside in their country of origin. Because this is a relatively recent phenomenon, it has not yet received much attention in the research literature.

International Migration Policies

International migration policies provide the legal context for social work practice with immigrants and refugees. These policies also provide the legal context in which intranational research is conducted. We highly recommend that intranational researchers be cognizant of the key policies that affect those international migrants involved in their research. These policies include both international laws that provide guidelines about how countries should treat citizens and aliens, as well as national laws that determine eligibilty for admission, public services, benefits, and protections. In planning, developing, and implementing research, it is necessary for the researcher to consider how and in what ways these laws affect decisions regarding the various steps of the research process.

SOCIAL WORK PROBLEMS

In her book *Best Practices for Social Work with Refugees and Immigrants,* Potocky-Tripodi (2002) focuses on problems that social workers deal with in providing services to immigrants and refugees. In particular, problems such as the following are discussed: economic adaptation, legal rights in the new country, language acquistion, domestic

abuse, health care access, differential treatment of minority clients, depression, somatization, guilt, anxiety, posttraumatic stress disorder, substance abuse, marital
conflict, intergenerational conflict, and so forth. In essence, international migrants
may present any and all of the problems that social workers deal with in addition to
problems that are specific to migration and displacement experiences.

We edited two special issues of the *Journal of Social Work Research and Evaluation:
An International Publication* that are pertinent to specific social work problems with
international migrants: "Human Trafficking" (Potocky-Tripodi & Tripodi, 2004)
and "Research on Refugees and Immigrants" (Potocky-Tripodi & Tripodi, 2001).
The following articles from those special issues illustrate the diversity of social work
problems in work with international migrants.

McDonald and Timoshkina (2004) examined service needs of trafficked women
from the former eastern European bloc in Canada. They focused on health services
and found that those women who were involved in the sex trade made limited use
of health and social services for these reasons: "cultural values (e.g., not being used
to actively seeking services), language problems, little knowledge about services,
no access to services, a nocturnal lifestyle, stigma, and fear" (p. 183).

Engstrom, Minas, Espinoza, and Jones studied the phenomenon of sex trafficking in Thailand, and derived the following conclusions and implications for social
work: "The intersection of globalization and international migration means that
increasing numbers of people find themselves working outside their country of
origin. Those who are trafficked are among the most vulnerable and exploited of
this unprecedented flux of people" (2004, p. 203).

> Globalization demands that social workers embrace more than just local and national
> perspectives, but an international viewpoint as well to understand the context and
> dynamics of human trafficking. . . . Social workers need to recognize that some of
> the thousands of trafficked women and children from Thailand and Southeast Asia
> will end up in the United States as our clients in emergency rooms, domestic vio-
> lence shelters, mental health facilities, and child welfare systems. (pp. 203–204)

Problems particular to international migrants are further noted in the following
articles by Ross-Sheriff (2001), Chambon et al. (2001), and Alaggia, Chau, and Tsang
(2001). Ross-Sheriff studied the adaptation of immigrant Muslim women to American society, and concluded that

> to attain their goals, the women require support from both their families and the
> Muslim community. The appreciation of education and a commitment to their fami-
> lies reflects a strong cultural value of Muslim immigrant families and represents a
> potential that ought to be realized with educational programs to allow the women
> to pursue their goals and reach their full potential. (p. 291)

Chambon et al. conducted an exploratory study with survivors of torture and
war who migrated to Canada. They were interested in studying the befriending
relationship and how it might be employed by social workers to help survivors re-
settle in Canada. The researchers noted that responses of the survivors were shaped
by whether or not they felt they would be granted legal status from the Immigration and Refugee Board and by their cultural backgrounds.

Alaggia et al. eported on the phenomenon of "Astronaut" Asian families in Canadian society:

> 'Astronaut' Asian families are those who immigrate to a new country while one or or both parents return to live in their country of origin leaving their children to pursue an education in the host country. . . . These families often migrate to Canada to attain a life with more political and social stability and to provide their children with a Canadian education. When parents return to their country of origin it is usually for economic reasons. (2001, p. 295)

The researchers studied a sample of youth who lived with their mothers only, with relatives, with their father only, or alone. They concluded that the astronaut family arrangement had an impact on family roles, patterns of communication, and developmental issues. The separation of family members led to role changes and different patterns of communication; and it was reported that "most of the youth struggled with issues of early independence and increased responsiblities in assisting the family unit" (p. 301).

THE RESEARCH PROCESS FOR INTRANATIONAL RESEARCH

We use the same categories of the research process for intranational research as were employed for discussing issues in the conduct and utilization of research for supranational research: problem formulation; instrument construction; research designs; sampling and study populations; data collection, data analysis, conclusions, and implications. International and national laws regarding immigrants and refugees provide a context in which researchers can study immigrants and refugees from another country who reside in a host country. Knowledge of these laws enables researchers to consider what factors might lead to participation or lack of participation in research as a result of legal definitions, legal requirements, and eligibility for social benefits. Moreover, such knowledge may indicate to the researchers possible ethical issues that might be involved in soliciting respondents for research, as well as what possible fears and concerns respondents might have, assuming they are aware of policies regarding them. In fact, questions about respodents' knowledge of policies affecting their status might be important to consider in developing studies regarding social needs, and more specifically in developing questionnaires, interview schedules, focus groups, and pilot studies.

International laws, notions of cultural competence, culturally sensitive research instruments, relevant populations from host and other countries, language and its translation, longitudinal research, and participatory research are among the topics that should be considered in the various stages of the research process.

Problem Formulation

To study international migrants in the host country, it is important for researchers to have knowlege about the country from which those persons emigrated. One should review the literature regarding the history of migration and the characteristics and concerns of migrants. More specifically, information should be obtained about the potential problem for research, whether it deals with poverty, mental health, social services, and so forth. One would form tentative questions and hypotheses to guide the literature review, being careful to note whether it is feasible to research the problem. This would include obtaining information on cultural and national characteristics about the use of language, customary ways of responding to questionnaires and interviews, and ethical considerations regarding informed consent and voluntary participation. In reviewing the literature, the researcher would also seek methodological knowledge related to the research problem, asking questions such as these:

- Are there any available instruments that are reliable and valid for gathering information from this migrant population?
- If the migrants have a native language that is different from the primary language in the host country, are there research instruments that have been cross-validated with both languages?
- What form of data collection appears to be more culturally appropriate: structured, semistructured, or unstructured questionnaires, face-to-face interviews, or observations?

Narrative reviews of available research and books and articles about migrants' experiences serve to sensitize researchers to the expectations, fears, and concerns that migrants might have. This in turn would help researchers to devise and use research instruments that are culturally sensitive to the migrants and their families. Metaevaluations and metaanalyses (see chapter 2 for a discussion of these review strategies in problem formulation) are useful, assuming research studies are available, for discerning the extent to which there is generalizable knowledge regarding the potential questions and hypotheses that are developed for research.

Questions such as these should be considered in reviewing literature about international migrants and the host country:

- Are there research studies that are concerned with the interactions of migrants and people in the host country?
- Does it appear that the topic of the research would be understandable to the potential participants?
- Would interpreters or bilingual persons have to be used in research studies?
- Do the migrants know what rights they have with respect to research in the host country; for example, as in the United States, the rights of informed consent, voluntary participation, freedom from injury, and confidentiality?
- Can hypotheses that are formulated be tested with the migrant population?
- Is knowledge available regarding living arrangements, migrants' socioeconomic characteristics, and patterns of migration that might affect the questions and hypotheses that could be investigated?

After having perused the literature, the researcher should develop guiding questions or hypotheses. However, prior to embarking on a study, it is helpful to secure some information from the migrants themselves, as well as some perceptions of the migrants from those who have been in contact with them, such as workers and other community members. The researcher may seek to arrange to interview a few migrants and service providers individually or in focus groups. The purpose of this would be to ascertain whether notions from the literature appear to be relevant to a small, convenience sample of migrants and those who might have been in contact with them. This process enables the researcher to solidify or modify questions and hypotheses for research and to assess the feasibility of subsequent research. Questions that are asked would be framed around the proposed research. If, for example, the researcher is interested in forming questions or hypotheses about employment, she or he might ask about the migrants' experiences in seeking employment, types of jobs, salary, difficulties in seeking and maintaining employment, and so on.

Cultural Competence

An important consideration for all social work researchers is the extent to which the researchers themselves are culturally competent. Sensitivity to other cultures and ethnicities is important in all phases of the research process. We discuss some notions of cultural competence in problem formulation because it is in this phase of the research process that researchers not only develop hypotheses and questions but also consider the extent to which they are researchable, which involves all phases of the research process.

According to Rubin and Babbie (2005, p. 497), cultural competence in social researchers "means being aware of and appropriately responding to the ways in which cultural factors and cultural differences should influence what we investigate, how we investigate, and how we interpret our findings." Moreover, Rubin and Babbie believe that in the United States, researchers should strive to include as research participants representatives of minority groups and to obtain information on socioeconomic factors (2005). With respect to problem formulation, they advise that in studying minority and oppressed groups, social work researchers should review the literature regarding historical, economic, family, traditional, and cultural factors that affect these groups. In obtaining knowledge about minority, ethnic, and oppressed groups, it is also important to consider and be knowledgeable about the migration and acculturation experiences that affect the particular group one is studying. At the same time, it is incumbent on researchers to avoid the biases of ethnocentrism, that is, placing one's culture as the point of reference in studying other cultures. It is extremely important for researchers to recognize that there are individual variations within cultures as well as between cultures, that is, not all members of a particular international migrant group are exactly alike (Harper & Lantz, 1996; Potocky-Tripodi, 2002; Rubin & Babbie, 2005). The researcher should also obtain experience with representatives of the cultural group being studied by seeking advice from members of the culture, participant observation, and focus groups (Rubin & Babbie, 2005).

Hurdle (2002, p. 183) believes that "the combination of personal awareness, knowledge of different cultures of clients, and the development of appropriate skills allows mental health profesionals to ably provide services to clients that are culturally different from themselves." She indicates that the culturally competent social worker understands cultural factors and cultural practices; and is able to apply that knowledge in working with clients and their cultural environments. Although social work researchers are attempting to obtain information rather than provide direct services to clients, they, too, can benefit from knowledge of cultural groups and skills in communicating with them, such as interviewing and participant observation. Harper and Lantz (1996) believe that it is extremely important for social workers to be aware of and free from their biases in order to help clients cross-culturally. They list a number of factors derived from naturalistic studies of the helping process, singling out worldview respect as the most important cross-cultural curative factor in existential treatment; the treatment process must be compatible with the client's cultural beliefs. This notion is important for researchers involved in planning to interview people from cultures different from their own.

Potocky-Tripodi (2002) provides a comprehensive discussion of culturally competent social work practice with refugees and immigrants, pointing to a number of principles that can also increase the cultural competence of social work researchers. Above all, she notes that cultural competency is not static; it is a process that the social worker is continually developing. We provide these suggestions for increasing cultural competence of social work researchers (Potocky-Tripodi, 2002, pp. 133–137):

- Become aware of one's ethnic background and how it has shaped one's outlook and experiences.
- Identify one's own negative attitudes, beliefs, and behaviors toward other ethnic groups.
- Realize that one may have negative attitudes toward members of one's own group.
- Value and respect and be nonjudgmental about cultural differences (as long as one doesn't harm others).
- Enhance one's valuing and respect of others by increasing contacts with members of different ethnic groups.
- Value the social work profession's commitment to social justice and to empirically based (evidence-based) practice.
- Recognize one's own limitations.

In essence, social work researchers need a broad base of attitudes, knowledge, and skills to conduct competent research. Attitudes include those listed here. Knowledge includes multiple theories, self-knowledge, characteristics of different ethnic groups, environmental influences, evidence-based practice, and the cultural basis of social work research. Skills include engaging participants in research, communication and interviewing, and selecting and developing culturally sensitive research instruments that are reliable and valid across cultures.

Instrument Construction

We present three interrelated approaches to the construction and utilization of culturally competent research instruments: (1) constructing a cultural competency inventory, (2) adapting an instrument from one langue to another, (3) developing original cross-cultural instruments.

Constructing a Cultural Competency Inventory

The work of Cornelius, Booker, Arthur, Reeves, and Morgan (2004) illustrates a process for constructing a consumer-based cultural competency inventory for a population of adult recipients of public mental health services. The population includes both native-born residents and international migrants; thus this is an intranational study. The methods used for instrument construction, assessing content and construct validity, and assessing reliability are as follows.

> The empirical examination of the validity and reliability of this instrument followed the administration of a 52-item scale to mental health consumers across the state of Maryland in January, 2002. In addition to developing the scale in English, the scale was translated into Spanish and Vietnamese using a process called forward and back translation. . . . The process of forward and back translation requires that the instrument first be translated from English to a second language. In the second stage, independent translators translate the instrument from the second language back to English. In the third stage, all the translators are brought together to reconcile the two versions of the document. In this study, two pairs of independent translators (two for Spanish and two for Vietnamese) were used to ensure comparability with the English version. For the Spanish translations translators from Spanish-speaking Central American countries were used because the Latinos targeted for this study were predominantly from Mexico and Central America. Following the translation of the scale into Spanish and Vietnamese, the 52-item scale was administered to a purposive sample of 238 adult consumers . . . across the state of Maryland who received public mental health services in psychiatric rehabilitation programs. Latino and Vietnamese American administrators were used to adminster this scale to Latino and Vietnamese respondents. Latinos and Vietnamese Americans were especially targeted based on the demographics of adult users of the public mental health system in the state of Maryland. These methods were used to minimize some of the translation errors that can occur in administering an instrument to multiethnic populations. (pp. 201–202)

Cornelius et al. (2004) assessed the reliability of the instrument by using Cronbach's alpha to measure interitem consistency. Validity was assessed by examining correlations of eight subscales that represented different aspects of cultural competence in providers of mental health services: language fluency or interpreters, understanding of indigenous practices, acceptance of cultural differences, awareness of patients' culture, respectful behaviors, patient-provider-organization interactions, consumer involvement, and consumer outreach. Examples of some of the items are: "Some of the office and support staff are from my racial or ethnic group" (Awareness of Patients' Culture Subscale); "The staff here treat me with respect" (Respectful Behaviors Subscale); "If I need it, there are translators or interpreters easily available to assist me and/or my family" (Language Interpreter Issues Subscale); "Staff are willing to be flexible and provide alternative approaches or services to meet my cultural/ethnic treatment needs" (Understanding of Indigenous Practice Subscale); "The staff here understand that I might want to talk to a person from my own racial or ethnic group about getting the mental health help I want" (Consumer Involvement Subscale); and "Staff here understand that people of my racial or ethnic group are not all alike" (Acceptance of Cultural Differences Subscale) (p. 205).

Validity was also assessed qualitatively by examining the content validity of the items. The process of assessing content validity involves the use of a panel of experts to make judgments on the extent to which the items of the inventory are regarded as relevant to the concept of cultural competence. A 2-year process involved the selection of a panel of experts (mental health practitioners, consumers, and researchers) who formed a battery of questions based on their review of the literature, interviews with local and national experts, and their own knowledge of cultural competence. Having discovered in 1999 that there were no available instruments that measured cultural competency, a 20-person panel of consumers, therapists, and administrators who advise the state of Maryland regarding the delivery of mental health services to multicultural populations developed the cultural competency inventory. Four focus groups were convened to review different iterations of the inventory. The panel of experts developed 61 questions that were reduced to 52 questions and organized into the eight subscales of cultural competency that were tested for construct validity.

The approach by Cornelius and colleagues was essentially a participatory process in which stakeholders developed a series of questions regarding the provision of mental health services, and then translated them for use by Vietnamese and Latino consumers. The researchers reported an overall alpha of .92 and modest intercorrelations among the subscales.

Adapting an Instrument from One Language to Another

Alvelo, Collazo, and Rosario (2001) provide an illustration of a cross-cultural equivalence model that "integrates the translation and adaptation into Spanish and validation of the MPSI with a sample of Puerto Ricans" (p. 700). This is a national, cross-cultural study; an instrument used with one cultural group (residents of the mainland U.S.) is adapted for use with another (residents of Puerto Rico), yet both groups are part of the same country. Although used in a national study in this case, the instrumentation method described is highly relevant to intranational research.

The Multi-Problem Screening Inventory (MPSI) has been used to measure different areas of personal and social functioning of social work clients. The cross-cultural equivalence model employs both emic (folk or indigenous, within cultures) and etic (common or universal, across cultures) perspectives (Alvelo et al., 2001; Burnette, 1998). The methods employed by the researchers were "translation and back translation by professional translators, the use of a bilingual committee, and empirical studies to assure equivlaence between the English and Spanish versions of the MPSI." The reliability and validity studies were integrated in this approach.

> Equivalence was assessed along four ... dimensions ... defined as follows: *semantic equivalence*—each item has similar meaning in the languages involved; *content equivalence*—the content of each item is relevant to the population under study; *technical equivalence*—similar effect is obtained when the same measuring technique is used with the different cultures; ... and *conceptual equivalence*—the theoretical concepts being assessed are the same in the different cultures involved. (Alvelo et al., 2001, pp. 701–702)

The adaptation of the MPSI into Spanish involved translation, back-translation, and a bilingual committee. First, an experienced translator provided the initial translation of the MPSI. Second, a bilingual committee reviewed the translation to assure the items were understandable and meaningful in the Puerto Rican context. Substitutions of inappropriate items were made, and documented. Third, a different bilingual translator back-translated the items. Fourth, "the bilingual committee compared the back-translated version with the original English version to identify discrepancies, determined the cause of the discrepancies, consulted the author of the MPSI scales, and made corrections as necessary to the targeted Spanish version" (Alvelo et al., 2001, p. 704). Fifth, a sample of 25 veterans who received outpatient services from a Veterans Administration medical center in San Juan, Puerto Rico, volunteered to participate in testing their comprehension of the translated MPSI items. Items that were difficult to understand were discussed, and a summary was presented to the bilingual committee for further modifications. Sixth, a Pureto Rican linguistics professor reviewed the MPSI for correct grammar.

With respect to equivalence studies, comparisons were made between studies of the MPSI in the mainland United States and the researcher's studies in Puerto Rico on background variables, means and standard deviations of 27 MPSI scales, and factor loadings. In addition, alpha coefficients and standard errors of measurement were computed for the mainland and the Puerto Rican samples. Content validity was established, in that 13 judges rated 98% of the items content relevant. Similarities of means and standard deviations between mainland and Puerto Rican samples indicated technical and conceptual equivalence. The researchers concluded that

> the application of the cross-cultural equivalence model . . . to the adaptation of the MPSI into Spanish for use with Puerto Ricans permitted the evaluation of the psychometric properties of an instrument that was conceptualized and tested with a United States Mainland (USM), non-Hispanic population. The results indicated that by using this conceptual model and its techniques, acceptable levels of reliability and validity were obtained in adapting the MPSI to another culture and language. The bilingual committee approach and a conscious effort to avoid the use of Spanish regionalisms are expected to provide an assessment tool that can be tested with other Hispanic groups. (Alvelo et al., 2001, pp. 721–722)

Developing Original Cross-cultural Instruments

Tran and Aroian (2000) describe a comprehensive, multistrategy, multistage procedure for developing research instruments that can be used cross-culturally, in all apsects of international research. Their procedure consists of nine steps: defining the concept to be measured in emic terms; obtaining cultural consensus; developing measurement items; peer validation; pretesting items with prospective study participants; seeking additional peer input for revising items; pilot testing; psychometric evaluation; and evaluating efficacy.

Tran and Aroian discuss their procedure in reference to the concept of depression. The first step, defining the concept in emic terms, involves the establishment of the cultural meaning of the concept in question. It is suggested that a technique that can be employed is that of "in-depth qualitative interviews with a sample of individuals from the ethnocultural group. . . . Interview questions should focus on eliciting emic or culturally relevant descriptions of the concept of interest, asking for typical as well as contrary and borderline examples; and identifying anteced- ents and consequences" (2000, p. 37). The intent of interviews is to delineate the entire range of experiences regarding the concept to be measured; hence sampling is conducted to represent variations in factors that potentially affect empirical de- scriptions of the concept, for example, age, gender, family income, religion, and so on. Interviews are conducted until there is saturation of descriptions, that is, when no new information is provided in subsequent interviews.

Step 2 involves obtaining cultural consensus regarding the information procured in step 1. This is accomplished by "using focus groups of representative members of the ethnocultural group to reach consensus about the core or essential defining elements of the concept" (Tran & Aroian, 2000, p. 37). It is suggested that focus groups consist of 6 to 10 people for promoting group interaction. The focus group should contain members who are representative of the population being studied and who have had personal or professional experience with the concept, for example, having experienced or worked with people who were known to be depressed. In step 2, categories of the concept are developed, and consensus is determined by calculating the extent to which group members agree (percentage agreement) on aspects of the concept, for example, symptoms of depression, such as loss of appe- tite, crying uncontrollably, and so on. The result of step 2 is a delineation of indica- tors of the concept.

In step 3, developing measurement items, a pool of items is specified for each of the indicators of the concept. That is, in the case of depression, items for each of the symptoms of depression are developed. Tran and Aroian suggest that 10 to 15 items should be developed for each hypothesized subscale (symptom), noting that these items will be pared down in further steps of the process. Peer validation, step 4, involves the use of a panel of experts to systematically review the item pool for content relevance. Experts are provided with individual items and a theoretical definition of the concept they are intended to measure, and they are asked to rate each item with respect to its degree of content relevance. Three or more experts are used to rate the items. According to Tran and Aroian (2000, p. 38),

> the minimum number of experts who must agree for each item to be assessed as content valid is established by (1) calculating the proportion of the number of ex- perts who might agree out of the total number of experts involved, and (2) setting the standard error of the proportion to identify the cutoff for chance versus real agreement. . . . Items that do not receive the minimum agreement among the ex- perts are eliminated or revised. Revised items are reevaluated for content validity.

Step 5 involves the pretesting of items with prospective study participants. These items are administered to a sample of people from the ethnocultural group of inter- est. After respondents complete their ratings, they are asked to indicate how they interpreted the questions, noting possible ambiguities.

> After each respondent completes the measure, the data collector elicits and audio- tapes the participant's explanations about his or her choices for a set of randomly preselected items. Specifically, the data collector asks the respondent to "explain a

little of what he or she had in mind when they chose the response." Explanations are used to evaluate respondents' interpretations and the meanings intended by the research team. (Tran and Aroian, 2000, p. 40)

Responses to these random probes are then evaluated with respect to the clarity and consistency of the explanations.

Step 6 involves obtaining information about revising questionable items discerned from step 5. Focus groups that are representative of the ethnocultural group are asked how to revise items so they are not ambiguous. Revised items are subjected to the procedures of steps 4 and 5.

Steps 7, 8, and 9 are procedures typically followed after a researcher or research team has created an instrument comprised of a series of items. Pilot testing is carried out with a sample of the study population to determine the length of administration time and the extent to which respondents are willing and able to complete their responses to the items. Psychometric evaluation involves the securing of information about interitem consistency and temporal stability, construct and convergent validities, and the internal factor structure of the instrument. Step 9, evaluating efficacy, involves classifying respondents who exhibit or do not exhibit the characteristics of the concept, that is, depression. This essentially refers to known-groups validity, another psychometric criterion for evaluating the measurement of a concept, such as depression.

The issues regarding the conduct and utilization of instrument construction revolve around the extent to which cross-cultural measures are actually equivalent and whether instruments comprised of the same items but translated in different languages can be confidently used in comparing minority poulations within a country and for eliciting information from international migrants in a host country. The procedures that were presented here are attempts to deal with those issues.

Research Design

As in other types of international research, a variety of research designs can be used in intranational research. Survey techniques and qualitative methods are more likely to be used than experiments, especially due to the difficulties in locating, engaging, and retaining populations of international migrants for participation in research. Since international migrants living in a host country are in transition and subject to the pressures of acculturation, longtitudinal research techniques are appropriate, particularly for the study of individual and group change. In addition, since there is often the issue of cultural competence involved in recruiting and retaining research participants, participatory research is a recommended procedure.

Longitudinal Research

In distinction from cross-sectional research, which is a study of variables within a sample at one period of time, longitudinal research

is research in which (a) data are collected for each item or variable for two or more distinct time periods; (b) the subjects of cases analyzed are the same or at least comparable from one period to the next; and (c) the analysis involves some comparison of data between or among periods. At a bare minimum, any truly longitudinal design would permit the measurement of differences or change in a variable from one period to another. (Menard, 1991, p. 4)

There are several types of longitudinal research: prospective panel design, retrospective panel design, single-subject design, and replicated cross-sectional design. The prospective panel design involves the measurement of variables over two or more distinct time periods, for example, measures of identity with the host country may be taken over two time periods to discern whether there are changes in indices of acculturation. Retrospective panel design can only be employed if there are repeated measures that have been recorded in files of public or private agencies, or if there are questions that can be asked of the respondents that require them to remember their behaviors over past periods of time. For example, immigrants may report on their past employment-seeking behaviors. Retrospective research is fraught with difficulties, and is not recommended for studying attitude changes, the perception of which may be altered over time; even the recall of behaviors can be problematic. The prospective panel design can be employed in the evaluation of social programs intended to create changes over time, as well as in the study of changes due more broadly to socioenvironmental influences. Single-subject design that involves the study of repeated measurements over time without and with the influence of interventions can be considered a special case of prospective panel design. Prospective panel design can also be considered to be a longitudinal case study, as utilized in the disciplines of anthropology and sociology. Single-subject design, having its origins in experimental psychology, can also be considered a longitudinal case study, as opposed to a cross-sectional case study that involves measurement at one period of time.

In prospective panel studies, longitudinal studies, or single-subject designs, individual changes can be studied, since the same persons are measured over different points in time. A research design that involves the study of group changes, but not individual changes, over time is the replicated or repeated cross-sectional design. At the first time of measurement, a random sample is drawn from the population of interest, and measurements are taken, say, of the immigrants' uses of social and health services. Average measures of service utilization can be calculated. At a later point in time, the second measurements are taken from another random sample drawn from the same population of immigrants. Group changes between time 1 and time 2 can be studied, but not individual changes, since the persons drawn in sample 2 are not necessarily the same as those drawn in sample 1. Obviously, this design is more useful when there is a large known population.

These designs provide more information than does a cross-sectional survey or case study. However, an issue that confronts social work researchers is the retention of participants over time, particularly in prospective panel designs and single-subject designs where the same persons are used as respondents. Rubin and Babbie (2005) suggest a number of procedures that may help in recruiting and retaining participants from minority and oppressed groups for research. Culturally sensitive approaches such as the following might be useful: employ local members of the group being studied as research staff; if there are community leaders of the population being studied, obtain their endorsement of the research; provide some payment as an incentive for research participants; employ culturally competent research staff as interviewers; train the research staff to be more culturally competent; use bilingual staff, if necessary; use tracking methods (telephone and agency reminders, for example) for locating persons for second, third, and/or repeated measurements over time.

The use of large-scale survey and panel designs depends on available population lists of large numbers of potential respondents. Without known population lists, random sampling procedures are impractical. Many researchers who deal with minority and oppressed populations indicate that snowball and purposive sampling might be useful for engaging participants, and disproportionate stratified sampling (i.e., sampling larger proportions of minority and oppressed populations) might lead to the study of larger numbers of minority groups (see Potocky & Rodgers-Farmer, 1998, for a detailed discussion of methodological issues and innovations involved in social work research with minority and oppressed populations).

Participatory Research

A research design that is more focused on the engagement of minority immigrants is that of participatory research. This approach is described in the research of Gellis (2001). He studied 84 immigrant family caretakers in Canada (35 Vietnamese, 29 Koreans, and 20 Jamaicans) to determine how they dealt with mental health services for their mentally ill relatives. The overall goal was to provide data that could increase cultural competency of mental health service providers. More specific goals were (p. 268):

- To encourage the active participation of ethnic minorityimmigrants in defining and addressing their problems.
- To document the barriers that confront immigrants from non-English-speaking backgrounds.
- To indicate courses of action that will overcome potential barriers to effective service delivery.
- To make recommendations on how findings may be incorporated within the provision of culturally sensitive programs in mental health.

According to Gellis (2001, p. 270), participatory research (PR) "is perceived as a methodology of action oriented research that is developed with and in support of groups that historically have been excluded from knowledge generation and utilization." It involves the use of quantitative and qualitative data that may assist in the solution of community problems. Participatory research is described as a process whose

distinguishing characteristics are (a) extensive collaboration between traditionally defined researchers and the community in each research stage from identifying the problem to applying and disseminating results; (b) a reciprocal educational process between community and resesearcher with an emphasis on taking action on the issue under study. Collaboration takes place between people within the community whose interests lie in changing the status quo and one or more technically trained researchers whose interests lie in developing knowledge. (p. 270)

The goals of participatory research are to generate knowledge, achieve community goals, and improve local services by the use of methods such as qualitative interviews, focus groups, home and institutional visits, and community analyses. Activities in the research process include field experience, recruiting members, developing coalitions and alliances, and attempts to influence service systems and political systems (Gellis, 2001). Whereas in the typical research process researchers attempt to take an objective posture and control their relationship to research participants, in PR the researcher is an adviser, "participants take ownership of study," and objectivity is enhanced "through critical inquiry and reflection" (p. 271). The final outcome of PR studies is the generation of knowledge, social action, and a report for stakeholders.

The approach employed by Gellis was to use snowball sampling methods to identify, within a large city in Ontario, Canada, three groups of immigrant families of caretakers whose relatives were mentally ill. Data were gathered from

focus groups, field interviews, community and demographic analysis, and documentary evidence. . . . Three focus groups met early in the study to provide in-depth understanding of Korean, Vietnamese, and Jamaican immigrant participant concerns. This strategy also served to link and enhance social networks among the three ethnic caregiver groups. Both Asian and Jamaican participants bonded during the focus group experience as a result of similar negative interactions with the mental health system. (Gellis, 2001, p. 271)

Focus groups included 20 to 30 members and provided discussion regarding these questions: "What barriers are you encountering in the mental health system?" and "How would you improve the mental health system?" (p. 272). Contents of focus groups and interviews were categorized into issues, general themes, and more abstract categories. Transcripts of interviews were coded and analyzed, with interrater reliability ranging from 85% to 90%. Among the major findings of the study these were included (pp. 275–276):

- One of the most common barriers delineated in the study was communication.
- The presence of mental illness raised a major taboo issue with all three immigrant ethnic groups.
- Language and cultural misunderstanding were consistently reported as common barriers to the effectiveness of mental health services.
- Immigrant caregivers were concerned with the behaviors of their mentally ill relatives because it was in a manner that was not culturally accepted.
- All participants reported high levels of mistrust of psychiatrists and other mental health providers.

These PR methods were used to develop an immigrant family caregiver council project: literature review, community analysis, collaboration with participants, and collaboration with mental health practitioners. The purpose of the council was to increase involvement of the caretakers in mental health service delivery decision-making, thereby reducing their isolation from the mental health services delivery system. Through the council, participants expressed their perceived needs of education for service providers regarding knowledge of their cultures, as well as the need for educational materials for interpreters and caregivers. Moreover, partnerships were developed between practitioners and participants as a result of meetings between immigrants and mental health service providers. These concluding statements were made:

> Participatory research has been chosen as the methodology for implementing the Immigrant Family Caregiver Council because it promotes the active participation of the community in addressing actions directed toward achieving its goal. This was achieved by ensuring that members of the immigrant communities were recruited into the research activities and given control over how the research problem was conceived and examined. These characteristics are consistent with social work practice of collective research, reflection and rational problem-solving, community education, and social actions for improved quality of community life. (Gellis, 2001, p. 278)

Sampling

Generalization to relevant populations is an issue that besets intranational research. Representative sampling methods are useful when population lists are available. Such lists can be generated with respect to current recipients of services from social agencies, but they would exclude those who have not made contact with social agenices. For these defined populations, representative sampling methods include the census (where the entire population is enumerated) and probability sampling methods such as simple random sampling, stratified random sampling, and so on. When multiple service agencies are involved, area probability sampling can also be employed.

It is important for intranational researchers to keep in mind the relevant population from which samples are drawn, for these populations serve to restrict the generalizability of research studies. Figure 4.1 depicts several different subpopulations of a host country. First, there is the larger population of all who reside in the host country. Second, there is the population of nonmigrants and a smaller population of migrants. The migrant population can also be subdivided into populations of immigrants, refugees, asylum-seekers, and so on. As depicted in figure 4.1, the migrant population includes migrants from all other countries. This can be further specified to migrants from one particular country. And an even smaller population can be delineated in reference to those migrants from a particular country who have resided in the host country for a specified period of time. Obviously, there are many possible variations on these patterns. The main point illustrated here is that even the most representative of sampling techniques can only be deemed representative of the population from which samples are drawn. Hence samples of Vietnamese migrants are not representative of other Asian migrants; samples of migrants who receive social services are not necessarily representative of those who do not receive services; samples of refugees are not necessarily representative of voluntary migrants; and so on.

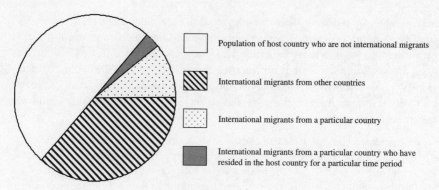

Figure 4.1. Population of the host country.

Throughout this chapter, it has been emphasized that migrant populations who are from ethnic minorities and oppressed populations are difficult to locate, recruit, and retain for participation in social work research. This is especially the case for those who are undocumented immigrants and may be fearful of deportation or of cooperating with social work researchers due to the expectation of reprisals from others, such as slave masters in human trafficking, families from the country from which they migrated, immigration officials, and so forth. Techniques that seek to assume anonymity and confidentiality are useful, as well as snowball sampling, which depends on the identification of people through other migrants or by means of others who have had contacts with migrants. These methods lead to purposive or convenience samples that are not necessarily representative, particularly if one is seeking to provide descriptive facts and correlations within the population being studied. However, these methods are useful for generating ideas and developing hypotheses for future study. Since research studies can be costly and time-consuming, it is recommended that studies be more comprehensive in their knowledge objectives, that is, seek new hypotheses and questions as well as providing information pertinent to the testing of hypotheses. Therefore, it is further recommended that, to the extent possible, research studies should specify different relevant populations and then include sampling methods that are geared to those populations. For example, one might use probabilistic sampling methods for studying migrants who received family services from specified agencies and snowball and anonymous sampling for locating and interviewing migrants who live in the same geographic area but have not received family services.

Data Collection and Data Analysis

Although it is recommended that researchers strive to be culturally competent, it is also recommended that there be methodological studies pertaining to the validity of cultural competence measures. For example, there should be studies that indicate the relationship between perceived cultural competence and the accuracy of obtained information. With respect to the use of interpreters, one should avoid using respondents' family members or friends as interpreters, since their own interests would bias the interview data (Potocky-Tripodi, 2002). One should not assume cultural competence because one person is of the same ethnicity as another. Methodological studies can be conducted with respect to measures of cultural competence and racial and ethnic identities to verify whether or not common assumptions such as this are true in various types of data collection. Given that a culturally competent researcher should be aware of and control her/his biases regarding minorities and oppressed groups, it is also possible that the researchers themselves may be biased toward or against their own groups.

Instruments that are constructed for use with international migrants should be pilot tested on a sample that is representative of the group that will be studied. It is insufficient to have translations and back-translations by professional researchers and their colleagues; the translations need to be understood by the intended participants in the research. In developing cross-cultural instruments, it appears to be more fruitful to use confirmatory factor analysis than exploratory factor analysis. This is because confirmatory factor analysis involves an indication of theoretical relationships between the measured variable and other variables, which is more directly related to the procurement of information regarding construct validity. In addition, there should be more efforts to obtain information regarding the cross-cultural equivalency of research instruments. In particular, there should be efforts devoted to translating and testing instruments developed in other countries for potential cross-cultural uses in the United States, as well as the obverse situation, in which instruments developed in the United States are translated for use in other countries.

In research that involves migrants, minorities, and/or oppressed populations, researchers should make efforts to analyze within-group differences of cultural groups, as well as making comparisons between cultural groups. Knowledge of within-group variation can be beneficial, in that it would help us to avoid making stereotypic impressions of our own as well as other cultural groups. In addition, it is important to study changes over time by means of longitudinal research. Not only can migrants change with respect to the ways in which they acculturate and their degrees of acculturation but also the people in the host country can change in their perceptions of migrants. Thus, more dynamic research that looks at changes in perceptions of different migrant groups over time is recommended. Changes in perceptions of migrants by the host country can be a result of public policy changes, political propaganda, geopolitical changes, socioeconomic environmental changes, and so forth. However, knowledge regarding the extent of these possible changes needs to be obtained and tested in further research.

Conclusions and Implications

Conclusions of data from a particular research study should be considered in the context of change. Data from cross-sectional studies provide important information about descriptive facts and the relationships of variables at one point in time; in other words, the data are from a sample of one time period and may not necessarily be reflective of the past or of the future. Therefore, appended to the conclusions of a time-constrained study should be the discussion of possible changes over time and suggestions for further research in that regard.

Conclusions based on exploratory research often include recommendations in the form of implications for social work practice. It is important for both research-ers and utilizers of research knowledge to understand the level of knowledge that is produced, as well as the extent of its generalizability. Often the results of these studies are in the form of hypotheses that are conceptually but not substantively general-izable; that is, the hypotheses need to be tested in situations other than where the research was conducted. Recommendations about changes in social services and suggested reorganizations of services need to be evaluated in other contexts. In addition, suggested interventions also need to be evaluated for use in practice by methods of program evaluation or practice evaluation.

The methods of participatory research are directly geared to the generation of data by researchers and participants, and for the implementation of interventions in the local context. Even for recommendations from those studies, as well as from action research in general, it is crucial for the interventions that are implemented to be evaluated to determine their effectiveness and efficiency. Although evalua-tion may be implicit in participatory research, it is suggested that evaluative efforts be included more formally as a part of the approach. Researchers and research par-ticipants and other stakeholders should be involved in participatory evaluation, where they decide on the objectives for the intervention, criteria for effectiveness and efficiency, necessary data that need to be gathered, and criteria for evaluating the data.

INCENTIVES AND BARRIERS TO INTRANATIONAL RESEARCH

Among the barriers to conducting intranational research are the following: costs, lack of collaboration, lack of time, difficulties in recruitment and retention, lack of cross-cultural instruments, and lack of resources to meet participants' needs.

There are costs involved in many aspects of intranational research. The more translators are used, the greater the costs for translation. Costs increase as a func-tion of time spent in the research per se, that is, longitudinal reearch is more ex-pensive than cross-sectional research. Costs also rise as a result of data collection and data analytic procedures. Interviews and the recording and coding of data are more costly than questionnaires. Employing consultants for data analysis as well as the data analyses and computer packages used can be costly. Costs for recruitment and retention that involve transportation and means of communication need to be considered in the budget for research, as well as the costs for the compensation of research assistants. Moreover, developing original cross-cultural instruments fol-lowing procedures discussed in this chapter can be expensive.

Incentives to overcome these cost barriers are the possible availability of research grants from governmental or private agencies. These require the development of research proposals. Social and health agencies may have monies set aside to use for research; thus, an incentive for research might be available through such agencies. A resource for research is universities, that is, professors and students who are interested in conducting research and who volunteer their time to do so. Academics might collaborate with social agencies, who may provide access to participants and the use of agency resources, including records of transactions with potential participants. Agency workers might donate a small percentage of their time for collecting data, particularly if the data, such as client needs, are relevant to their concerns.

If there is a lack of collaboration, however, this can be considered a barrier to research. With collaboration comes the investment of time and resources. Even if social agencies and other community organizations do not choose to collaborate in research, their cooperation is necessary. Agencies would need to give permission to researchers regarding access to data. Moreover, permission also needs to be received from potential participants to engage in the research. Issues of confidentiality, voluntary participation, informed consent, and other ethical concerns need to be approved by institutional review boards or their equivalent and by the social agencies themselves if they are to participate in the proposed research. Steps can be taken to overcome these barriers. It is up to the researchers and the research team to indicate why the research is necessary and how it might result in benefits for the participants, either in terms of knowledge that will be of value to other members of the population and/or in actual benefits received. Persuading agencies to collaborate in the research is helpful to the research enterprise. If there is a pooling of resources from the research team, say, of academics and social agencies, the costs can be reduced. In addition, the discovery of mutual benefits from the results of research would enhance the collaboration. There may be research grants, as in the United States, that are especially geared to collaboration between child welfare and/or mental health agencies, for example, and research teams.

Another barrier is lack of time. Sponsors of research, agency executives, and other stakeholders may exert pressures to have the research completed within a specified time period. This may, for example, reduce the likelihood of having extensive time available to conduct longitudinal research or to develop reliable and valid cross-cultural instruments. To overcome this barrier, it is necessary for the research team to demonstrate that the extra time devoted to the research is necessary to provide knowledge that is valid and useful, as opposed to inapplicable, invalid knowledge. Or there might be compromises of certain aspects of the research; for example, longitudinal research may involve fewer points in time, or interviews might involve a greater number of structured and fewer open-ended questions. However, the standard should be new knowledge that will be useful for research participants and for those who might provide social services for those participants.

A barrier that affects research with minorities and oppressed populations, including international migrants, is that of recruitment and retention. As we prevously indicated, locating migrants, particularly illegal immigrants, some of whom might be involved in illegal activities such as the sex trade, is extremely difficult. Potential research participants may be reluctant to be involved in resarch because of fears of deportation, fears for their lives, and other fears that affect them and their families. Researchers should be in a position to guarantee confidentiality, but at the same time refer them to agencies or persons that might be able to educate them about their legal rights. Incentives for participation are paramount, whether it be by some small payment (which obviously increases the costs of the research), or in some equivalent form such as coupons for food, free language lessons, discussion with interpreters about legal rights, and so forth. Or the research method itself, such as participatory research, may increase for participants the likelihood that their concerns might be heard, thereby leading to more favorable outcomes for them. The location of potential participants may be enhanced with sampling methods such as snowball sampling and anonymous sampling; however, it is unknown whether the obtained samples would be representative of the population under consideration.

Nonavailability of cross-cultural instruments may be a barrier to research. Obviously, this can be overcome by the use of interpreters and/or the development of cross-cultural instruments. This, of course, requires more time and money. The methods employed by Cornelius et al. (2004), previously described in the section on instrument construction, are instructive. They used a participatory process in which stakeholders (mental health practitioners, consumers, and researchers) collaborated to develop an instrument to measure cultural competence. Their collaborative process for developing instruments can serve as a model that others might follow in the development of instruments. Time and money become less of an issue when the stakeholders believe it is important to develop an instrument, taking the necessary time, that can better serve their purposes.

Resources can be increased through collaboration between researchers and key stakeholders as described here. Researchers can assist social agencies by engaging in research on needs of clientele and resources for helping to meet those needs. In turn, agencies can assist researchers by making available some of their resources, for example, computers, case records, a portion of social work time, lists of migrants who receive services, and so on. Resources can also be made available through small university research grants and the activities of students and professors in joint research projects.

SUMMARY

We began the substantive portion of the chapter by defining intranational research as international research that studies a population from one country residing within another country, and uses literature from both countries to formulate the research problem and to interpret the data in deriving conclusions and implications. In addition to having the same characteristics as supranational research, intranational research is distinguished by studying two or more countries, the host country as well as migrants from another country. It was also noted that intranational research often involves more than one language. A hypothetical example of intranational research was presented, involving the research process in a study of Russian migrants' uses of mental health and family services.

We discussed social work problems that confront research participants in intranational research. Social workers who work with potential participants in intranational research, as in all international research, deal with problems such as these: human rights, migration, displacement of persons, provision of services for youth and older persons, poverty, social/economic development, and social justice. Problems faced by international migrants include the following: economic adaptation, legal rights, language acquisition, domestic abuse, health care access, differential treatment of minorities and oppressed persons, depression, somatization, guilt, post-traumatic stress disorder, meeting social and health needs, education, communication, separation of family members, and so on.

We illustrated the type of information social workers should have about migrant populations in order to have a comprehensive perspective that affects the potential research participants. This was done by providing key conceptual definitions pertaining to international migrants. Included were definitions of various categories of voluntary and forced, and permanent and temporary, migrants. We briefly described the classical theory of the causes of migration and factors included in more complex theories, as well as stages of migration: premigration and departure, transit, resettlement, and repatriation. We noted the importance of international migration policies in forming a context for intranational research.

We discussed issues regarding different aspects of the research process. In problem formulation, we discussed literature reviews, and we emphasized what factors are necessary for cultural competence to be achieved by social work researchers. In instrument construction, we illustrated a participatory process that was involved in devising a measure of cultural competency (Cornelius et al., 2004). In addition we presented a cross-cultural equivalence model that assessed semantic equivalence, content equivalence, technical equivalence, and conceptual equivalence in translating a mainland U.S. instrument into Spanish for Puerto Rican participants (Alvello et al., 2001). In addition, we described a comprehensive, multistrategy, multistage procedure for developing research instruments (Tran & Aroian, 2000).

Two major research strategies that can be used for intranational research were described: longitudinal research and participatory research, which involves the collaboration of researchers and participants in developing research knowledge and creating a structure for community organization. We represented the problem of generalizability as serious, and distinguished different relevant populations from which samples could be drawn; and we recommended combined approaches to sampling. For example, the use of disproportionate stratified random sampling combined with snowball or purposive sampling.

With respect to data collection and data analyses, we emphasized cultural competence in the development of cross-cultural instruments, and the use of confirmatory factor analysis for investigating construct validity. We continue to emphasize critical thinking and care in deriving generalizations from research; and we pointed out that implications for social work are often in the form of hypotheses, and as such should be tested when implemented in social work practice. We concluded the chapter with a discussion of incentives and barriers to intranational resarch, considering factors such as these: the costs of research; the advantages of collaboration regarding sharing of resources; how available time affects the type of research design and data collection methods used in intranational research; and the need for cross-cultural instruments and their development by means of collaboration of researchers and stakeholders.

5

ISSUES AND EXAMPLES
OF INTRANATIONAL RESEARCH

We present five intranational studies in this chapter. Within the section on each study, we describe it with respect to the research process: problem formulation and knowledge objectives; instrumentation and data collection; relevant populations, sampling, and research design; and data analyses, conclusions and implications. We indicate why each study is classified as intranational; then we present issues that are discussed or referred to in the research, and consider research and utilization issues that arise from the study. We conclude with a summary of the issues presented in the five studies.

Selection of the Studies

We used the same criteria, with the exception of the study's classification as intranational as opposed to supranational, for selecting research studies as were employed in chapter 3:

- Excellence of study
- Presentation of a range of research methods
- Studies are from several social work journals
- Studies are from different countries
- Studies evoke pertinent issues in the conduct and utilization of research

As in chapter 3, the selected studies are intended to be illustrative, rather than representative or exhaustive of all studies that meet these criteria.

The studies in this chapter were selected from these journals: *Social Work, International Social Work, Journal of Social Work Research and Evaluation: An International Publication*, and *Research on Social Work Practice*. The research studies took place in Nicaragua, Canada, the United States, and Israel; and they were concerned with Korean Americans, Iraqi refugees, forced and voluntary migrants in Nicaragua, Ethiopian Jews, and Vietnamese immigrants. The studies involved a field experiment, longitudinal research, focus groups, semistructured interviews, qualitative analyses, random sampling, qualitative description, analyses of variance, regression analyses, and bivariate analyses. Issues involved such topics as sampling and representativeness, age as a variable in studying adolescents, attrition in panel studies, training of staff in field research, implementation and evaluation of recommendations, and exploratory data analyses.

STUDY 1: "EFFECTS OF CULTURALLY RELEVANT PSYCHOEDUCATION FOR KOREAN AMERICAN FAMILIES OF PERSONS WITH CHRONIC MENTAL ILLNESS," BY SUN-KYUNG SHIN (2004)

Study Description

Problem Formulation and Knowledge Objectives

The author reviews notions about mental illness for Korean Americans, indicating cultural obstacles and misunderstandings that affect treatment for the mentally ill. The purpose of the study is to specify culturally relevant treatment and to evaluate the effectiveness of a psychoeducational intervention with Korean American parents of children who are mentally ill. The hypotheses to be tested were framed as causal hypotheses:

Hypothesis 1: Participants in the psychoeducational treatment groups would describe experiencing less stigma associated with mental illness than the control group.
Hypothesis 2: Participants in the psychoeducational treatment group would increase their empowerment more than those who were in the control group.
Hypothesis 3: Participants of the psychoeducational treatment group would improve their efficiency in coping with their problems more than nonparticipants.

(Shin, 2004, p. 236)

The rationale for conducting the study was as follows.

- The author indicated that in a previous study it was shown that "compared to a control group that received only individual supportive therapy, an experimental group of clients that received a culturally sensitive psychoeducational program in addition to the individual supportive therapy showed significantly reduced symptom severity and perception of stigma and increased coping skills after the treatment" (Shin, 2004, p. 231).
- In the author's literature review, a number of studies indicated that educating families about the mental illness of their relatives and how to manage the illness could be beneficial for the clients as well as for their families. The psychoeducational approach employed was based on three theoretical approaches: social learning, family systems theory, and stress theory. The social learning approach "emphasizes the learning of adaptive skills while increasing the knowledge of illness. Educational models generally include information on the epidemiology and nature of illness, diagnosis and symptoms, etiology, course and outcome, and medication. In addition, psychoeducation provides a cognitive framework for clients and their families to understand the illness and rationale for treatment" (p. 232). Family systems theory emphasizes how interactions of family members can have direct and

indirect influences on the treatment of the mentally ill. In addition, the psychoeducational approach incorporates ideas from stress theory, focusing on the reduction of stress in families and using them as allies in the process of treating their relatives.

- Previous research studies did not incorporate knowledge about cultural values that are unique to Korean Americans. Hence the researcher identified culturally relevant treatment methods that could be employed in psychoeducation.
- Extrapolating from studies in Mainland China, it was inferred that Asians (Koreans) are more likely to be affected by their family interactions than non-Asians. Therefore, it is justifiable to focus treatment methods on the family of the client as well as the client.

Instrumentation and the Process of Data Collection

Forty-eight parents of children who were mentally ill received a series of measurements before and after 10 weekly psychoeducational group sessions (for 24 parents in an experimental group) or 10 individual supportive sessions (for 24 parents in the control group). According to Shin,

> the instruments were initially translated by the author and subsequently reviewed by two Korean American psychiatrists who are bilingual and bicultural. The Korean versions of instruments were then translated back to English by a bilingual and bicultural social worker. The retranslated versions were compared with the original English version, and ambiguities thereof were corrected. (2004, p. 234)

The measures were comprised of demographics such as age, sex, education, marital status, employment status, and so on, of which the data were gathered by questionnaire; and the stigma/devaluation scale, the family empowerment scale; and the family crisis oriented personal evaluation scales, which were employed as dependent variables in the three hypotheses of the study:

Stigma/devaluation (STI). Stigma was measured using Link's (1987, 1989) Stigma Devaluation Scale (alpha = .88). The scale consists of 12 items that assess the extent to which respondents believe that most people devalue or discriminate against a person with a history of psychiatric treatment.

Family Empowerment Scale (FES). The Family Empowerment Scale (FES) consists of 34 items designed to measure empowerment in families with a child who is emotionally disabled (Koren, DeChillo, and Friesen, 1992). Subscale scores are available for three levels of empowerment, that is, Family, Service System, and Community/Political. The scale has very good evidence of reliability. Validity in the ratings is seen with kappa coefficients of agreement for multiple raters of .83, .70, and .77, respectively.

Family Crisis Oriented Personal Evaluation Scales (F-COPES). The Family Crisis Oriented Personal Evaluation Scales (F-COPES) was created to identify problem-solving and behavioral strategies utilized by families in difficult or problematic situations (McCubbin, Olson, and Larsen, 1991). . . . The instrument includes 30 coping behavior items that focused on two levels of interaction: (a) from individual-to-family system, or the ways a family internally handles difficulties and problems between its members; and (b) from family to social environment, or the ways in which the family externally handles problems or demands. The F-COPES has very good validity with a kappa coefficient of .86. Individual scales have alphas that range from .63 to .83.

(pp. 235–236)

Sampling, Relevant Populations, and Research Design

The immediate, relevant population in this study is that of the parents of Korean American children who are diagnosed as mentally ill and are receiving outpatient services in Queens, New York. A broader population might have been Korean American families in the United States over a span of time much more extensive than that which is noted in accidental or convenience sampling. The sample in this study is itself the relevant population, and that is the population to which generalizations should be restricted:

Either the mother or the father from each family of individuals with chronic mental illness was recruited from a pool of 110 Korean Americans who were receiving services at an outpatient mental health clinic in the borough of Queens in New York City. The ethnic designation of Korean American was made only when a father and a mother from each family were Korean by origin. Anyone who had a child with a diagnosis of schizophrenic, schizoaffective, or schizophreniform disorder set forth in the DSM-IV was eligible for the study. The current study combined purposive and convenience sampling procedures. Among 65 parents whose child met the diagnostic criteria, 48 consented to participate in the study, a response rate of 73%. Before the first session, the 48 participants were provided with a brief description of the study and were asked to sign an informed consent form, following an approval of the protocol by an Institutional Review Board. (Shin, 2004, p. 233)

The research design was a pretest-posttest experimental design, with 24 Korean American parents randomly assigned to the experimental group and another 24 Korean American parents randomly assigned to the control group. The experimental group received 10 weekly psychoeducational group sessions, each session lasting for 90 minutes; and they received "individual supportive sessions on an as-needed basis, although it was subject to the psychoeducational sessions" (Shin, 2004, p. 233).

The author, who is a Korean-speaking social worker specializing in mental health, led the psychoeducational sessions. "These sessions were conducted in Korean and . . . included a variety of culturally oriented educational techniques designed to enhance the participants' learning and to maintain their attention. The first part of each session was conducted in lecture form and was followed by question and answer and discussion" (Shin, 2004, p. 234). A curriculum manual was used that compiled material from other psychoeducational programs that were concerned with biological and environmental determinants of mental illness. Moreover, Shin (p. 234) reported that

the conventional curriculum manual was properly modified to consider the culturally unique characteristics of Korean American values. For example, discussion of traditional disease concepts commonly shared by the Koreans was integrated into the sessions because many Koreans tend to attribute their psychiatric illness to hav-ing been haunted by a ghost or to a misfortune destined to be carried with them on their birth.

Members of the control group did not receive the psychoeducational treatment, but they received 10 individual supportive sessions, each lasting approximately 45 minutes. All participants were given questionnaires that included the measures for the study just before treatment was instituted and one week after treatment was completed. The experiment occurred between January and March 2000.

Data Analysis, Conclusions, and Implications

The author first presented reliability analyses using Cronbach's alpha of the three dependent variables tested in the study's hypotheses: stigma devaluation scale, .89; family empowerment scale, .96; and F-COPES, .87. Then, 2 x 2 analyses of variance were conducted (the experimental and control groups, before and after treatment) for each of the three dependent variables. All three hypotheses were supported. There were significant main effects for time, indicating that for the entire sample, there was a decrease of stigma regarding mental illness, an increase in empowerment, and an improvement in coping strategies during family crisis from before treatment to after treatment. Moreover, interactions were found between time and treatment for all three dependent variables, indicating that over the 10-week period of time, the experimen-tal group decreased their sense of stigma about mental illness, gained in family em-powerment, and increased coping skills to a greater degree than the control group. The presentation of findings for Hypothesis 1, or stigma/devaluation (STI), is illus-trative of presentations for all three hypotheses, with similar findings:

> There was a significant main effect for time, $F = 543.70$, $p < .001$, proportion of variance explained (PVE) $= .226$, indicating that for the sample as a whole, there was a lessening of STI regarding mental illness from pre- to posttest. An interaction was also found between time and treatment ($F = 145.48$, $p < .001$, PVE $= .168$), dem-onstrating that over the course of treatment, the experimental group decreased their stigma about mental illness when compared to the control group. (Shin, 2004, p. 236)

The author made the following conclusions.

> An existing psychoeducational approach, wherein the actual curriculum manual thereof was slightly modified to incorporate the culturally unique characteristics of Korean American values was adapted and used to enhance the treatment of Korean American families whose children were mentally ill. The results of the current study showed that Korean American families can benefit from a culturally relevant psychoeducational program; that is, psychoeducation enhanced the participants' attitudes about mental illness and increased their empowerment and coping skills in dealing with the crisis. . . . To improve the quality of mental health care for Korean Americans, service delivery systems should be developed based on a comprehen-sive mental health care model that emphasizes the importance of culturally relevant care. In the case of the Korean Americans, such a desirable service delivery system requires valuing their families as allies for the social work practitioners to be more effectively engaged in the treatment of individuals with mental illness. (p. 238)

The knowledge produced in this study included descriptive facts about the Korean American families and supported hypotheses of a causal nature, the generalizability of which is restricted to the local context in which the research occurred. Implications for mental health care are hypothetical and subject to further implementation and evaluation.

Classification of the Study

The study is classified as intranational research for these reasons:

- Literature from more than one country is used to frame the research problem: the United States, Korea, China, England.
- The research is focused on Korean immigrants in the United States whose children are mentally ill.
- Implications are presented for other countries as well as the United States, where the research occurred.

Issues Addressed in the Study

Group Equivalence in Experimental Studies

Randomization in experiments has the purpose of controlling for unknown variables and distributing them in such a way that there are no significant differences between experimental and control groups. It is always a good experimental procedure to check on the results of a randomization process. The author did this by comparing the experimental and control groups on variables, other than the dependent variables, for which there was available information. The idea is that if there are no statistically significant differences with known variables, it increases the researcher's confidence in presuming the randomization procedures are effective. Shin tested for equivalence on these variables, employing chi square tests on nominal classifications, such as marital status, and two sample t-tests on variables that are represented by ratio scales, such as age, number of children, and years in United States. There were no statistically significant differences on any of these variables, confirming the equivalence of experimental and control groups.

Equivalence of Experimental and Control Groups over Time

The utilizer of research should pay attention to the extent to which experimental and control groups are equivalent over time, that is, in this research, between the pretest and the posttest. If there is attrition in either of the experimental or control groups, the randomization procedures are affected with unknown changes in probability. The greater the attrition, the less likely it is that the randomization procedure would be effective, that is, producing equivalent groups. In such an instance, the randomized pretest-posttest experimental design would become a quasi-experimental research design, namely, a nonequivalent control group design (Shadish et al., 2002).

With attrition, the researcher should again check on the distribution of variables on experimental groups. If the variables remain equally distributed between experimental and control groups, the researcher can increase the confidence in equivalence. In this study by Shin, there was no reported attrition; hence the randomization process remained in effect, and the experimental and control groups can be regarded as equivalent.

Issues Arising from the Study

Experimental Equivalence in Research Design

The author conducted the 90-minute psychoeducational sessions for the experimental group; and individual supportive sessions, subject to the psychoeducational sessions, were given as needed over the 10-week period. A social work student who was closely supervised by the author gave supportive sessions for the control group. The logic of the experimental design was apparently to compare the treatment for the experimental group (psychoeducational treatment = X plus supportive treatment = Y), symbolized as X + Y, with that for the control group (who received only the supportive treatment, Y). Assuming that Y in the experimental and control groups is equivalent, the changes in the control group, Y, can be subtracted from changes in the experimental group, X + Y. This serves as an approximation to an experimental group, X, compared with a no-treatment control group, with no X and no Y. In this experiment, it appears that the Y in the experimental and control groups is not the same. First, the length of each total session in X + Y is approximately 90 minutes versus 45 minutes for the control group Y. Second, in Y, the treatment was administered by different persons. The interactions with parents might have been different. Third, the person who provided X for the treatment group also provided Y. Hence it appears quite possible that Y in the experimental and control groups is not equivalent. If this is the case, the experimental design becomes a design comparing two treatments rather than an experimental design with a no-treatment control group. In subsequent experimentation, it would be recommended that the Y portion of supportive treatment be equated as much as possible for both groups. If that would be impossible to do a priori, then it is recommended to detail the nature and amount of the treatment under the rubric of Y so as to more clearly be able to discern the effects of the treatment, X.

Implications as Hypotheses to Be Tested

Often in research studies, authors derive implications for social work. These implications are often requested by editors of social work journals to indicate the utility and relevance of the research for social work. With the constraints of providing implications, the authors of research studies may speculate and develop hypotheses based on their experiences and preconceived notions and not necessarily on data produced in the studies. The utilizer of research, in general, should determine to what extent the implications are based on data from the study, and the level of knowledge and generalizability of the implications. Hypotheses, for example, are in need of further testing. They are the results of studies that have no degree of generalizability. A study confined to a local area, a few clients, and a local treatment provider would not be generalizable; hence the results of such a study would be at the hypothetical level.

The development of hypotheses from the research is illustrated in the penultimate paragraph of Shin's discussion of applications of the research:

> A consideration of culture or ethnicity in formulating treatment plans may enhance the process of therapy and prevent premature termination. The underutilization of mental health services by Asian Americans, including the Korean population, will not be resolved unless a restructuring of the mental health system is linked to more comprehensive and culturally specific service delivery. Thus, to improve the quality of mental health care for Korean Americans, service delivery systems should be developed based on a comprehensive mental health care model that emphasizes the importance of culturally relevant care. In the case of the Korean Americans, such a desirable service delivery system requires valuing their families as allies for the social work practitioners to be more effectively engaged in the treatment of individuals with mental illness. (2004, p. 238)

Obviously, there are implicit hypotheses in that paragraph. For example, "restructuring of the mental health service delivery system" linked to "more comprehensive and culturally specific service delivery" will result in increased utilization of "mental health services by Asian Americans, including the Korean population." This is a plausible notion, but it is not based on data from the study. Further research, for testing this hypothesis, should focus on its implementation and program design, followed by an evaluation of the effectiveness and efficiency of the program in increasing utilization rates of mental health services by Asian Americans.

STUDY 2: "THE CHALLENGES OF RESETTLEMENT AMONG MALE, GOVERNMENT-ASSISTED IRAQI REFUGEES IN CANADA," BY JOSEPH H. MICHALSKI (2001)

Study Description

Problem Formulation and Knowledge Objectives

Providing a context for his research, Michalski (2001, p. 207) reported that

> in July 1996, the Government of Canada responded to a United Nations Appeal by agreeing to accept more than 300 of the thousands of Iraqi citizens who had been living in the Rafha refugee camp in Saudi Arabia since 1991 as a result of the Gulf War. The difficulties for Iraqis in adjusting to Canadian life after their experiences at Rafha were expected to be enormous, even with Citizenship and Immigration Canada's case management assessment approach and the financial support of the

Adjustment Assistance Program. The Iraqi refugees were primarily single males, Muslim, under the age of 30, and had only a limited or no capacity to speak English. Many men had been in the Iraqi military.

Concerned about the extent to which Canada could provide significant assistance to aid Middle Eastern refugees in adaptation and adjustment, the researchers developed a thesis suggesting

> that the Canadian government had only a limited capacity to meet the settlement needs of the Iraqi refugees who were expected to experience both structural and cultural barriers to successful integration in Canadian society. Additionally, at that particular time, many community-based agencies providing services to refugees and newcomers in general suffered cuts to their funding that further reduced their capacity to respond effectively to the plight of the Iraqi refugees. (p. 208)

In light of the author's theses, the purpose of his research was to study how government-assisted refugees from the Rafha camp settled in Toronto, Canada. Michalski was interested in presenting

> the strengths and potential problems with the resettlement program for government-assisted refugees from the perspectives of the Iraqi refugees, as well as Citizenship and Immigration Canada officials and service providers. In cooperation with the Settlement Directorate of Citizenship and Immigration Canada (Ontario region), researchers tracked and interviewed an initial sample of 59 Iraqi refugees from the Rafha camp in Saudi Arabia at roughly four-month intervals throughout their first year in Canada. (2001, p. 211)

Essentially, the researcher was interested in providing quantitative-descriptive information about the settlement of Iraqi refugees by means of questionnaires and providing correlational knowledge of factors potentially related to the satisfaction of Iraqi refugees with their settlement experiences. In addition, from interviews with Canadian officials and service providers, the author sought to elicit recommendations for improving services to the refugees.

The rationale for the study was derived in reference to an extensive literature review of refugees and immigrants from a number of countries resettling in the United States and Canada:

- There has been very little research regarding the relocation of Middle Eastern refugees in Western countries that focuses on the settlement needs and expectations of refugees.
- "The research literature consistently highlights problems of learning the host language and assessing labour markets as among the most important challenges to settlement and adjustment" (Michalski, 2001, p. 209).
- Economic survival and occupational adaptation are important considerations in the settlement of refugees.
- It is important for refugees to understand the cultural and social norms of the host society.
- There are different models of intervention to assist refugees, but no uniform model. A challenge for social services is to develop effective interventions.

Instrumentation and the Process of Data Collection

Two sources of data were collected: (1) interviews with Iraqi refugees over four successive time periods: September 1996; January 1997; May 1997; and October 1997; and (2) interviews with key informants.

The interviews with Iraqi refugees were conducted in Arabic, with the interviewers recording responses on the interview schedules. An extensive set of questions was included in the interval schedules. These questions focused on the following: demographics, housing and employment; sources of income and economic support; assistance in finding a job; social and community supports; access to community programs for assistance; general settlement experiences and future plans in Canada; and "refugees' goals, their satisfaction with life in Canada, their future plans, and their sense of belonging to Canadian Society" (Michalski, 2001, p. 216).

To obtain information about the perceptions and recommendations of key informants regarding the settlement of Iraqi refugees, a semistructured interview schedule was administered to settlement service providers and immigration officials. According to Michalski, the

> interviewees included key personnel at each of the three Reception Centers in Toronto . . . orientation counselors, Citizenship and Immigration Canada settlement counselors and immigration officers in Toronto, London, and Calgary, and a service provider from a community center. Nearly everyone interviewed had at least eight years experience working in the area of settlement or with immigration in general. Finally, the principal investigator informally discussed with various Citizenship and Immigration Canada officials a variety of issues pertaining to these refugees, as well as obtained additional feedback from the two Arabic-speaking interviewers. (Michalski, 2001, pp. 218–219)

Sampling, Relevant Populations, and Research Design

The sample in this study was taken from a population of 161 adult Iraqi refugees who landed in Ontario in 1996 and were from the Rafha camp in Saudi Arabia. This represented 161 out of 341, or 47% of all of the Iraqi refugees from the Rafha camp who arrived in Canada in 1996. The study sample was narrowed down to those government-assisted Iraqi refugees who arrived in Toronto between mid-August and mid-October 1996, for a sample size of 89 Iraqi refugees from the Rafha camp in Saudi Arabia who stayed in one of the three reception centers in Toronto. Of this sample, 79 were adults, of whom 59 agreed to participate in the research. And of those 59 refugees, 35 remained for the complete study. Hence the relevant populations were restricted to Iraqi refugees from the Rafha camp in Saudi Arabia who arrived in Canada in 1996 (n = 341), in Ontario (n = 161), in Toronto (n = 89), as adults in Toronto (n = 79), as those who agreed to participate in the study (n = 59), and finally those who remained in the study for the fourth set of interviews, that is, the final wave of a panel study with four successive waves (n = 35). Broader relevant populations would include all Iraqi refugees from the Gulf War who resettled in different areas throughout the world. The sample for the study is a convenience or accidental sample, and the response rate depends on what relevant population is included in the calculation. For example, in the initial phase of the research (n = 59), the response rate is 59 out of 79 (74.7%), 59 out of 89 (66.3%), 59 out of 161 (36.6%), or 59 out of 341 (17.3%), depending on which relevant population is the focus of discussion. The author referred to the response rate of the study as 59 out of 79, that is,74.7% of the adult Iraqi refugees from the Rahfa camp in Saudi Arabia who arrived in Toronto within a two-month period of 1996.

The research design was a panel design for the Iraqi refugees conducted in four waves of interviewing: September 1996, January 1997, May 1997, and October 1997. A team of researchers conducted the interviews. Within the panel design, for example, in obtaining responses regarding satisfaction of life in Canada, 1996–1997, the sample size was reduced from 56 to 49 in wave 2, from 49 to 42 in wave 3, and from 42 to 34 in wave 4.

Relevant populations for the key informants included "key personnel at each of the reception centers in Toronto, orientation counselors, Citizenship and Immigration Canada settlement counselors and immigration officers in Toronto, London, and Calgary" (Michalski, 2001, p. 219), as well as service providers from community centers. The sample size consisted of 14 key informants. No information was provided on population sizes. The research design of key informants was a cross-sectional survey comprised of semistructured interviews at one point in time.

Data Analysis, Conclusions, and Implications

For analyzing responses from the refugees, the researcher systematically presented information in terms of percentages regarding demographics and the set of questions that were asked of the respondent. It was, for the most part, a straightforward presentation of quantitative descriptions. With respect to demographics, in the first wave, 94.9% were male; the average age was 30.0 years; 74.2% were single; 18.6% shared household accommodations; 20.3% had graduated from high school; 88.5% had been in the Iraqi military; and 76.3% had poor English language ability. The largest changes observed in the fourth wave were that sharing accommodations increased from 18.6% to 70.6%, and poor English language ability decreased from 76.3% to 11.8%.

Some of the major findings from interviews with the Iraqi refugees are as follows (Michalski, 2001, pp. 213–216):

- The interviewees indicated that there had been only three sources of financial support in their households in the past 12 months: Adjustment Assistance Program (AAP) income, which everyone received; social assistance, which most turned to as a primary means of support once their AAP payments had ended (69%); and wages and salaries from paid employment opportunities (26%).
- More than half (55%) of the respondents indicated they had received help in finding jobs.
- Most respondents reported they had family or close friends available (85.7%)
- The respondents rarely accessed community programs. Those that were most often used were community programs for English (42.9%), programs

to find housing (25.7%), food banks (20.0%), and programs for other settlement tasks (11.4%).

- The most common responses in answer to the question "Based on your
experience, what are the three most important things that you have learned
to help you deal with the challenges of settling in Canada?" were "learn or
improve upon their knowledge of the English language (62%)"; "become
acquainted with Canadian customs and laws (38%)"; and "be independent"
or "self-reliant (21%)."
- 75.0% of the respondents were very satisfied or satisfied with life in Canada
in wave 1, while 67.6% were very satisfied or satisfied in wave 4. The apparent main reason for dissatisfaction was the inability to find a job (33%).

The researcher conducted a series of bivariate correlations between various factors and satisfaction. For the most part, demographic variables were not related to
satisfaction. The only factors apparently related to satisfaction were identity with
Canada as one's home, current attendance at a mosque, or the number of times one
had moved.

The key informants indicated that these were the main challenges faced by Iraqi
refugees in trying to settle in Canada (Michalski, 2001, p. 219):

- Language barriers
- Inability to access paid labor market or market their skills effectively
- Housing stability/high geographic mobility
- Prioritization of work at the expense of schooling
- Lack of understanding with respect to Canadian culture
- Overcoming trauma of one's previous experience
- Lack of discipline in young men's lives
- Single males who have felt somewhat isolated

The key informants, particularly immigration officials and settlement counselors, viewed the overall program as successful in helping the refugees to survive
economically and in the provision of language training. However, key informants
suggested that "more needed to be done prior to the refugees' arrival in Canada,
particularly around issues of cultural adjustment and language acquisition, as well
as routine or systematic follow-up with information once here in Canada" (Michalski,
2001, pp. 222–223). They also indicated that the Canadian government should have
taken a more active role in providing and disseminating information to the refugees, and more attention should have been paid to issues of family reunification.

The author concluded that the services provided to Iraqi refugees were inadequate and underutilized. He noted that "the Canadian Council for Refugees (1998)
has argued for the establishment of national standards to ensure that newcomers
are guaranteed certain minimum levels of service wherever they may settle"
(Michalski, 2001, p. 223). In addition, he further speculated that

the most innovative settlement practices likely transcend universal standards as such,
but rather lie somewhere within the efforts to bridge the gaps in community-based services and increased access to informal support systems available to those of particular
cultural backgrounds. The process of successful resettlement and integration seemed

to be tied most strongly to the ability to identify a cultural (and physical) "home" in a foreign land with a clear sense of a connection to an Iraqi community. (p. 224)

Classification of the Study

The study is classified as intranational research because:

- The research problem is framed by using literature from other countries regarding immigrants and refugees: Iraqi, Polish, Bosnian, Ethiopian, Czech, Salvadoran, Somalian, and Vietnamese. In addition, literature from the host country, Canada, is used.
- The study focuses on Iraqi refugees from the Gulf War who were resettling in Canada.
- Implications were discussed in relation to the literature from other countries as well as Canada regarding the challenges faced by Iraqi refugees.

Issues Addressed in the Study

Attrition in Panel Studies

In longitudinal research and panel studies, the initial panel typically has more people in the original sample than at later points or waves of the panel. Attrition refers to the loss of people over time. In the study by Michalski, there was attrition in the second, third, and fourth waves. As reported by the author, the sample of refugees included 59 people at time 1 and 35 at time 4. There is also attrition due to missing data. For example, with respect to responses of the refugees concerning their satisfaction with life in Canada, there were 56 people at time 1, as opposed to 49 at time 2, 42 at time 3, and 34 at time 4.

Michalski gives the following reasons for attrition in his study:

> Eight of the nonparticipants could not be contacted because their current addresses and telephone numbers were unknown even to Citizenship and Immigration Canada officials. Indeed, unpublished reports indicated that some of the Iraqi refugees were having difficulty in following through with administrative procedures regarding ongoing notification of their current addresses. By the end of the study period, most of the refugees had completed the Adjustment Assistance Program and were under no obligation to continue to notify Citizenship and Immigration Canada officials of their whereabouts. The interviewers learned that another reason for nonparticipation had to do with a general mistrust of the entire process. Some potential interviewees reported that they had learned from newspaper accounts that an Iraqi had been hired by Canadian intelligence to "spy" on other Iraqis in their mosques and other locales, thereby generating a considerable cloud of suspicion. Finally, at least one individual expressed the sentiment that after spending several years in a refugee camp, he no longer wanted to be "interrogated" further. His desire to be left alone reflects an attitude consistent with other survivors of torture. (Michalski, 2001, p. 211)

As the number diminishes from wave to wave in a panel study, it is quite possible that some of the characteristics are not the same as in the original sample, for two possible reasons: the same people are not represented, and changes are made due to a number of factors over time. This is illustrated in the author's presentation of data from the first wave in September 1996 (n = 59) compared with data from the fourth wave in October 1997 (n = 35): In September 1996, 94.9% were male, 74.2% were single, and 88.5% had been in the Iraqi military, compared to 97.1% male, 77.1% single, and 78.1% Iraqi military in October 1997. To illustrate the possible interaction of different sample sizes and time, in September 1996, 18.6% shared household accommodations and 76.3% had poor English language ability, in contrast to 70.6% sharing household accommodations and 11.8% reporting poor language skills in October 1997. To discern whether or not the changes are due to different subjects or time, the researcher can reanalyze the data with the same 35 people at times 1 and 4. In this way, only the effects of time are considered in the analysis.

Utilizers of panel research should pay careful attention to the numbers of people represented in different waves of the research. If the numbers are identical, it is clear that the different waves are comprised of the same people. On the other hand, if there is attrition, one cannot assume that the panels are equivalent on certain characteristics such as sex, age, and so on; equivalence or nonequivalence has to be demonstrated by further analysis, using the same people in each panel over time. Otherwise, the research design changes from panel research to that of replicated cross-sectional surveys, and one can only assess group changes over time, not individual changes.

Disclosure of Income

Disclosure of income refers to the extent to which refugees are willing to indicate all of their sources of income. In particular, it refers to the possibility that refugees may have boosted their available income by other means, often illegal. The research strategy is to obtain information from other sources such as key informants and the observations of others. This was demonstrated by the observations of Michalski in reporting the problems of disclosure and in attempting to make inferences about it.

With respect to reporting and analyzing data from the refugees, Michalski (2001, p. 214) said:

> These refugees reported only work in the formal economy or government assistance as sources of income. If there were other sources of financial support available to the study participants, then no one actually disclosed such information to the interviewers. The fact that some former Rafha camp refugees living in Alberta had been the subject of criminal investigations for fraud by working without declaring their incomes (while receiving AAP checks) undoubtedly affected the interviewees' willingness to be forthcoming in describing other "informal" means of financial support.

Michalski believed that inferences might be made about the possibility of refugees obtaining other sources of income by analyzing monthly housing expenses in combination with total incomes reported. Therefore, he calculated a summary statistic of "post-shelter monthly income" as "the sum of Adjustment Assistance Program payments, social assistance, and/or employment earnings minus net housing costs per person (that is, housing costs divided by household size)" (2001, p. 214). It was reported that the refugees in the study had a median amount of $253 cash each month to meet all other costs. Those who had jobs had approximately $600 more available each month. Although Michalski did not indicate how inferences could be made as to whether the refugees had other sources of income, one might surmise that if observations suggested the standard of living were the same for those employed and those not employed, those who were reportedly not employed may have had other sources of income.

Combining information from interviews with the refugees and from observations of key informants, Michalski reported (2001, p. 220):

> The Iraqi group, however, appeared to rely much more extensively upon informal networks (particularly friends) rather than accessing formal search clubs or other employment services. The apparent independence of the Iraqi refugees has produced mixed results. Although some were able to find work or moved to areas where others had "broken ground," the insular nature of the community did not promote a more active engagement with groups that might have facilitated their transition to working in the mainstream economy. Thus some evidence suggests that perhaps refugees worked "on the side" or in the "informal economy," though the interviews with the men did not elicit an admission of any such activity (earlier interviews did indicate that several had at least thought about such work). In light of their financial difficulties associated with the Adjustment Assistance Program and social assistance payments, combined with their possession of many commonplace Canadian goods (televisions, VCRs, and microwaves) and the desire to help families abroad, one should expect that at least some men had been working "on the side" to earn extra money as a supplement.

Issues Arising from the Study

Representativeness of Key Informants

In this study, it was reported that key informants had differences of opinion regarding the psychosocial adjustment of Iraqi refugees with whom they had come in contact. Moreover, it was indicated that the 14 key informants were from reception centers, were orientation or settlement counselors, and included one service provider. The issue posed here is to what extent the key informants in the study are representative of the possible number of key informants that could have been interviewed. If the sample of key informants is by convenience, it is possible for biases to occur. In other words, to what extent are the opinions of key informants representative; would a different sample of key informants have produced different results?

We recommend that the same care and thought should be devoted to the selection and representation of key informants as is typically devoted to the selection of other study participants. First, the areas from which key informants are to be selected should be specified, for example, service providers, settlement counselors, and so on. Second, the difference in perspectives of those groups as well as the rationale for their inclusion should be articulated, and the available numbers of their populations should be indicated. Third, samples should be selected, and the extent to which they can be regarded as representative should be indicated. Fourth, in questionnaires and interviews conducted with the key informants, a section should be included that asks about experiences and biases, if any, they believe they might have about the group they are reporting on, for example, Iraqi refugees.

Validity of Interviews

Michalski reported that the interviews with the Iraqi refugees

> were conducted in Arabic and the responses to each question were translated into English. The interviews were not tape recorded, but rather the interviewers wrote down individual responses directly on the interview schedules. Once they agreed to participate, everyone completed the full interviews with only an occasional refusal to answer specific questions. Most interviews required 45 to 90 minutes, with an average of just under one hour. (2001, p. 212)

The validity of information from the interviews depends on factors such as these: the accuracy of the translation from Arabic to English; the skill of the interviewers and the extent to which they might have influenced responses in accord with their possible biases; the degree to which written responses produce the same information as an analysis of tape-recorded responses; and with more than one interviewer, the reliability of their written recordings.

As indicated previously in chapters 2 and 3, issues of accurate translation and procedures for doing it, as well as reliability and validity of information from interviews, can be enhanced by pretesting the interview procedures with a small sample (in this instance, of Iraqi refugees). The added costs of a research study by retesting the research protocols are not extensive and provide the researchers with some control of the accuracy of the study. More costly, but more effective, in discerning possible biases, are methodological studies that focus on the reliability of the interviewers and the accuracy of data processing. For example, an actor might be employed to pose (with the knowledge of the research participants) as an Iraqi refugee, speaking in Arabic. Those who would conduct interviews in an actual study could interview the actor. The interviewers would record responses to their questions in writing, and the interviews would be tape-recorded. Information obtained by separate interviewers would be compared for their reliability with respect to the information obtained, by written recordings and by their analyses of the tape-recorded information. Tape-recorded information could be compared with written responses. Similarity of information obtained by interviewers with that obtained by recording methods would satisfy the assumption that equivalent information would be obtained irrespective of the interviewer or of the methods for recording and analyzing information. Criteria for analysis would be specific to each of the questions posed in the semistructured interviewers.

Recommendations as Hypotheses

Several recommendations arose from interviews with Iraqi refugees and key informants. These are examples of some of the recommendations provided by respondents:

- Counselors should be more active in helping refugees find employment and
  affordable accommodations.
- More emphasis should be placed on issues about cultural adjustments and
  language acquisition prior to the refugees' arrival to Canada.
- More direct information regarding housing and available resources should
  be made available at reception centers when refugees first arrive to Canada.

The author also indicated that his research confirmed the importance of some
of the guidelines proposed by the Canadian Council for Refugees as key areas
for integration. For example: "achieving financial independence through access to
employment and thus contributing to Canadian society with their skills and experience"; "learning the cultural orientation of the host society, which in turn needs
to have greater sensitivity toward the values and patterns of behaviors that the
refugees bring with them"; "bringing families together through family reunification
[which] appears to be critically important in terms of the health and well-being
of refugees, particularly if separated from spouses and children" (Michalski, 2001,
p. 224).

The recommendations from refugees and key informants in the study as well as
guidelines from the Canadian Council for Refugees are essentially hypotheses. It is
assumed that if the recommendations are followed, there will be greater degrees of
integration of the refugees into Iraqi society. If one is interested in testing these
hypotheses, research might be undertaken that follows steps such as these:

- Specify the hypotheses more clearly, for example, indicating what kinds of
  programmatic activities and services as independent variables would result
  in increased integration, as the dependent variable.
- Operationally define criteria of integration and their indices, for example,
  in terms of increased income, language acquisition, employment, and so on.
- Design a program to implement the suggested activities and services.
- Analyze the extent to which the program is implemented.
- Devise an evaluation design to assess the effectiveness and efficiency of the
  program.

We cannot help but emphasize to utilizers of research that the results must be
considered in terms of the levels of knowledge produced. If recommendations are
hypotheses, rather than verified and generalizable facts, they need to be tested in
further research. Although recommendations might appear to be plausible, they do
need testing. One cannot assume they will achieve the desired result. For example,
one can recommend that increased cultural sensitivity with refugees would lead to
increased integration. But what is cultural sensitivity? Its meaning and operationalization would need to be specified and carried out programmatically, and then tested.
Is it possible that one concept of "cultural sensitivity" might be incompatible for

refugees, perhaps leading to even less integration? Answers to questions like this are the raison d'être for further intranational research.

STUDY 3: "CRITICAL ASSUMPTIONS IN PROVIDING AID TO FORCED AND VOLUNTARY MIGRANTS IN MANAGUA, NICARAGUA," BY JOHN H. NOBLE, JR., AND FREDERICK L. AHEARN, JR. (2001)

Study Description

Problem Formulation and Knowledge Objectives

The authors addressed assumptions about migrants and refugees that were promulgated in an international conference in Amsterdam in 1991: "it makes little sense to separate the problems of refugees, stayers, internally displaced people and returnees in a particular crisis area," and "ongoing gender-blindness in the practice of refugee-aid.... The model of 'the refugee' as an adult male too often feeds policies" (Noble & Ahearn, 2001, p. 125). They believed that the first assumption was based on the need to make the most of limited resources, while the second assumption was premised on the notion that gender-specific interventions may be cost effective.

To test these assumptions, the authors planned to collect data from heads of households whose lives were "disrupted by the 1981–1990 civil war in Nicaragua and had since resettled in a Managuan barrio" (Noble & Ahearn, 2001, p. 125). Three related theoretical frameworks were reviewed, with the purpose of selecting variables that are involved for reducing stress in adapting to adversity:

- The model by Beiser, Dion, Gotowiec, Hyman, and Nhi (1995) viewed adaptation in relation to physical and mental health, considering it a "complex function of (a) certain precursor variables, such as personal characteristics and pre- and post-migration stressors, and (b) several mediating variables encompassing a variety of personal and social resources" (p. 126).
- The McCubbin and Patterson model of family stress and adaptation deals with mechanisms employed by families to cope with different forms of stress.
- Folkman and Lazarus (1988) "conceptualize problem-focused and emotion-focused coping mechanisms as operating in parallel to produce either positive or negative emotions. In their paradigm, emotion-focused coping influences the person-environment encounter, whereas problem-focused coping changes the person-environment relationship itself" (p. 128).

The authors used these theoretical frameworks to select variables for examining the different kinds of stress experienced by their sample of forced and voluntary migrants in Managua, Nicaragua, and the degree to which the migrants utilized material and emotional help from available sources. Their generalized hypotheses were (Noble & Ahearn, 2001, p. 128):

- There are no differences between forced and voluntary migrants in variables that could be controlled by would-be providers of aid.

- There are no differences between males and females in variables that could be controlled by would-be providers of aid.

More specifically, the authors planned to (1) study the differences between forced migrants and voluntary migrants on variables pertaining to personal characteristics, pre- and postmigration stress, personal and social resources, and anxiety, depression, psychosocial dysfunction, and so on, and (2) study the relationships between predictor variables (such as self-esteem, size of support network, life events, material support, economic support, religion, number of moves, age, gender, etc.) and these dependent variables: frequency of receiving help, general stress, economic stress, relationship stress, and depression. In essence, the researchers sought correlational knowledge regarding those factors that could alleviate stress; and then, although they did not operationally define controllable and noncontrollable variables by would-be providers of aid, they inferred which of the variables were controllable. For example, the provision of material support and education were deemed controllable, while gender and self-esteem were not. Furthermore, the researchers were interested in generalizing the results of their correlational study to heads of households of forced and voluntary migrants who resettled in a Managuan barrio.

Instrumentation and the Process of Data Collection

According to Noble and Ahearn (2001, p. 130),

seven staff members with degrees in sociology or social work were recruited both to maintain a presence in the neighborhood and to collect qualitative data for five months prior to the design, testing and implementation of the study questionnaire. Each received a week of orientation, intensive practice and daily supervision in the field. After an interview, a supervisor returned to each respondent's home to inquire about satisfaction with the interview. Clerical staff keyed collected data into an Excel spreadsheet, which then was checked for accuracy by another clerical worker and one of the authors.

The questionnaire was comprised of these instruments: a chronic stress scale (alpha = 0.69–0.85), a social readjustment rating scale (alpha = 0.55), a self-esteem scale (alpha = 0.78–0.85), a social support scale (alpha = 0.72), a general health questionnaire (alpha = 0.91), and a self-rating scale of current general health status (no reliability reported) (Noble & Ahearn, 2001). The authors reported that "all instruments that lacked a Spanish version underwent a standardized process of translation, back translation, discussion, critique, and final adjustment by the Nicaraguan staff before and after pretest" (p. 130). Their questionnaire also included demographic information and information related to religion, income, and war-related experiences.

Sampling, Relevant Populations, and Research Design

The most relevant population for this study is the census universe of 528 households living in a marginal neighborhood, Barrio 3–80, located in Managua, Nicaragua. An unequal probability sample was randomly drawn from five household strata consisting of: (1) 41 repatriated refugee families; (2) 69 families of demobilized soldiers; (3) 21 families who were uprooted by the war; (4) 153 families who had voluntarily moved from the countryside for economic reasons; and (5) 244 families who had voluntarily moved from another location in Managua. (Noble & Ahearn, 2001, p. 129)

The first three groups were considered to be forced migrants and the last two groups were considered to be voluntary migrants. The sample that was drawn consisted of 235 households, of which 118 were drawn from 131 forced migrants, and 117 were drawn from 397 voluntary migrants. This resulted in a disproportionate stratified random sample of 235 households living in Barrio 3–80. A larger relevant population was the authors' reference to 72,000 refugees, 350,000 displaced persons, and demobilized soldiers as a population most affected by the 1981–1990 civil war in Nicaragua. And a still larger relevant population is that of migrants in crisis areas. With respect to generalizations from the study regarding correlational data, the relevant population of interest is that of 528 self-defined heads of households. The forced migrants "experienced substantial duress and coercion during the civil war, which by their own accounts, motivated their eventual move into Barrio 3–80," and the voluntary migrants "were the lucky ones whose lives were less affected by the war. They chose to move from the countryside to Barrio 3–80 to improve their economic circumstances or to move from another location in Managua for the free-rent status of squatters" (p. 129).

The research design employed was a cross-sectional survey research design. After drawing the disproportionate stratified random sample and designing the study questionnaire, the authors and their staff arranged for interviews at one point in time for the Spanish-speaking respondents. The respondents provided information pertinent to the study's instruments and recalled information prior to their resettlement retrospectively. No direct data regarding change over different points of time, as could be provided in a panel study, are possible with this design.

Data Analysis, Conclusions, and Implications

To analyze differences between forced and voluntary migrants on the study variables, the authors tested for statistically significant differences using two sample t-tests and Bonferonni adjusted probabilities. There were no reported differences on variables pertaining to personal resources, on dependent variables such as anxiety and depression, and on social resources, except that the voluntary migrants were more satisfied with the help they received. There were more males (57% vs. 29%), more war victims (69% vs. 33%), more prior residential changes (2.18 vs. 1.52), and more economic stress over the past 3 years (9.84 vs. 9.07) for the forced migrants as compared to the voluntary migrants.

In attempting to predict the frequency of receiving help, the authors employed

undifferentiated and gender-specific regression equations. The procedure permitted identification of possible interactions between gender and the statistically significant predictors in the undifferentiated regression equation. A difference in the sign of one or more regression coefficients in the gender-specific equations from those in the undifferentiated equation would signal the existence of interaction effects ... receipt of more frequent help was predicted by larger size support network, lower self-esteem, suffering more stressful life events, and voluntary migrant status. ... None of the signs of the regression coefficients in the gender-specific equations changed in indication of the existence of an interaction between gender and any of the predictor variables. ... Regardless of gender, the single most powerful predictor of receiving help is the support network. (Noble & Ahearn, 2001, p. 131)

The authors employed the same analytic procedures of undifferentiated and gender-specific regression equations for examining the relationships of predictor variables to four different manifestations of stress: general stress, economic stress, relationship stress, and safety stress. There were no interaction effects of gender in any of the analyses. According to the authors,

regardless of gender, the single most powerful predictor of general stress is receipt of less material support. ... The two most powerful predictors of interpersonal stress are receipt of less material support and more frequent prior changes in residence. ... The three most powerful predictors of stress from living in a perceived unsafe environment are lower self-esteem, younger age, and receipt of less material support. (Noble & Ahearn, 2001, pp. 133–135)

The authors also studied correlates of depression. They noted that women had higher levels of depression symptoms than men. However, self-esteem and year moved appeared to be more predictive of depression. Nevertheless, the amount of variance explained by eight predictor variables (including gender, self-esteem, and year moved) was 20%, a relatively low degree of predictability.

The authors concluded that the only controllable variables from their analyses that aid providers could use are education to reduce depression (although the relationship between education and depression is apparently very weak) and the provision of material aid to reduce stress that forced and voluntary migrants have experienced. In relation to the questions posed at the outset of their study, the authors make these conclusions:

Returning now to the original questions—does it make sense to separate the problems of refugees, stayees, internally displaced people and returnees in a particular crisis area? This study provides substantial evidence that such separation would make little sense in providing aid to the people who struggle for survival in Barrio 3–80. Does gender-blindness in the provision of aid somehow impede meeting basic human needs? This study offers no support for providing gender-specific aid, except in the delivery of health care where the protection of the privacy and modesty of all patients is the universal practice norm. The data contain nothing that would argue for delivery of gender-specific aid in the areas of economic development, education, or social services. (Noble & Ahearn, 2001, pp. 137–138)

The authors and their research team essentially produced quantitative-descriptive and correlational knowledge that could be generalized to the forced and voluntary migrants living in Barrio 3–80. There is no basis for generalizing that knowledge to other relevant populations other than in the form of hypotheses that remain to be tested.

Classification of the Study

This study is classified as intranational research for these reasons:

- Literature was used about the civil war in Nicaragua; and refugees in Nicaragua, England, Canada, and Cambodia, and the United States; and theoretical models from the United States regarding social support and stress. The literature was employed to frame the research problem and to analyze the implications of the study.
- Among the forced migrants were repatriated persons who had lived as refugees in Honduras.
- Persons moved to Managua from other parts of Nicaragua due to displacement as a result of the civil war and for economic or geographic reasons.
- Implications were derived at the level of hypotheses regarding how providers of aid might be helpful to people involved in crisis situations such as civil war and issues regarding resettlement.

Issues Addressed in the Study

Incomplete Psychometrics

The authors indicated that they used Cronbach's alpha measure of internal consistency or reliability for five of the instruments they used. For two of the instruments, the alpha measures were relatively low. The social readjustment scale had an alpha of .55, and the social support scale an alpha of .72. Moreover, it was reported that "none of the measures is known to have predictive validity to the study's dependent variables," that is, indices of stress, depression, and help frequency; and that "all instruments that lacked a Spanish version underwent a standardized process of translation, back-translation discussion, critique, and final adjustment by the Nicaraguan staff before and after pretest" (Noble & Ahearn, 2001, p. 129).

The issue here is whether more psychometric information should have been obtained prior to implementing the survey. Reliability coefficients for Spanish versions might be different from non-Spanish versions, and further reliability tests might lead the utilizer of such information to have more confidence in the data. Although there were no data on predictive validity, there appeared to be face validity in the instruments selected. During the pretesting stage, it might have been possible to obtain measures of validity, particularly of concurrent validity where the selected dependent variables should differentiate between those migrants who were known to be successfully resettled, as opposed to those who were not. The study itself provides evidence of the predictability of independent variables, but, according to the authors, "behavioral outcomes based on interventions designed to modify the study's controllable predictor variables would seem necessary to document their predictive validity" (Noble & Ahearn, 2001, p. 130).

Training and Monitoring of Staff in Field Research

The authors indicated that seven staff members received an orientation, guidance, and supervision. A supervisor checked on the satisfaction of respondents by visiting them after staff members had interviewed them. This procedure of checking at pretest is a good device for assuring accuracy of data reporting, as well as satisfaction of the respondents.

Such a procedure can also be employed in the actual survey; but rather than check each interview, a random selection of, say, 10% of the sample can be spot-checked. And in the spot check, the supervisor would ask about satisfaction and repeat a small number of questions to ascertain the agreement between the responses to the supervisor and the responses to the staff member. Obviously, if there were great variation between the staff and the supervisor as well as among the staff members, the accuracy of the data collection process would be questionable.

Issues Arising from the Study

Conceptualization of Controllable Variables

In this study, theory was applied to select variables related to stress and health. The authors then inferred which variables could be controllable, that is, manipulated by providers of aid to forced and voluntary migrants with respect to predicting changes in the dependent variables of the study. The question initially raised in the study about whether or not different strategies should be employed in helping forced or voluntary migrants was not answered with any degree of certainty.

One could conceptualize controllable variables, for example, as those that could be manipulated to either relate directly to the dependent variables or to relate to other variables that might serve to mediate relations between independent and dependent variables. Moreover, a family or universe of dependent variables might include direct provision of material sources and education, as conceptualized by the authors; but they might also include case management and brief therapy approaches, as well as a system of referral, medication, and so on. The controllable variables should be practical and easily manipulable by providers of aid. Those variables should bear relationships to dependent variables of interest; for example, obtaining jobs and places to live, relief from depression and anxiety, reduction of domestic violence, and acquisition of knowledge about health and social resources. Mediating variables would be variables that could be affected by the independent variables, which in turn would influence dependent variables. For example, variables such as self-esteem and reduction of depression (which could also be conceptualized as a mediating variable as well as a dependent variable) as mediating variables may lead to an increased desire to seek jobs, a reduction in spouse and child abuse, and greater efforts to acquire knowledge about resources. Provision of training in skills related to available jobs, brief supportive therapy, medication, and so on, in turn, may effectuate self-esteem and reduction of depression and anxiety, which could lead to changes in the dependent variables.

The issue pertains to the conceptualization of independent, mediating or intervening, and dependent variables; and whether or not the conceptualization is sufficient to represent the possible universe of relevant variables for studying the phenomenon of aid provision to forced and voluntary migrants. The authors' selection of controllable variables and their outcomes appears to be a sample of possible variables that could have been utilized in the study. Consideration of what is possible for aid providers to do in situations of disaster, such as war, appears to be an important step to take prior to the conceptualization of which variables to study. The notion here is that the sample of variables chosen should be representative of what can be possibly done and with what effects.

Analyzing Complex Interactions

The authors combined forced migrants and voluntary migrants into 235 migrants; and they studied the undifferentiated effects among the independent and dependent variables chosen for the study, as well as gender-specific effects. However, according to the authors, there were statistically significant differences beyond the .05 level between forced and voluntary migrants on variables such as help satisfaction, past three years economic stress, prior residential changes, being a war victim, being a participant in the civil war, gender, and age. From an analytic point of view, it is quite possible that there are second- and third-order interactions among these variables. For example, relations between economical reason for moving and general stress may not show an interaction with gender (as indicated in the study), but in further analysis might show a secondary interaction with gender and with the migrant status (forced or voluntary). The idea is that one might explore whether it makes a difference in separating migrant status by gender with respect to the obtained relationships in the study. By combining forced and voluntary migrants in their analyses, it appears that the authors assumed there were no differences between them. The variables in which there were differences might not be controllable per se, but they can serve as moderating variables that can interact with more controllable variables. For example, different strategies may be differentially effective for providing aid to male forced migrants, female forced migrants, male voluntary migrants, and female voluntary migrants. Rather than assuming no differences, it is preferable that the researchers provide more evidence that this is the case, given the data they have.

STUDY 4: "FACTORS IN THE INTEGRATION PROCESS OF ADOLESCENT IMMIGRANTS: THE CASE OF ETHIOPIAN JEWS IN ISRAEL," BY SHOSHANA RINGEL, NATTI RONELL, AND SHIMCHA GETAHUNE (2005)

Study Description

Problem Formulation and Knowledge Objectives

The authors were interested in studying the process of acculturation of Ethiopian immigrant adolescents in Israel. Noting that "most of the Jewish Ethiopian community lives in Israel," they articulated the purpose of their study as follows: "This pilot study examines the different attitudes and perceptions of the Israeli adolescents and Ethiopian immigrant adolescents concerning their process of mutual adjustment and integration, and makes recommendations to help enhance the integration process based on the views of the adolescents themselves" (Ringel et al., 2005, pp. 63, 66).

On the basis of their review of Israeli, American, and international literature regarding acculturation of Ethiopian Jews in Israel, the authors indicated that the following factors played a part in difficulties experienced by the Ethiopians in the process of integration and acculturation:

- There are wide cultural differences between Israelis and Ethiopian immigrants, including education and hostile Israeli attitudes toward Ethiopian culture.
- "There have been few efforts to maintain the cultural continuity of Ethiopian immigrants because of a lack of cultural and religious sensitivity among the Israeli public and professional people, and because most Ethiopian children are educated in boarding schools, separated from their families which live in immigrant housing sites" (Ringel et al., 2005, p. 64).
- A number of studies cited the darker skin color of Ethiopian Jews, prejudicial attitudes of some Israelis, particularly Russian immigrants, and a lack of social relationships between Israelis and Ethiopian Jews as factors that make acculturation difficult.
- Racism and discrimination were noted in the majority of studies reviewed.
- There are differences in communication styles. In particular, "Ethiopian culture emphasizes nonverbal communication, indirect expression, silence, and soft-spokenness, and this has frequently led to misunderstandings with their Israeli caregivers, mental health professionals and others" (p. 65).

The focus of the study was to develop qualitative information that is descriptive of adolescents' perceptions of the integration process of Ethiopian Jews. Moreover, the authors aimed to develop hypotheses that are conceptually generalizable regarding the enhancement of "integration, self-esteem, and academic performance" of Ethiopian Jewish adolescents (Ringel et al., 2005, p. 23).

Instrumentation and the Process of Data Collection

The data were collected from semistructured group interviews comprised of open-ended questions. The interviews took place in an Orthodox Jewish junior high school in central Israel in 1999. According to the authors,

> the interviews . . . were based on problems identified in the literature review and on the objectives of the study. They lasted approximately 1.5 hours each and were manually recorded in Hebrew by a recorder and later translated into English. In order to maintain confidentiality, participants' names were not included. (Ringel et al., 2005, p. 66)

Different sets of questions were asked of the Ethiopian Jews and the Israelis (non-Ethiopian Jews). Examples of questions posed to two focus groups with Ethiopian adolescents are as follows:

> How did you adjust to living in Israel? . . . Do you feel that you need to adjust your behavior to the Israeli Environment? How? . . . How do your Israeli peers relate to

you? Do they invite your over? . . . In your opinion, what are the problems between Ethiopian and Israeli students? What are the causes? . . . What can be done, in your opinion, to improve the integration process between the Ethiopian immigrants and Israeli society?" (Ringel et al., 2005, p. 75)

Examples of questions posed to a group of non-Ethiopian adolescents are:

How do your Ethiopian peers relate to you? Do they invite you over? . . . Are you involved in mutual activities with Ethiopian students? . . . In your opinion, are there problems between Ethiopian and non-Ethiopian students? What are the causes? . . . What can be done, in your opinion, to improve the integration process between Ethiopian immigrants and Israeli society?" (p. 76)

Sampling, Relevant Populations, and Research Design

The relevant populations for this study were the total number of Ethiopian Jews in Israel (reported by the authors as 88,900 in 2002), the number of adolescent Ethiopian Jews in Israel, the number of adolescent Ethiopian Jews in Israel enrolled in junior high schools, and the number of adolescent Ethiopian Jews enrolled in one Orthodox Jewish junior high school in central Israel during the spring of 1999.

The sample was a convenience sample comprised of three focus groups: one group consisted of 13 male Ethiopian adolescents, seventh and eighth graders, 12–15 years of age; a second group included 11 female Ethiopian adolescents of the same ages and grades; a third group was made up of seven male and nine female non-Ethiopian adolescents, also of the same ages and grades. Administrators of an Orthodox Jewish junior high school in central Israel recruited the participants.

The research design was that of a qualitative, exploratory research study. It employed focus groups that were interviewed. Questions, as previously described, were designed to secure opinions of the Ethiopian and non-Ethiopian adolescents from an Orthodox Jewish junior high school. There was no empirical basis to generalize the results of the study, in the form of qualitative descriptions, to any of the relevant populations except for the sample itself, although it was possible to make conceptual generalizations in the form of hypotheses.

Data Analyses, Conclusions, and Implications

According to the authors,

content analysis was used as a data analysis method. The investigators initially translated the manually recorded interviews into English. The data were then analyzed starting from raw data and moving to aggregate data and to basic content questions. These were given names and codes and the codes were then organized into major themes after the data had been saturated. The data were analyzed by two of the investigators, who then compared their results with each other and consulted with the third investigator in order to provide an inter-rater reliability. (Ringel et al., 2005, pp. 66–67)

The authors organized their findings into three major themes that reflected the perceptions of the study participants regarding the integration of Ethiopian immigrant adolescents into Israeli culture: racism and discrimination, intergenerational conflicts, and differences in verbal and nonverbal communication styles. These are some of the results of the study reported by the authors:

- Generally there seemed to be a consensus between ... groups that their teachers did not treat the Ethiopian immigrant students equally and that they favored the Israeli students (Ringel et al., 2005, p. 67).
- Initially, the Israeli students denied the existence of any racial problems at all. However, eventually, they suggested that racial tensions ... did exist (p. 68).
- The Ethiopian immigrant students ... stressed the significance of intergenerational conflicts with their parents during their adjustment and integration process.... They expressed a strong desire to mend any intergenerational conflicts through mutual discussions with their parents and by learning the native Ethiopian language (Amharic) and culture (pp. 68–69).
- It appeared that the communication styles between the Israelis and the Ethiopian immigrants ... differed, but not as greatly as previous research indicates. In general, the Ethiopian participants seemed more soft-spoken and shy compared with the Israeli group which was more verbally expressive (p. 73).

The authors suggested the following implications from their study.

- Problems depicted in the major themes of their findings need to be addressed in order to improve the process of integration and acculturation for Ethiopian immigrants.
- Teachers should be given training to be more culturally competent.
- The creation of a bicultural identity, including aspects from their parents' culture as well as Israeli culture, might increase the self-esteem of Ethiopian adolescents.
- School social workers who receive cultural competency training are more likely to successfully interact with adolescents from immigrant countries.
- An intervention model should be developed to enhance further "the integration, self-esteem and academic performance of Ethiopian youth" (p. 73).

These implications are essentially hypotheses that would require further specification, implementation, and evaluation in Israeli settings. The findings of the study were compared with other studies to highlight similarities and differences with the authors' study. It was clear that the qualitative descriptions pertained to the sample in their study, and that further research would need to be conducted in order to enhance the generalizability of the findings.

Classification of the Study

The study is classified as intranational for these reasons:

- Literature was reviewed about Israeli and Ethiopian Jewish adolescents from U.S., Israeli, and international sources to frame the research problem.

- The study focused on immigrant Ethiopian Jewish adolescents residing and attending an Orthodox Jewish school in Israel.
- Literature from Israel, the United States, and international journals was used to provide a context for discussing implications for immigrants in Israel and in other countries.

Issues Addressed in the Study

Group Interviewing versus Individual Interviewing

The authors indicated that peer pressure within the three focus groups might have affected the accuracy of their findings. Participants might have given different responses if they were interviewed separately. The issue involves the relative accuracy of individual versus group interviewing. Would the same results be produced by either method? This can only be answered by methodological studies comparing the two approaches. For example, in a focus group of, say 10 persons, 5 would be picked randomly to have individual interviews before participating in the focus group, and the others would be individually interviewed after participating in the focus group. The purpose of this would be to counterbalance the effects of previous information experienced by the participants, that is, order of presentation. If the same results are obtained from each half, it can be inferred that the effects of order are minimal. The interviews, group or individual, would contain the same questions, and the responses would be recorded, analyzed, and compared with each other.

If the extracted themes from content analyses were similar for both group and individual interviews, then the group interviews would be more cost effective. But if, in a focus group, the results are dominated by a few members and are not representative of all of the individuals in the group, individual interviews would be preferred. In that way, in an exploratory study of this type, a greater number of themes might be extracted from the data.

Analyzing Within- and Between-group Differences

The authors indicated that there were differences between the Israeli and Ethiopian adolescents, and that there were also differences within the two groups as well. They essentially point out that it is worthwhile to study within- as well as between-group differences. It is quite possible that within-group differences, say with respect to racial attitudes, may vary to a greater extent than between-group differences. We believe that whenever two groups representing different cultures (for example, an immigrant culture versus a host or the dominant culture) are compared on the same sets of data (e.g., racial attitudes) that in addition to studying between-group differences, within-group differences for both groups should also be studied. Emphasizing the differences between cultures without studying within-group differences can lead to cultural stereotypes that are simply not true, particularly if the within-group differences show greater variation than the variation between groups. For example, with respect to racial attitudes, there may be a greater degree of racism and nonracism toward each other expressed within the immigrant group, or within the group from the dominant culture. Within- and between-group variances are, of course, the basis of statistical analyses, but the issue here is that they should also be explicitly examined in qualitative analyses such as those of this study.

Issues Arising from the Study

Cross-sectional versus Panel Studies

The authors collected data at one point in time by means of semistructured interviews in three focus groups. They referred to the significance of intergenerational conflicts between the adolescent Ethiopians and their parents. The information was obtained retrospectively from the point of view of the Ethiopian adolescents. To study the phenomenon more precisely, it might be advantageous to conduct panel studies, that is, gathering information with the same groups of respondents in order to study any possible changes over time with respect to conflicts with parents. Correspondingly, it might be useful to conduct panel studies with parents at the same points in time to determine whether the perceptions of the adolescents and parents are consistent. In studying the conflicts between adolescents and their parents, it might be possible that the conflicts are due in part to adolescent-parent conflicts that might occur in any culture. A more complete study would then include both Israeli parents and adolescents in panel studies (with the ages of the Israeli adolescents matched with those of the Ethiopian adolescents). This would allow for a comparison of immigrant and nonimmigrant issues between adolescents and parents. Hence some information would be provided on the extent to which intergenerational issues are over and beyond those that may occur between adolescents and parents in a host culture.

Age as a Variable in Research Studies

The authors point out in their discussion that their sample of adolescents was younger than adolescents who were involved in previous research. It is important for the utilizer of research studies to keep in mind that comparing the results of studies may lead to inconsistent information due to differences in ages among the participants. We recommend that the researcher, when studying groups that may exhibit developmental stages over time, as in adolescence, should include age cohorts in panel studies. In this way changes in specific age groups over time can be studied as they relate to such phenomena as perceptions of racism, intergenerational conflict (among immigrants, among nonimmigrants), and so on. From the study presented here, since it was exploratory at one point in time with a convenience sample, the authors could only speculate about adolescent changes in development with respect to the phenomena of racism, intergenerational conflict, and communication styles.

Recommendations as Hypotheses

The authors made many recommendations suggesting changes that may facilitate the integration of Ethiopian adolescents in Israel. The following represents a recommendation for social work education.

> The authors found some acculturation among Ethiopian adolescents, but also a wish to maintain their native culture. These findings suggest that Ethiopian adolescents are in the process of creating a new cultural identity of being Ethiopian-origin Israelis, which includes components from both their parents' cultural identity and from the prevailing society, and at the same time is different from both. The findings also suggest that the creation of this bicultural identity is an empowering experience that may improve self-concept and self-esteem. It includes active resistance to the racist attitudes that Ethiopian youth encounter, rather than an attitude of passivity and despair. These findings differ from previous findings that emphasized the difficulties of Ethiopian adolescents in maintaining a positive sense of ethnic identity . . . and suggest that the development of a bicultural identity, combining features of the ancestral culture as well as the dominant social context, may enhance adolescent immigrants' integration in the prevailing society. Therefore, following the paradigm of partnership with oppressed populations . . . the authors recommend that this model of ethnic identity development be taught in social work education. (Ringel et al., 2005, p. 71)

Although the notion may have merit, prior to teaching the model of ethnic identity development, there should be research that focuses on the implementation and evaluation of that particular model. Should components of two different cultures be equal, or should components of the host or immigrant culture prevail? Depending on the mix of cultural components and the developmental stages of adolescents, could a bicultural identity lead to increased integration and acculturation? Questions such as those would need to be answered; for example, in a field experiment comparing instruction in developing a bicultural identity with a control group in which no particular cultural instruction occurs. Recommendations should clearly specify whether they are based on evidence or untested hypotheses. If recommendations based on the latter are implemented, they must be evaluated in order to provide further knowledge.

STUDY 5: "KIN AND NONKIN SOCIAL SUPPORTS IN A COMMUNITY SAMPLE OF VIETNAMESE IMMIGRANTS," BY ZVI D. GELLIS (2003)

Study Description

Problem Formulation and Knowledge Objectives

According to the author, the purpose of his research was

> to investigate the role of social support networks on depressive symptoms among a community sample of Vietnamese immigrants. On the basis of earlier research, this

study examined the relationships between demographic variables (including age, gender, education, income, years in new country, marital status, and income) and psychological distress as measured by level of depression. A unique feature of this investigation was the focus on two types of social support mechanism (that is kin and nonkin social networks). (Gellis, 2003, p. 249)

The rationale for conducting the study was as follows.

- The author found few studies that dealt with the relationship of kin and nonkin social support with mental distress.
- There was little research examining the role of culture "in the expression and experience of psychological distress" (Gellis, 2003, p. 249).
- The profession of social work is now more interested in "mental health services research for ethnic minority groups" (p. 249).
- Previous research provides data indicating that Asian American immigrants have a relatively high degree of mental health problems.
- "The social science literature suggests that the mental health needs of ethnic minority groups are largely unmet and that services are culturally flawed and misguided" (p. 249).
- The author believes his study is the first empirical study that examines the relationships between kin and nonkin social support and depression.

The author derived notions of social support in a cultural context from literature dealing with psychological and psychiatric symptomatology among various groups of Asian refugees and immigrants. Moreover, he reviewed a number of research studies that examined the relationship between social support and mental health, and defined social support as an "interactive process in which emotional, instrumental, or financial aid is obtained from a social network and can be positive, negative, or both in effect" (Gellis, 2003, p. 249). These are some of the key ideas abstracted from the literature that provide a background for his research (p. 250):

- Size and membership are key dimensions of support networks.
- When studying immigrants, the role of social support needs to be assessed in a multidimensional fashion. By definition, the migratory experience involves disruption of immigrants' social interactions and networks.
- Asian Americans share a common thread of family-centered social support systems ... maintained through a cultural sense of family loyalty and the predominance of group over individual concerns. There is also great respect and obligation offered to family members, especially parents.
- The social support system in Asian American families incorporates both shame and harmony in giving and receiving help ... these concepts reinforce and maintain cultural values that help shape their support systems.

The intent of the author appears to have been the provision of quantitative-descriptive data and testing correlational hypotheses about demographic variables, social support, defined as kin and nonkin, and depression. Since the research was focused on a convenience sample, the knowledge obtained could only be generalized as hypothetical to contexts other than that in which the research took place.

Instrumentation and the Process of Data Collection

Data were gathered in one-hour semistructured interviews over two time periods in the summers of 1996 and 1997. According to the author, "all measures were translated into Vietnamese and then independently translated back to English to ensure their validity. Questionnaire data were collected at one month (time 1) after the participant's discharge from the hospital and six months later (time 2)" (Gellis, 2003, p. 251).

The measures employed in the study were:

- *Demographics:* this included age, gender, marital status, education, employment status, number of years in new country, income, and length of hospital stay.
- *Psychological distress:* "the Center for Epidemiologic Studies Depression Scale (CES-D) was used to assess psychological distress. This is a widely used, reliable, and valid 20-item scale that assesses current level of depressive mood in the general population, and has been used with Vietnamese samples" (p. 51).
- *Social support:* conceived as sources of support and satisfaction with the support received, social support was subdivided into kin social support, nonkin social support, and satisfaction with support. These were measured as follows. Kin social support was operationally defined as the "sum of the number of living parents, spouse, relatives, children, and Vietnamese friends" living in the same country as the research participants. Nonkin social support was defined as "the sum of the number of non-Vietnamese co-workers, friends, and formal mental health, social services, and church organizations used. Overall satisfaction with social support networks was measured using one question, 'How satisfied are you with the overall support you have?' . . . The item is rated on a scale ranging from 6 = very satisfied to 1 = very dissatisfied" (p. 251).

Sampling, Relevant Populations, and Research Design

The relevant populations funnel down from approximately 10.1 million Asian and Pacific Islander Americans (in 1999) to an estimate of 768,000 Vietnamese (in 1998) to the criteria for inclusion in the research: men and women who received services from a public mental hospital in the United States, are "between 18 and 65 years of age, foreign-born Vietnamese, and had one of the following primary DSM-IV diagnoses: major depressive disorder, dysthymia, or adjustment disorder with depressed mood" (Gellis, 2003, p. 251). From one hospital in the northeastern United States, the investigator found 93 clients who met the criteria for inclusion in the study; 14 were not included for these reasons: "five refused to participate at time 1, two could not be contacted because of a change in address, four dropped out between time 1 and time 2, and three had incomplete data" (p. 251). In this study, a convenience sample of 79 was taken from the population of one northeastern U.S. hospital at one particular time period.

The research design was that of a longitudinal survey taken at two points in time: time 1, after the patient was discharged from the hospital, and time 2, 6 months later.

Data were obtained by semistructured interviews with the 79 Vietnamese patients in the sample.

Data Analysis, Conclusions, and Implications

According to the author, in his analysis of the sample of 79 Vietnamese patients compared to the 14 who did not participate in the research, "the diagnostic subgroups did not differ with regard to either severity of depression or sociodemographic characteristics . . . nonparticipants were similar to the participants on all demographic variables" (Gellis, 2003, p. 251).

Means, standard deviations, and bivariate correlations between times 1 and 2 were calculated and reported for depression scores, kin network size, satisfaction with support, and nonkin network size. Regression analyses of depression scores at time 2 were conducted with predictor variables of demographics and social support at time 2. Gellis says he

> estimated the stability of the CES-D depression scores over time by regressing CES-D time 1 scores on CES-D time 2 scores, while controlling for the sociodemographic variables. Control variables that were incorporated into the analyses included age, gender, marital status, education, employment status, and years of residence in the new country. All control variables were measured at time 1. Because this analysis is cross-sectional, it cannot inform us of causal direction. (2003, p. 252)

Characteristics of the sample were as follows: the mean age was 45.3; the mean length of hospitalization was 1.7 months; 72% were diagnosed with major depression; the mean number of years in the new country was 14.2; 72% were married; 83% were unemployed and were receiving welfare benefits; 77% were female; and 71% were high school graduates.

The major findings of the research included the following.

- Age, gender, and length of residence in the new country were related to initial level of depression, but were not related to the change in depression (Gellis, 2003, p. 253).
- Increases in social support from kin networks (that is, family, relatives, and ethnic friends) contributed to higher CES-D scores, although nonkin network support (that is, nonethnic coworkers, friends, mental health workers, and social service providers) had the opposite effect of decreasing psychological distress. Satisfaction with support received had no effect on depression scores (p. 253).

On the basis of his review of the literature and the findings of the research, the author suggested several guidelines for social work practice with the population studied. These guidelines can be the basis of further hypotheses that need to be explicated, implemented, and evaluated (Gellis, 2003, p. 256):

- Social workers need to adhere to fundamental concepts of universality of human behavior and cultural relativity.
- Unique language, cultural, and family values need to be considered for culturally competent interventions.

- Kin and nonkin support networks need to be assessed for therapeutic alliance.
- Social workers need to assess the presence of familial conflicts.
- Culturally appropriate mental health information and follow-up services need to be offered.

Classification of the Study

This research is classified as intranational for these reasons:

- Literature regarding depression and social support with Chinese, Hmong, and Vietnamese populations was used to frame the research problem. Sources of the literature were from cross-cultural psychology and English and American journals and books.
- The study focused on Vietnamese immigrants who resided in the United States
- Literature form several countries was employed to analyze the findings of the study.
- Implications in the form of concepts and hypotheses could be applicable to more than one country.

Issues Addressed in the Study

Response Bias

The author described the Center for Epidemiologic Studies Depression Scale (CES-D) for assessing depression, indicating that these dimensions were measured: depressive affect, somatic activity, positive affect, and interpersonal relations. Referring to the literature, the author identified potential response biases on the part of Asians that could affect the validity of the measurement of depression. Once a potential source of response bias is located, the issue for researchers is whether or not corrections for response bias should be made in the context of new research studies. The author deleted the four items of positive affect, and then reanalyzed the revised CES-D scale for alpha coefficients (interitem reliability):

> Lin (1989) identified a potential source of response bias on the "positive affect" dimension of the CES-D measure. Asian responses to this dimension should be interpreted with caution because of the cultural tendency to report unusually low levels of positive affect. According to Lin (1989) this phenomenon is indicative of a dysphoric response pattern that is related to cultural factors and independent of psychiatric morbidity. Lin (1989) recommended two methods to eliminate this response bias: rephrasing the positive affect items with negative content or discarding the four positive items. (Gellis, 2003, p. 251)

Reporting Limitations of the Research

It is customary for researchers to report the limitations of their studies, often at the request of editors of journals to which the research is submitted for publication. For example, the author of this study reported that the convenience sample that was employed limits generalizability; and that he did not, in his analyses, distinguish between respondents with and without spouses, noting that marital status could be an important moderating variable.

The issue is whether or not to incorporate limitations into implications for future data analyses and research studies. In our opinion, it would be worthwhile for researchers to indicate how they might overcome the limitations and what suggestions they might have for other researchers investigating the phenomenon.

With respect to sampling for generalizability, future research would depend on the conceptualization of what the relevant population is and what characteristics of it should be employed in representative sampling. In this way, decisions and the type of sampling employed could be considered, balancing cost and time considerations with the degree of representativeness expected. Subsequent research might focus on all of the psychiatric hospitals in the United States over extended periods of time, or it might concentrate on Vietnamese immigrants with symptomatology of depression, and so forth. The point being made here is that thought should be given to how to address the limitations in further research.

With respect to further data analyses, if the author had been able to identify those participating in the study who had spouses, he might have been able to do further analyses with the data already available. If the data were not available, it might have been possible to recommend what types of data should be collected to determine the role that spouses play in providing social support.

Issues Arising from the Study

Measures of Social Support and Their Validity

The measures of social support in this study were based on adding the number of identified sources of social support: living parents, spouse, relatives, children, and Vietnamese friends for kin social support; and non-Vietnamese coworkers, friends, and mental health, social services, and church organizations used for nonkin support. These measures appear to be proxies for the actual amount of social support based on positive, neutral, or negative interactions with people over time. The issues involved here are the extent to which the proxy measures are predictive of actual time spent with those providing social support, and the degree to which the interactions are consistently positive, neutral, or negative. Measures of social support could be validated in pretesting, or their validation could be built into the study.

Information for such an assessment would lead to measures that reflect change or lack of change over time, and would be obtained by means of a panel study, specifying the initial, static measures (numbers of social support) and subsequent, dynamic measures (e.g., positive and negative interactions for kin and nonkin members over time, including amounts of interaction). If the initial static measures are highly correlated with the subsequent dynamic measures, one could infer that they are valid to the extent of predicting more specific interactions with the providers of social support. On the other hand, if they are not highly correlated, the investigator may choose to conduct analyses with both types of variables (initial static and subsequent dynamic) as predictors of depression.

Incorporating Qualitative Research in Quantitative Research Studies

This study was a quantitative, correlational research study. In order to understand the findings in a quantitative study, it might be helpful for the utilizer of research to also obtain the findings of qualitative research in the same study. The issue is whether or not qualitative research should be incorporated in a quantitative study. We believe qualitative methods could be employed in a study such as this one to help explain why there was a negative correlation between kin social report and depression. The author speculates about several possible explanations of that correlation, for example:

> Another explanation is that acknowledging a mental health problem in the Vietnamese community can lead to shame for both the individual and the family. Demands and expectations from the family also can exert pressure on intergenerational relations to embrace cultural norms. A heavy reliance on family ties can place strains on familial relations, especially for depressed Vietnamese women, who have heavy responsibilities to nurture and promote the family's survival. (Gellis, 2003, p. 255)

These ideas could have been explored in a qualitative study of a sample of Vietnamese women who were participating in the study. Semistructured interviews of the women and their families might have included questions that focused on these issues: shame, demands and family expectations, strains on familial relations, and so on. The value of such research is that it could provide some evidence as to whether or not such a hypothesis is supported. If no evidence is provided, the speculation remains at the hypothetical level of knowledge. Utilizers of research should not treat such a hypothesis as supported, whether or not it is plausible.

Implementing and Evaluating Recommendations

We have indicated previously that recommendations based on hypotheses should not be implemented without attempting to test them. Implementation without evidence on which it is based and without an attempt to evaluate it through research and evaluative methods would be naïve and inappropriate. For example, this conclusion from the study was not based on any data within the study: "awareness of cultural validity in measurement tools is essential for greater accuracy in diagnosis of depressive symptoms" (Gellis, 2003, p. 256). Although plausible, it needs to be tested. A laboratory experiment could be conducted in which information regarding depression in the form of vignettes is provided with or without additional cultural knowledge to two randomly selected groups of psychiatrists and/or social workers: one group receives background information about clients; the other group receives background information about clients in addition to cultural information about them and their families. Both groups would classify the clients with respect to symptoms and degree of depression. In order for the hypotheses to be supported, the group who receive cultural information should be more accurate in their diagnoses than the group who do not receive cultural information. Again, we are making the point that recommendations based on hypotheses need to be tested before implementing them in practice.

SUMMARY

We presented five studies in this chapter that were illustrative of intranational research, particularly with respect to immigrants and refugees from Korea, Iraq, Ethiopia, and Vietnam resettling in the United States, Canada, Israel, and the United States, respectively, and former refugees repatriating in Nicaragua. As in chapter 3, all of the studies were described with respect to these aspects of the research process: problem formulation and knowledge objectives; instrumentation and the process of data collection; sampling, relevant populations, and research design; and data analysis, conclusions, and implications. Reasons for classifying the research as intranational were also provided.

Following the same framework as in chapter 3, issues pertaining to the conduct and utilization of intranational research were presented and briefly discussed. Issues that were considered by the authors were presented, as well as issues that we derived from a critical analysis of each study. The issues addressed in the studies were: group equivalence in experimental studies, equivalence of experimental and control groups over time, attrition in panel studies, disclosure of income, incomplete psychometrics, training and monitoring of staff in field research, group interviewing versus individual interviewing, analyzing within- and between-group differences, response bias, and reporting limitations of the research. Issues that arose from the studies were experimental equivalence in research design, implications as hypotheses to be tested, representativeness of key informants, validity of interviews, recommendations as hypotheses, conceptualization of controllable variables, analyzing complex interactions, cross-sectional versus panel studies, age as a variable in research studies, measures of social support and their validity, incorporating qualitative research in quantitative research studies, and implementing and evaluating recommendations. All of these issues were discussed within the contexts of the five research studies that were previously described.

6

TRANSNATIONAL RESEARCH

This chapter assumes that the reader has been exposed to the basic concepts about social research and international social work research that were presented in previous chapters. Notions about substantive and methodological knowledge and criteria for generalizability are fundamental for understanding different aspects of the research process. We distinguished national from supranational research and supranational research from intranational research. We also presented key concepts relevant to cross-cultural research and cultural competence that are essential for the conduct of transnational research. Moreover, we discussed social work problems pertinent to international social work research, and indicated the importance of understanding the laws and policies pertaining to international migrants in various countries.

We build on those notions in this chapter. First, we discuss and define transnational research, distinguishing it from supranational and intranational research. Second, we provide a special case of transnational research, and a hypothetical example of this type of research. This is followed by a consideration of some of the social work problems involved in this type of research. Different strategies of qualitative and quantitative descriptions are presented in a discussion of the research process, and then we discuss important issues that should be considered in transnational research for the various aspects of the research process. In problem formulation, we discuss the importance of standardized definitions of social indicators and consideration of cultural variations, as well as the sociopolitical context in quantitative and qualitative descriptions. In addition, we indicate the importance of collaboration, partnerships, and the involvement of key stakeholders in comparative studies.

We reaffirm the issues presented in previous chapters regarding instrument construction: care in translation and cross-validation of instruments. The value of pretesting is emphasized, and issues of reliability and validity are considered within countries as well as in comparisons between countries. In research design, we focus on designs that can be utilized in comparative research that aims to produce correlational and causal knowledge: randomized experiments, crossover designs, nonequivalent control group designs, and interrupted time-series designs.

In the section on sampling, we discuss the complex issue of relevant populations and sampling in comparative transnational research. In addition, we introduce notions of replication from one country to another, fitting models of data across countries, and the importance of making extra efforts to retain those selected in samples. We discuss several issues in data collection and analysis: the fact that techniques commonly used in the United States, such as telephone interviewing, mailed questionnaires, and payment to participants, may not be appropriate in other countries; the use of available data sets; the notion that categories such as race may not be equivalent, that is, have the same meaning, across countries; and the use of multiple data sources. In the section on conclusions and implications, we focus on problems of generalizability within and between countries, and we discuss notions of evidence-based practice that the utilizer of transnational research should consider.

We conclude the chapter by discussing incentives and barriers to transnational research, including the need for knowledge, costs, ethics, cooperation, sociopolitical contexts, and agreements on the purposes of research.

DEFINING TRANSNATIONAL RESEARCH

Prior to specifying our definition of transnational research in social work, we shall specify some notions of research that are related and are subsumed by our definition. These notions are basically those of comparative research. Oyen, in discussing theory and practice in international social research (1990b, p. 7), said:

> The vocabulary for distinguishing between the different kinds of comparative research is redundant and not very precise. Concepts such as cross-country, cross-national, cross-societal, cross-cultural, cross-systemic, cross institutional, as well as transnational, trans societal, transcultural, and comparisons on the macro-level, are used both as synonymous with comparative research in general and as denoting specific kinds of comparisons, although the specificity varies from one author to another. The confusion reflects the point that national boundaries are different from ethnic, cultural, and social boundaries. Within all countries, even the very old and fairly homogeneous ones, we may find several sub societies which on some variables may show greater variation than comparisons across national boundaries can demonstrate: that is, within-variation may sometimes be greater than between-variation.

Within social work and social welfare, Estes (1984, p. 1) refers to comparative social welfare as

> a discrete field of research inquiry aimed at understanding national and international patterns of social provision. The patterns that are of greatest interest to comparative researchers are those public and private systems of social care that emerge in response to recurrent human needs, that is, recurrent human needs that exist in all societies regardless of their particular forms of social, political, or economic organization. These needs include exposure to such recurrent social risks as poverty, hunger, illness, disability, early death, solitary survivorship, and so on.

In addition, Joyner (2000, p. 94), in discussing a lack of comparative social welfare research with respect to the study of family violence, alludes to cross-national research as "the systematic comparison of provision and intervention across a range of states."

As we indicated in chapter 1, transnational research is comparative research between populations of two or more countries; literature across populations is used for formulating the research problem and for drawing implications for the countries involved. As it deals with social work and social welfare problems, it is comparative social welfare research.

Transnational research shares these characteristics with supranational and with intranational research:

- It follows steps in the research process from problem formulation, sampling, and research design to instrument construction, data gathering, analyses, and conclusions.
- It uses literature from two or more countries.
- It generalizes substantive knowledge across countries or specifies differences between countries in formulating research problems.
- It may conceptualize generalizability of methodological knowledge across countries in formulating research problems.
- It seeks to generalize implications across countries.

These characteristics are shared by intranational and transnational research:

- Two or more countries are studied.
- These populations may be studied: the country of origin and those who have migrated from the country of origin to live in another country.
- Migration patterns may be studied over time.
- The research may be generalized across subcultural groups within the populations that are studied.
- Researchers seek to apply research findings to the populations that are studied.

Unique to transnational research are the following characteristics:

- Qualitative comparisons may be made between countries with respect to programs, policies, laws, social resources, social needs, and/or social interventions, and so on.
- Quantitative comparisons may be made with respect to social indicators, and/or to international standards regarding social and health needs, and so on.
- Quantitative comparisons may be made with respect to common stimuli, for example, professional reactions to a case vignette.
- Correlational and causal research designs are employed within two or more countries that are being studied.

A Hypothetical Example

Suppose Italian and American social workers are interested in disseminating information to social workers in Italy and the United States about drugs, especially the range of substances to which teenagers in both countries may become addicted. Moreover, suppose that these educators are interested in evaluating training workshops in both countries.

The educators must first discuss what type of program they wish to offer, to whom, and with what objectives of program effectiveness. They decide that they will offer in each country a one-day workshop that aims to provide knowledge about drugs, the pharmacology of those drugs, symptoms of substance abuse in teenagers, motivational interviewing to increase the likelihood that the teenagers desire to stop their drug usage, and counseling regarding relapse. It is decided that this information would be provided in the format of a workshop that includes lectures, demonstrations, movies, and a group project that involves the development of motivational interviews for adolescents who are substance abusers. The workshops would take place in continuing education programs offered in a school of social work in the United States and in the Zancan Foundation in Padova, Italy. Arrangements would have to be made to have similar contents in the programs in Italy and the United States. A panel of social workers, drug counselors, interpreters, and pharmacists would be formed to develop course contents and to ensure that the contents are equivalent in the Italian and the American workshops. A site would be selected in the United States, a continuing education program in New York City, for example, and one in Padova, Italy, under the auspices of the Zancan Foundation.

The objectives of each program would be to increase the participants' knowledge about substances that can be abused by adolescents and to determine whether the dissemination of knowledge can be imparted in each country. To measure the attainment of knowledge, the investigators would review the literature in Italy and the United States regarding substance abuse and its detection, treatment, and prevention in adolescents. The investigators would determine whether there are available tests of knowledge, and whether or not they could be used in the Italian and American continuing education programs. If not, they would develop a test made up of items in a multiple choice format, and pretest the instrument on samples of social workers who regularly attend continuing education programs in the U.S. and Italian sites. What would be assessed in pretesting is whether the items can be translated from one language to another with, to the extent possible, identical meanings; the clarity of the items and response systems; the number of items to include, say, 100; the interitem consistency of the instrument; and the content validity of the instrument, as judged by panels of experts in both countries.

Since the investigators are interested in determining whether their workshops can be effective with social workers in both countries, the sampling method is that of purposive sampling: groups of regularly attending participants of continuing education programs for social workers in the U.S. and Italian sites. Of course, if the researchers were interested in generalizability within each country, probabilistic sampling of identifiable populations of social workers could be obtained, and the workshops would be offered to them. In addition, multiple sites could be simultaneously employed, increasing the potential generalizability within each country. However, the costs for that broader approach are deemed exorbitant, and the response rate for enrolling in the workshops might be low, reducing the extent to which the results could be generalized. The investigators decide to offer the one-day workshop to continuing education participants and to conduct research on those participants who are interested in the workshop. The program will be conducted simultaneously at each site in each country.

After the investigators believe the workshop is developed for each country according to their specifications and the instrument is reliable (in addition to using Cronbach's alpha to test for interitem reliability, the researchers would also test for test-retest reliability), they devise a research design to use for each country. Suppose that there are 60 social workers in each country who wish to take the one-day workshop. If so, an experimental design could be employed at each site. Social workers would be randomly assigned to the workshop or a control group with no training. Prior to the workshop, persons in the experimental and control groups would take the knowledge test. The experimental group would participate in the workshop, and the control group would not. The next day both groups would again receive the knowledge test. If the workshop is effective, the experimental group should significantly increase its knowledge of substance abuse in adolescents relative to the control group. If the same results were obtained for both sites, then it would be observed that there is one replication of the experiment.

Employing a crossover design could increase generalizability further: those social workers in the control groups would receive the workshops the next day and be tested again after they completed the workshop. Prior to the experiment, the participants would be informed that they would participate in an experiment in which they would be randomly assigned to an experimental group or a control group. If they were assigned to the control group, they would receive the training program the next day. The participants' informed consent would be sought. Moreover, the researchers would have to ensure that the logistics of providing the program on two separate days was feasible. If the control group did not show increases in knowledge without training, but did show increases after receiving training, then there is evidence for a replication of the results within each site. The researchers would analyze the results and consider the implications of training for both countries.

To further determine the efficacy of the program, participants might also be interviewed or might respond to a questionnaire regarding their perceptions of the workshop, what they felt they learned, and whether the knowledge would be useful to them in their work. Comparisons of the quantitative results between each country would be made, as well as qualitative comparisons of the social workers' perceptions of the training workshops in each country. This, in turn, might lead to further streamlining and packaging of the courses if they are successful. They may, for example, be developed for transmission in films or in computers, whereby participants could gain knowledge about drugs without traveling to workshops.

A Special Case of Transnational Research

In the hypothetical example of transnational research, two experiments were conducted simultaneously in two different countries. A special case of transnational research exists when research is carried out in one country at one point in time; and when, subsequently, the experimental model is transported and implemented in another country at a later point in time, with a specific intent to compare the results from the two countries. For example, the experiment to evaluate the effectiveness of a drug-training program may first have been implemented in Italy at the Zancan Foundation. Suppose the results indicated that participants who received the training program increased their knowledge of drugs and its pharmacology with adolescents. United States investigators may have learned about the experiment and may have been interested in implementing it at a site in the United States. The investigators would need to understand the contents of the training program and be able to translate and transform its contents for usage in a training program for American social workers. Instruments would have to be cross-validated, and all the necessary arrangements for implementing the experiment at an American site would need to be made.

If the results of the experiment in the United States are identical to the results of the experiment in Italy, they represent a replication of the program results transnationally. On the other hand, the time samples of the two experiments might be discordant; the researchers would attempt to show that the separation in time does not affect the results. With respect to the variable of knowledge obtained by means of the training program, there should not have been a major problem. However, if the researchers were testing attitude change, there could be a serious problem. For example, attitudes regarding adolescent uses of drugs may be radically different between the two countries, and the attitudes within and between countries may be different over time. Hence the transportability of a training program to change attitudes toward drug usage may be problematic if the programs are separated by long periods of time, say, 20 years. Nevertheless, researchers may be able to demonstrate that the time differences are not a factor in explaining the results, particularly if they are identical for both countries.

Research that is transported from one country and applied to another would be supranational research if the results were focused only on one country. Transnational research exists when results or data from two or more countries are compared with each other. For example, a community training experiment in Peru (Young, Johnson, & Bryant, 2002, p. 90) developed a therapeutic communities (TC) model that consisted

> ... of a core curriculum in which trainees are taught how to use TC concepts and tools during six, 1-week training modules. The core curriculum includes a simulation exercise that lasts 7 days and nights in which participants assume the roles of either administrators or residents to create a TC model, using concepts and practices presented in the training. The extended TC training course includes the six core curriculum training modules plus two additional 1-week modules that focus on methods for managing organizational change.

According to Young et al.,

> seventy-four treatment organizations that provide substance abuse treatment or early intervention services in Peru participated in the TC training and evaluation. A randomized block design with repeated measures was used, and the organizations were assigned to three experimental conditions. Groups A and B received six weeks of training on the core TC curriculum modules. Group A received the two additional training modules on managing organizational change. Group C

served as the control group and received delayed core curriculum training approximately 16 months later. A total of 234 staff representing the 74 organizations participated in the experiment. Twelve separate data collection instruments were developed and translated into Spanish. Outcome data were collected via in-person interviews and a short, self-administered questionnaire from all participants at three points in time. (2002, p. 91)

Young et al. (2002) analyzed data from the experiment to evaluate the effectiveness of the treatment programs. Since their focus was on results from the experiment within Peru and not on any other country, we classified their research as supranational rather than transnational. It is classified as supranational because literature from several countries was employed to formulate the research problem and because the researchers drew implications for other countries besides Peru. If Young et al. (2002) did not use literature from other countries for framing the research problem or for deriving implications for their research, their study would have been classified as national rather than international research. In addition, if the study specifically sought to compare the Peruvian results with those of other countries, using a priori research questions or hypotheses about such international comparisons, the study would be classified as transnational.

SOCIAL WORK PROBLEMS

Social work problems studied in transnational research concern the same topics that were discussed in chapter 4 in relation to international migrants as well as other international phenomena such as women's issues, social work education, mental health and physical health, policy development, social services, and so forth. In particular, transnational research deals with problems such as these:

- The transportation of social work knowledge validated in one country to other countries with respect to social interventions, education, policy development, and methodological knowledge regarding the transmission and utilization of substantive information
- The identification and treatment of problems that occur across countries such as domestic violence, bullying, child abuse, elder abuse, and other forms of delinquent and criminal behavior
- The study of poverty, welfare, and welfare reform and the development of policies, programs, and services to reduce or eliminate poverty, across countries
- The study of cross-cultural phenomena regarding ethnicity, gender, sexual orientations, and minority groups; and their similarities and differences within and between countries in research on poverty, social policies, mental health, child welfare, and so on
- The cross-validation of instruments for collecting data in international social work research
- Comparisons of laws, policies, programs, practices, and services that deal with social work problems across countries

- Comparisons of social work professionals, students, training, and research across countries
- Comparisons of social workers' responses to standardized cases, vignettes, and other protocols regarding the assessment, prevention, and treatment of biosociopsychological problems with which social workers deal

Essentially, transnational research deals with the problems that social work practitioners and educators confront within and between countries.

THE RESEARCH PROCESS FOR TRANSNATIONAL RESEARCH

The same categories of the research process that are employed with supranational and intranational research are used for transnational research: problem formulation; instrument construction; research designs; sampling and generalizability; data collection and analyses; and conclusions and implications. Moreover, as discussed in previous chapters, researchers should keep in mind the following topics in the conduct and utilization of transnational social work research: international and national laws; cultural competence; culturally sensitive research instruments; relevant populations from the countries being studied; language and its translation; historical and political knowledge; economics; social and health services and their provision; and ethics.

In transnational research, which focuses on comparisons between countries, we have abstracted from the literature three basic strategies for comparisons: qualitative descriptions, quantitative descriptions, and comparative research designs. In this section, we shall describe comparisons by qualitative descriptions and by quantitative descriptions. In the section on research designs, we shall describe several comparative research designs that can be employed in transnational social work research.

Qualitative Comparisons

Qualitative comparisons across countries may be conducted in the following ways.

Review of previous research studies. Research studies that have occurred within and between countries are analyzed, and their findings are discussed. For example, Kazi, Blom, Moren, Perdal, and Rostila (2002) described realist evaluation for social work practice in Sweden, Finland, and Britain. They illustrated how the process of realist evaluation could be applied internationally on the basis of their descriptions of the research in those three countries.

Narrative comparisons of laws, policies, programs, and/or practices. Available documentation of laws, programs, and so on is described and compared within and between countries. For example, Faul and van Zyl (2003) compared the work-based welfare reform programs in the United States and South Africa, on the basis of data from program evaluations and data on the state of poverty in those countries. They concluded that the welfare programs in both countries were not sufficient to raise women out of poverty.

Content analyses. These can be employed to describe the themes in laws, policies, programs, and so on within countries; and the resulting themes can be qualitatively compared by narratives across countries. For example, Turner (1990) discussed how a comparative content analysis of biographies could be employed in international social research. Using verbal expressions as key indicators for change, he compared American and British biographies. Although frequencies and percentages were tabulated per theme, the results were discussed qualitatively.

Quantitative Comparisons

The following approaches may be used in the conduct of quantitative comparisons across countries.

Metaanalyses of the results of empirical research between countries. These analyses essentially compare effect sizes of the results of research. The reader should refer to our discussion of databases such as the Cochrane Library, which provides metaanalyses of studies in psychiatry and health care, in chapter 1, and our discussion of metaanalysis in chapter 2. Although metaanalyses are rare in international social work research, we believe that they would be useful in providing information on evidence-based practice for international social workers. Shlonsky and Gibbs (2004) provide a concise summary of how evidence-based practice can be taught in the helping professions.

Comparing social indicators. A common definition of a social indicator across countries is specified, and quantitative comparisons are made. For example, Christopher (2002) used poverty among women as a social indicator, comparing Australia, Canada, Finland, France, Germany, the Netherlands, Sweden, the United Kingdom, and the United States.

Comparing responses to a common stimulus. Professional workers in different countries are provided with a common stimulus, such as a case study, case vignette, and so on, and asked to provide responses to how they would deal with the stimulus. For example, Jergeby and Soydan in their comparative cross-national study provided a vignette "about a family in which the four-year-old child is reported as being exposed to hardship or abuse" (2002, p. 130). Professional social workers from Sweden, the United Kingdom, the United States, Germany, and Denmark were asked to provide responses on their assessment of the situation and to indicate what additional types of information would be needed to make a better informed assessment.

Comparisons against a standard. A standard is specified, and countries are rank ordered with respect to their adherence to the standard. For example, to compare global patterns of statutory unemployment social security provision, Dixon (2001, p. 415) indicated that

> a comparative methodology has been developed to assess a country's statutory intention with respect to unemployment programs, and using that methodology, to rank unemployment programs in 80 countries. This comparative program evaluation ... is one that evaluates the ... design features of all social security programs, social security financing arrangements and social security administrative arrangements.

Fitting a statistical model to two or more countries. Empirical data are obtained for two or more countries. A statistical model is applied to the data from each country, and the extent to which the model is applicable to each country is determined. For example, Barak, Findler, and Wind investigated this hypothesis across a sample of a high-tech company in Israel and one in California (2003, p. 147):

> Individuals with diversity characteristics are more likely to experience more exclusion, perceive the organization as less fair, and experience more job stress, less social support, lower job satisfaction, and poorer well-being than those who belong to the "main-stream" in work organizations.

In addition, they investigated two other hypotheses, and they concluded (p. 157):

> The primary goal of this study was to examine diversity and well-being in work organizations across two national cultures, and to test the applicability of an overall model of diversity, inclusion, and employee well-being. Taken together, the important finding of this study is that the model fits the data well across the two different national cultures. Despite cultural differences, the overall model accounts for half of the variance in the dependent variable in both the California and the Israeli samples.

Problem Formulation

The transnational researcher reviews literature from two or more countries to frame the problem for research. In doing so, she or he seeks information on cultural and national differences between countries, employing narrative review, metaevaluation, and/or metaanalyses of previous research as described in the section on problem formulation in chapter 2. In addition, the transnational researcher is sensitive to multicultural competencies required in the study of more than one country. Previous historical and political knowledge of countries as well as substantive and methodological knowledge and their generalizability are reviewed. In addition, laws and policies affecting research within and between countries are reviewed.

In chapter 4, we provided suggestions for increasing cultural competency of social work researchers, and we believe those suggestions could also be framed to increase not only cultural competency but also international competency, that is, a sensitivity to national and international issues regarding the countries being studied. Hence one can increase one's international competency as a transnational researcher by:

- Becoming aware of one's national background and how it has shaped one's outlook and experience
- Identifying one's own negative attitudes, beliefs, and behaviors toward other national groups
- Realizing that one may have negative attitudes toward members of one's own national group
- Valuing, respecting, and being nonjudgmental about national differences (as long as one doesn't harm others)
- Enhancing one's valuing of and respect for others by increasing contacts with members of different national groups
- Valuing the social work profession's commitment to social justice and to empirically based (evidence-based) practice
- Recognizing one's own limitations

Young et al. (2002), in discussing lessons they learned from the conduct of a therapeutic training experiment in Peru, provide transnational researchers with several issues to consider in problem formulation; creating collaborative relationships; putting together a research or evaluation team; understanding the historical, political, and economic context of the research; planning for the translation of instruments; and ethical considerations. Young et al. (p. 91) emphasize the importance of planning and creating collaborative relationships:

> The most consistent finding of previous studies of research use and planned change is that the key actors of a social experiment must be involved at every stage of the research process. . . . Cross-cultural researchers have also emphasized the importance of collaboration with constituencies . . . as a key element in the successful implementation of social science research. . . . Involvement of key players in the host country is important in order to obtain legitimation and endorsement. It is also essential for gaining an adequate understanding of the social, historical, and political context of the experiment.

Young and associates indicated that they developed a conceptual framework for their social experiment in Peru in collaboration with key Peruvians. A logic model was employed to design the study's methodology, and "the Peruvians provided input in developing the hypotheses and research questions, research design and interpretation of findings. They reviewed the instrument translations, assisted us in developing data collection strategies, and helped communicate with key officials in the Peruvian government" (2002, p. 92).

Young et al. also point out the importance of using skilled, bilingual native-speaking translators in developing instruments for use cross-culturally and cross-nationally. In particular, they suggest that international researchers should rigorously examine the "concepts, language, and data collection methods to ensure measurement equivalence across the culture of the investigator and that of the research subjects" (2002, p. 95). They also admonish international researchers to critically examine procedures they employ in their own country before implementing them in other countries:

> One interesting ethical issue that emerged during the final stages of data collection related to compensation of participants to reduce the rate of refusal or attrition. In the United States, people are surveyed so frequently that the use of "respondent fees" has almost become an expectation. In Peru, however, social surveys are not so pervasive, and our Peruvian data collection team was adamantly opposed to the idea of paying respondents to participate in the evaluation. First, they were very concerned about the safety of the field interviewers having to carry around cash to pay respondents. They also expressed a strong concern that to pay the participant for providing data for the evaluation would set a precedent and would make it more difficult for other research projects in Peru to obtain cooperation without some sort of compensation. (p. 99)

Kosberg, Lowenstein, Garcia, and Biggs (2002) discuss the conceptual and methodological difficulties in planning tansnational studies of elder abuse. Their observations are also pertinent to transnational researchers who are framing the problem for research in other substantive areas:

- "Not only is the comparative analysis of elder abuse adversely affected by conceptual and methodological challenges but also the sharing of preventive and interventive efforts to combat this problem is made more tenuous when there are differences in the definition of the problem within and between different countries" (p. 19).

- "The complexities of elder abuse studies result not only from variations in definitions of the phenomena but also from the cultural diversity of populations within a country. Elder abuse studies from such countries as the United States, Canada, United Kingdom, and Israel, in particular, have intentionally or inadvertently included subjects from different cultural backgrounds. In some instances, elder abuse studies have failed to identify the implications of the variations in cultural backgrounds of a sample in a particular country. But even when done, there is a need to be concerned about the cultural diversity within a cultural group. For example, Hispanic and Asian populations in the United States, Sephardic Jews in Israel, or those of Indian backgrounds in the United Kingdom are likely to be more dissimilar than they are likely to be similar, given variations in income, education, literacy, and so forth" (p. 20).

- "In studies of the influence of ethnicity or race on individual attitudes or behavior, it is necessary to determine whether it is the racial or ethnic background of a group that is predictive of negative attitudes and behavior toward older persons. Possible alternative explanations may be related to religion, religiosity, geographic location, family characteristics, social class, and degree of acculturation" (p. 21).

Dixon and Joyner (2000, p. 1), in a cross-national review of research on family abuse, indicate the difficulties in conceptualizing cross-national (transnational) research:

This multiplicity of research approaches and intervention strategies increases in complexity when we consider the field within a comparative context. Cultural, economic and institutional differences across states vary representations of violence within a family setting, and thus produce unique policy responses and practice strategies that can only be understood within their specific social, political and cultural contexts.

In addition, Taune (1990, p. 45), in discussing lessons learned from comparative, international research, makes a plea for transnational researchers to conceptualize and use theoretical concepts in their research:

What we have learned from all of this is that selecting countries and time points should be *theoretically justified*. The same holds true for single or pair-wise country case studies. If they are embedded in a theory, they are potentially theoretically relevant. Examples are comparisons of Poland and Mexico with single parties and different processes of political co-option, or Nigeria and Brazil with state-owned development corporations. And countries do not have to be compared at the same time point. Nigeria before "privatization" can be compared with Brazil today.

Instrument Construction

In chapter 2, we indicated the importance of cross-validation in the construction and utilization of instruments for international social work research. Moreover, in chapter 4 we presented three approaches to the construction and utilization of culturally competent research instruments: constructing a cultural competency inventory, adapting an instrument from one language to another, and developing original cross-cultural instruments. All of those ideas and procedures are applicable and relevant to transnational research.

Kosberg et al. (2002, p. 22) pointed out that "the general concern for cross-national research on elder abuse, or in any such comparative study, necessitates the existence of reliable and valid data, independent of its source." Moreover, they said:

> In the search for commonalities in the development of cross-national studies on elder abuse, reliable and valid instruments are imperative for use with populations not sharing common values, mores, and languages. Challenging the perceived contextual national character of elder abuse is the fact that the study of elder abuse cannot easily be measured by a common national "yardstick," because different subgroups exist within each nation having different as well as common values and norms. (p. 26)

Lane (1990, pp. 190–191), in his work on data archives in comparative research, cited the advantages and disadvantages of national archives:

> A good national archive is characterized by: (1) *quantity,* comprehensive data as well as of data of various kinds; (2) *quality:* a fairly precise elaboration of different variables and how they have been measured; (3) *access:* easily retrievable information at one central site stored by means of modern computer technology; (4) *overview:* knowledge about where to go in order to find relevant data, including what is available at other locations outside the central archive; (5) *communication:* improved transmission of data for research purposes from one central site to places elsewhere; (6) *development:* the detection of lacunae in existing data is facilitated by the centralization of available information; (7) *re-analysis:* the central storage of various data bases assembled in connection with special projects by different groups of scholars opens up an opportunity for other scholars to use the same data for renewed analyses in terms of others' questions or approaches. To sum up, a national data archive leads to more (quantity) and better organized (quality) empirical information.

Lane (1990) emphasizes that good social science theory is necessary for deciding on criteria for the selection of variables. In particular, there is the problem as to how to process information, that is, how to manipulate information so that it can be employed as data. In addition, there is the problem of measurement regarding the reliability and validity of data and the contextual problem:

> Data that have been assembled for certain research problems may not be suitable for other research questions. The empirical information could have been assembled by indicators that are dependent for their validity on the problems at hand. Or a new framing of the problem may require that additional variables be added or already existing ones be measured by different indicators. (pp. 191–192)

And, more specifically in relation to the translation of instruments, Young et al. (2002, p. 94) discussed the problems they encountered in translating an English version of a questionnaire into Spanish:

> One of the questionnaire items used the word "tradition" but the Spanish word for "tradition" has connotations that are not comparable to the English meaning of the word. As a result, the Spanish word for "customs" was substituted. Some questions used terms referring to TC behavioral management concepts such as "haircuts" and "pull-ups" that could not be literally translated. For these questions, a parenthetical explanation of the meaning was included in the wording of the item. Both the English and Spanish version of the instruments were pilot tested and the Spanish instruments were back-translated into English by an independent bilingual translator. These are just a few examples of some of the language equivalence issues encountered during the TC Training Experiment that illustrate potential problems in constructing data collection instruments for transnational studies.

Research Design

As with research designs in supranational and intranational research, research designs for transnational research depend on the knowledge objectives that are sought. Cross-sectional group study and longitudinal group study designs (i.e., case studies as well as participatory research that includes techniques such as participant observation) are employed for developing researchable hypotheses; and cross-sectional surveys and replicated cross-sectional surveys, for example, are used to provide quantitative descriptions (Tripodi, 1983). Since transnational research involves comparative research within and between countries, we will focus on selected research designs that aim to provide correlational and causal knowledge: experimental and quasi-experimental designs as described in detail by Shadish et al. (2002). In particular, we will illustrate how these designs can be adapted for use in transnational research: randomized before/after group design, nonequivalent control group design, and interrupted time-series design.

Randomized Before/After Control Group Design

This is the classical experimental research design in which subjects are randomly assigned to either an experiment group, X, or to a control group, X_0. Both groups are administered research instruments before the intervention, X, is delivered to the experimental group, and both groups are given posttests after the intervention has been administered. This is symbolized in the diagram, where R represents random assignment; O_1 pretest observations for the experimental group; O_3 pretest observations for the control group; X the experimental stimulus or intervention; X_0 the absence of an experimental stimulus; O_2 posttest observations for the experimental group; and O_4 posttest observations for the control group (Shadish et al., 2002; Tripodi, 1983):

$$R \quad O_1 \, X \, O_2$$
$$R \quad O_3 \, X_0 \, O_4$$

The process of randomization controls for biased selection on known as well as unknown variables; each subject has an equal chance of being included in the experimental or control group.... Since randomization doesn't guarantee equivalence between groups. ... it is necessary for the evaluator to check the comparability of experimental and control groups on relevant variables. Variables that are not comparable are used as covariates in an analysis of covariance for observing the statistical significance of changes between the experimental and the control group.... The combination of randomization and a comparison group controls for statistical regression, effects of previous measures, measurement instability, history, and maturation. However, experimental mortality cannot be controlled, particularly in open settings where clients may drop out of experimental programs and control group members may seek social-program interventions elsewhere. Hence the evaluator carefully monitors the dropout rates, checking the see whether the randomization procedure is altered ... Experimentation is intended to produce cause-effect knowledge. It is especially likely to do so when there is a low dropout rate and when there are no extensive periods of time between preprogram and postprogram measures. (Tripodi, 1983, pp. 140–141)

STRATEGIES FOR USING THE RANDOMIZED BEFORE/AFTER CONTROL GROUP DESIGN IN TRANSNATIONAL RESEARCH   In conducting comparative research within and between two countries, we recommend the following.

Strategy 1. A randomized before/after control group design is implemented within each country. Care must be taken to ensure that the experimental stimulus is identical in both countries. Procedures for language equivalence and for obtaining cooperation between researchers from both countries are employed (Young et al., 2002). Moreover, as recommended by Corrigan and Salzer (2003, p. 109), design strategies to deal with some of the problems of treatment preference are employed:

> Random assignment raises other, unanticipated threats to internal validity as a result of failing to consider treatment preference in research participant behavior. Treatment preferences arise from an individual's knowledge and appraisal of treatment options. Treatment preferences impact: (1) the recruitment phase because people consider whether they want to participate in a study that involves the possibility of receiving an undesirable treatment or waiting for treatment, (2) degree of engagement in the intervention condition, and (3) attrition from the study.

Design strategies to reduce the impact of treatment preferences are to pilot test assumptions about randomization to enhance enrollment and engagement of participants, and to use partially randomized preference trials. These procedures are explained in detail by Corrigan and Salzer (2003).

Within each country, each experiment can also employ a crossover design (Tripodi, 1983), in which those in the control group receive the intervention after the experimental group has received the intervention. In this way, there is an experiment with one replication in each country; and each country's experiment is a replication of the other. Hence generalizability is increased as a result of possible replications within and between countries.

Strategy 2. The first strategy relies on the implementation of field experiments within each country. This heavily depends on the collaboration and cooperation of researchers from both countries. For complicated, time-intensive interventions, the problems of dropouts and attrition are likely to occur. In contrast, there is less of a problem with short-term interventions such as teaching knowledge about drugs, social resources, and so on. The second strategy we propose is for such short-term interventions. Suppose one is interested in transmitting knowledge about drugs and alcohol. A test can be devised to test for such knowledge, and it can be, with careful attention to cross-validation of the instrument, translated, if necessary, for use for two or more countries. Second, an intervention of short duration can also be devised and translated for use by both countries. The knowledge test and the intervention can be computerized, that is, put online. Participants would be selected, for example, by randomized procedures from pools of possible participants within each country. Then the experiments would be conducted online, with each participant taking a knowledge test before and after the short-term intervention designed to increase knowledge about drugs and alcohol. Within each country, the crossover design can also be employed, where those in the control group receive the intervention after the experimental group has received it. Hence an experiment and a replication can be conducted within each country, and the experiments within each country are replications of each other. In addition, by putting the test and the interventions online, the data can be easily processed. Moreover, the costs of field experimentation could be considerably reduced since the experiments would be conducted online.

Nonequivalent Control Group Design

If the randomization in an experiment is not successful, for example, with attrition in experimental and control groups, the randomized before/after control group design becomes a nonequivalent control group design. The nonequivalent control group design depicted in the diagram aims to produce correlational knowledge and to approximate causal knowledge:

$$O_1 \; X \; O_2$$
$$O_3 \; X_0 \; O_4$$

In the Nonequivalent Control Group Design, an experimental group receives an intervention, X, while a comparison group does not, X_0. . . . Measurements (O_1 and O_3) on the dependent variable are made for both groups of clients before the intervention (X) is delivered to the experimental group and again (O_3 and O_4) after the intervention is delivered. Differences between the experimental and comparison groups are compared with respect to their relative degrees of effectiveness. The comparison group controls for the possible effects of history, maturation, and multiple treatment interference. The two groups are regarded as potentially non equivalent because possible selection bias is not controlled, as in the randomized Before-After Control Group Design. . . . Biased selection means that the clients in the experimental and comparison groups probably are not comparable on relevant variables (variables that are either theoretically or empirically related to the dependent variables). Three different strategies can approximate control of selection biases: control by definition, control by individual matching, and control by aggregate matching. . . . Control of selection biases is a simple procedure. The practice-researcher selects one or more variables and specifies the levels of the variables be included in the research. For example, gender has two aspects or levels, male and female. It is controlled by definition if only males (or only females) are included. . . . Control of selection biases by individual matching of subjects is a procedure by which pairs of individuals are identified with respect to one or more relevant variables and each individual is arbitrarily assigned to the experimental or comparison group. . . . The third strategy for controlling selection biases is aggregate matching. This involves identifying the percentage or proportion of experimental group clients who have a particular characteristic on a relevant variable. Then a comparison group is constructed such that its members have the same percentage or proportion of the particular characteristic as do the members of the experimental groups. (Blythe, Tripodi, & Briar, 1994, pp. 192–193)

STRATEGIES FOR USING THE NONEQUIVALENT CONTROL GROUP DESIGN IN TRANSNATIONAL RESEARCH   The same strategies that are employed for the randomized before/after control group design in transnational research can be used with the nonequivalent control group design. The basic difference in the designs is that one employs random assignment and the other does not, although it (nonequivalent control group design) attempts to obtain equal distributions of the experimental and control group on relevant variables. Again, replications with the crossover design can be employed in each country; and the results of each country can be a replication of the other. It is important to point out that these are potential replications. If the potential replications provide consistent, repeated results, then there are actual replications, and generalizability is enhanced.

This design can also be used to evaluate the effects of short-term knowledge-increasing interventions online. It is, of course, possible to also register attitude and behavior changes online; however, the data would more likely rely on self-reports of participants and would not be as valid as behavioral data collected independently of the participants.

Interrupted Time-Series Designs

These designs aim to produce correlational knowledge regarding an intervention and its outcomes (Shadish et al., 2002; Tripodi, 1983). This design is symbolized as

$$X_0 \ 000 \ X \ 000$$

Interrupted Time-Series Designs for evaluating programs are symbolically identical to interrupted time-series designs for evaluating individuals. First it is established that there is no intervention, X_0. This is followed by three or more baseline measurements, 000, until there is a stable pattern. Next, the intervention or program is introduced, X, and measurements are taken while the program is operative, X 000. When used for evaluating groups or programs, the interrupted time-series design focuses on organizational variables or those that represent aggregates of individuals.

Hence measurements in a set of observations, 0, are typically comprised of numbers, averages, and proportions; for example, the number of referrals made by an agency, the average weight of clients in a weight-watcher program, and the proportion of clients who are employed. ... This design controls for most internal validity factors; however, it cannot rule out factors of contemporary history that change simultaneously with program exposure. ... Therefore, an evaluator should obtain information from program participants, significant others, or both regarding potential historical influences. ... Data can be obtained by questionnaire or interview after participants have completed their programs. Although the potential effects of contemporary history cannot be completely ruled out, data may suggest that their influences are relatively minimal. When there is an extensive baseline period, the influence of historical events can regarded as not very plausible. (Tripodi, 1983, pp. 133–134)

STRATEGIES FOR USING THE INTERRUPTED TIME-SERIES DESIGN IN TRANSNATIONAL RESEARCH   Interrupted time-series designs can be employed when there are social indicators or behavioral measures that can be obtained repeatedly over time. It is imperative that the measurements be valid and stable over time. They can be employed on a large scale when policy changes are made that might impact such social indicators as poverty, unemployment, proportions of people with health insurance, and so forth. In addition, these designs can be employed to evaluate the effectiveness of programs dealing with issues such as weight reduction, use of condoms, cessation of smoking, and so on. For example, researchers of two or more countries might be interested in introducing an intervention (say, a didactic presentation about smoking and its relation to health risks and hazards), and studying its effects on smoking within and between countries. Researchers may decide to use the number of cigarettes smoked each week as a dependent variable. The researchers may decide to use self-reports of smoking behavior as the basic source of data, after having determined in pretesting in both countries where the research is to take place that self-reports are highly correlated with the independent reports of significant others. In each country, a baseline would be established in which the average number of cigarettes smoked per week is stable. The baseline measures need not be equivalent in both countries, since the basic control in each country is the stable baseline for its participants. The same intervention, to the extent possible, is provided for the participants in each country. The interventions should be identical with both countries, and its presentation—either by film, computer, or live instructors—should be made for the same length of time. If there are significant changes in smoking behavior after the intervention is introduced for each country, it can be observed that there is a replication of results across countries.

Sampling and Relevant Populations

All the sampling methods that were presented in chapters 2 and 3 can also be employed in transnational research. In comparative research, it is necessary to think of relevant populations within each country so that the researcher knows whether or not the comparison samples are representative of the relevant populations. If the samples are accidental and not necessarily representative of each country being compared, it is difficult to know what is actually being compared, other than the samples themselves. By employing the strategies for replication that we presented in the previous section on research design, it is possible to increase the generalizability of the research through replications. This is an alternative to representative random sampling (Shadish et al., 2002).

In field experiments, Young et al. (2002) indicated that stratified random sampling enables an efficient allocation to experimental and control groups; they randomly assigned organizations to experimental conditions, and then selected individuals for training within the organizations. Regardless of how a sample is initially selected, there is often attrition, particularly in longitudinal research. Cotter et al. (2005, p. 15) indicated that "the success of longitudinal studies depends entirely on the sustained co-operation of its participants. Often, participants are difficult to contact or locate for follow-up assessments, and searching for such participants may require the exploration of a variety of resources." Cotter, Burke, Stouthamer-Loerber, and Loeber (2005, p. 15) examined "the impact of restricted persistence on participant retention and selective attrition in longitudinal research." They collected data from a longitudinal study of the development of disruptive behavior disorders in clinic-referred boys who were studied from childhood to adulthood; and they concluded that it was cost effective to put in extra effort to retain the participants in their sample by systematic and comprehensive efforts in making contacts, participant tracking, interviewer persistence, as well as payments to the participants.

In addition to replication as an alternative to representative sampling, the work of Barak et al. (2003) suggests another aid to generalization. They utilized data from two high-tech companies in California (U.S.) and Israel to test a model whose premise was "that individuals from diverse backgrounds experience greater exclusion, more job stress, less social support, and a sense of unfair treatment, all of which lead to reduced job satisfaction, and ultimately, a significantly poorer sense of well-being in comparison to those in the mainstream" (Barak et al., 2003, p. 145). Their samples of the workers in the two companies were purposive and not necessarily representative of workers in Israel on the United States However, by employing regression equations based on their theoretical model, they concluded that the model fit the data from both countries. Hence, they showed the existence of similar relationships between variables of the model for both countries.

Data Collection and Analysis

Transnational researchers often use multiple models of data collection. Kazi et al. (2002), in their evaluation of practice in Sweden, Finland, and Britain, give examples of how the perspective of critical realism combines types of data: studying changes in outcomes in intervention models, in mechanisms, and in contexts of service. Kazi et al. (2002), for example, combine interview data from different sources and analyze available documents. In addition, Jinkerson et al. (1992), in discussing an approach to collect and analyze data in an international business setting, describe how they used document review, personal interviews, and survey techniques. Of particular importance, they used one data collection modality to check and verify another; they indicated that they used telephone calls as a follow-up to interview notes that were taken during and after interviews in order to clear up ambiguities.

We previously referred to the importance of ethical considerations in data collection, as reported by Young et al. (2002). Moreover, we emphasize notions presented by Kosberg et al. (2002) regarding differences in meanings for such categories as race that vary by definitions and perceptions in terms of skin color, religion, social class, income, and so on; essentially, they indicate that care should be taken to assure that transnational definitions of categories are equivalent. Kosberg et al. (2002, p. 212) also comment on data collection techniques used in studying child abuse and elder abuse:

> In a book on child maltreatment, Knudson (1992) identifies specific limitations with various data collection techniques that can have ramifications for cross-national studies. Data from self-reports depend upon recall and truthfulness (and cognitive ability). Data from observations of maltreatment may reflect professional biases (or ignorance of the adversity). Data from reports resulting from professional or lay person observations allow for a broad definition of adversity but depend on a willingness to report and include only observed acts. Finally data from investigated reports are dependent upon recorded information, limited by observations of the phenomenon and influenced by investigator turnovers, and permit only a short-term view. Ogg and Munn-Giddings (1993), writing about research methodologies in studies of elder abuse in Great Britain and the United States, identify similar challenges resulting from different data collection techniques.

Christopher (2002, p. 66), in examining poverty rates of U.S. women compared to other affluent nations, illustrates how some transnational researchers utilize available data sets:

> I use the Luxembourg Income Study (LIS). The LIS is a consortium of data sets that includes surveys from 25 industrialized countries. It provides comprehensive information on household income sources. All data sets include nationally representative samples of the population in each country. My sample includes: Australia (1994), Canada (1994), Finland (1994), France (1994), Germany (1994), the Netherlands (1994), Sweden (1995), the United Kingdom (1995), and the United States (1994). I select those countries because they have complete information on marital and parental status, employment, and social transfers and taxes.

It is incumbent on the transnational researcher who uses existing data sets to examine the categories of data with respect to available information on their reliability and validity when they were first gathered. In particular, the investigator should check for equivalencies of definitions across countries, as well as the completeness of data.

With respect to data analyses, it is important for transnational researchers who are making comparisons between countries to provide evidence that the samples within countries are representative of their relevant populations and that those in the samples are sufficiently retained in the research. Then, the researchers should analyze the results within countries comparatively by determining the extent to which the research results are consistent; for example, whether they are replicated results, whether regression models are equivalent, and whether factor structures are equivalent across countries. Moreover, the instruments for collecting data should be reliable and valid, and they should be cross-validated so they can be used transnationally.

Data can be analyzed by different methods; and multiple means of analysis help to increase the researchers' confidence in the results. Christopher (2002, p. 675) provides an example of the use of multiple methods:

> I use several different methods to analyze data: logistic regression analyses and regression decomposition techniques to assess how family status affects poverty; the calculation of employment rates and poverty rates based on one's market income to assess how employment affects poverty and the comparison of poverty rates before and after social transfers and taxes are included in income to assess how social assistance programs affect poverty. Regarding the former, because the dependent variable in my analyses (poverty) is dichotomous, the logistic distribution is the appropriate functional form. I run a logistic regression analysis for U.S. women. I report the results of this analysis, along with U.S. women's means on these variables. . . . I use a regression decomposition technique to simulate U.S. women's hypothetical poverty rates if they had the same rates of single motherhood as women in other nations. The regression decomposition technique first uses U.S. women's means and the coefficients from their logistic regression equations of poverty to predict U.S. women's actual poverty rate. Then I substitute the rate of single motherhood found in the other eight nations for that of the U.S. rate (one nation at a time), keeping the means and the coefficients for all other variables the same. The hypothetical poverty rates that result indicate what U.S. women's poverty rates would be if they had the rate of single motherhood found in the other eight nations.

Conclusions and Implications

It is important for any researcher to ensure that conclusions derived from research studies are based on quantitative and/or qualitative data, not on hunches and predilections. This is more difficult for transnational researchers, since they must attend to data from two or more countries, as well as to comparisons between countries. Transnational researchers must attend to these considerations:

- Decide on and provide evidence regarding the extent to which samples from each country included in the research are representative of the countries.
- Decide on the mode of comparison, whether it be by quantitative and/or qualitative methods; for example, consistency and replications of experimental results, similarity of factor structures and explained variance, statistical fit of regression models, comparisons to a standard, rank ordering of countries on social indicators, and so forth.
- Ensure that the definitions of dependent variables and social indicators are equivalent across countries.
- Provide evidence from previous research or within a research study that the variables being measured are reliable and valid within countries and cross-validated between countries.
- Provide evidence on appropriate forms of reliability; for example, Cronbach's alpha, which indicates interitem consistency in an instrument,

is not an indication of stability or test-retest reliability. In intervention studies seeking change after the introduction of an intervention, evidence of stability in the dependent variables is required; otherwise, it is possible that observed changes are due to the instability rather than to the effectiveness of the intervention.

When accidental samples are employed and comparisons are made across countries, including the notion of consistent data within countries, the conclusion should be that the existence of similarities or differences are shown but that future research would be required with additional samples of relevant populations. These findings, since they are not representative, would be at the level of research hypotheses awaiting testing. Care must be taken to indicate whether or not implications are based on data. If they are not, then it should be indicated in the research that these are hypotheses. It is incumbent on research utilizers to not simply attempt to apply and adapt recommendations without first discerning what level of knowledge is represented; that is, untested hypotheses or evidence from tested hypotheses.

The researcher and the utilizer of research can consider the research results of a study in relation to what is known about the phenomenon under investigation. This is facilitated by the internet. Shlonsky and Gibbs (2004, p. 139) indicate that

> according to survey data, 97% of members of the National Association of Social Workers have access (either at home or work) to the Internet (O'Neill, 2003). Anyone who has access to the Internet can access many useful bibliographic databases for free (e.g., PubMed, ERIC (Education Resources and Information Center), Cochrane Library abstracts (but not full reviews), Campbell Collaboration, the National Criminal Justice Reference Service (NCJRS). Agencies that have the funds can subscribe to many of the most useful databases through single-source vendors such as Ovid (www.ovid.com/site/index.jsp).

Shlonsky and Gibbs (p. 139) point out that

> emerging methods for synthesizing studies make it easier to stay current. . . . These procedures employ rigorous methods for locating published and unpublished studies and synthesizing them with respect to their methodological rigor, findings, and implications in practice. The leading sources in this area are the Cochrane Library (www.update-software.com/abstracts/mainindex.html) and Campbell Collaboration (www.campbellcollaboration.org).

INCENTIVES AND BARRIERS TO TRANSNATIONAL RESEARCH

We indicated in chapter 2 that barriers to research included the problems of availability and accessibility of translations of literature from other countries, the time needed to thoroughly review the literature, and the costs involved in reviewing the literature and discussing the results and their meaning with social workers from a country other than the one in which the research was conducted. In addition, supranational research includes all the barriers that are faced in national or domestic research, including all of the issues involved in the research process, such as sampling, ethical considerations involved in institutional review boards, cross-cultural considerations, and so forth. Incentives for supranational research include knowledge for the profession, helping the population in need, individual prestige, use of the internet, use of bilingual investigators, and available grants.

We further indicated in chapter 4 that the barriers and incentives in supranational research were also cumulated in intranational research. We discussed barriers to intranational research as including lack of knowledge about international migrants, lack of resources to meet the needs of participants, difficulties in recruitment and retention, lack of validated cross-cultural instruments, lack of collaboration, additional costs, and additional time. We suggested that those barriers could be met or diminished by the use of resources such as university researchers and professors, the demonstration of the significance and importance of knowledge, the use of incentives for migrants to participate in the research, use of diverse sampling methods, and attempts to increase the ownership of the research results by the participants.

All of these barriers and incentives are cumulated in transnational research, which we regard as the most difficult type of international research, essentially because more types of knowledge and more countries and people are involved, leading to a greater need for collaboration. Cooperation is paramount when investigators and/or participants from two or more countries are involved. This barrier can only be met by desire, awareness of the need to increase transnational knowledge, willingness to cooperate in defraying costs, and having the necessary time for the research. The need to increase comparative knowledge has increased since the effects of globalization and internationalism have permeated the professions, including social work.

Agreement on the research purposes and methodologies is paramount in transnational research. When one investigator makes comparisons of countries on selected social indicators, other investigators and practitioners in the countries involved might question the results. Panels of international reviewers could serve as an incentive for the countries involved to enhance the reliability and validity of research results.

The perceptions of ethical considerations and incentives for participation may vary from country to country. This means that the investigators should learn what are the best research practices involved in countries being compared and attempt to incorporate, if necessary, compromises in research strategies. If, for example, one country employs payment to participants and another doesn't, when comparing the countries, these differences may lead to unknown biases, making comparisons less valid. A compromise position might be the provision of gifts to participants in the countries involved rather than cash.

There are sociopolitical differences and sensitivities between countries that could aid or hinder international research. To the extent possible, researchers should attempt to understand these differences for the countries involved and more particularly for the sites chosen for the research.

Experimental research with replications can provide a great deal of knowledge about the transportability and effectiveness of social work interventions and programs. However, the costs can be exorbitant. We suggest the possibility of increasing international research, particularly experiments on short-term interventions and surveys of knowledge, attitudes, and beliefs by means of online computer participation. There is no question that the use of e-mail and the Internet has led to more instant international communication in the dissemination and utilization of knowledge. We believe the use of online surveys and experiments could decrease the costs of transnational research considerably.

SUMMARY

We defined transnational research as comparative research between populations of two or more countries; and literature across populations is used for formulating the research problem and for drawing implications. We distinguished transnational from intranational and supranational research, indicating common characteristics shared by these types of research. Then we indicated unique characteristics of transnational research with respect to quantitative and qualitative comparisons that can be employed, as well as strategies for employing correlational and causal experimental designs for purposes of comparisons between countries.

We presented a hypothetical example of transnational research involving Italy and the United States in which a training program on adolescent substance abuse was evaluated in both countries by a classical experimental design and by a crossover design. We also indicated the possibility of a special case of transnational research when an experimental model is first tested in one country; then at a later point in time it is transported and replicated within another country.

Problems confronted in transnational research were discussed as those that social work practitioners and educators confront within and between countries. These include the transnational validation of instruments, as well as various types of comparisons: of laws, policies, programs, practices, and services; of social work professionals, students, training, and research; and of social workers' responses to standardized cases, vignettes, and other protocols involved in the assessment, prevention, and treatment of the many problems worldwide with which social workers deal, such as domestic abuse, bullying, poverty, welfare, discrimination, and so forth.

Within the research process, we described qualitative and quantitative comparisons that could be made in transnational research. Qualitative comparisons include: review of previous research studies; narrative comparisons of laws, policies, programs, and/or practices; and content analyses. Quantitative comparisons include these approaches: metaanalysis; comparing social indicators; comparing responses to a common stimulus; comparisons against a standard; and fitting a statistical model to two or more countries.

Under problem formulation, we discussed various principles that transnational researchers could employ in increasing international competency, that is, sensitivity to national and international issues regarding the countries being studied. Seven principles such as these were presented: becoming aware of one's own national background and how it has shaped one's outlook and experiences; identifying one's own negative attitudes, beliefs, and behaviors toward other national groups; and so on. These issues were also considered: creating collaborative relationships; putting together a research or evaluation team; understanding the historical, political, and economic context of the research; planning for the translation of instruments; and ethics. Moreover, concepts of issues such as definitions of social indicators, cultural diversity of populations, and the use of theory were considered.

We discussed the potential uses as well as problems associated with using national archives for selecting variables as instruments in research. In addition, we continued to emphasize the necessity for valid and reliable information in international research. Moreover, we emphasized the need to obtain language equivalence across countries in the construction of instruments for transnational research.

We illustrated how experimental and quasi-experimental research designs could be utilized in transnational research. These designs were discussed: randomized before/after group design, nonequivalent control group design, and interrupted time-series design. In addition, we proposed strategies for the use of these designs. For both the randomized before/after group design and the nonequivalent control group design we proposed two strategies: to increase generalizability by building in replications within countries and considering results from each country as possible replications; to conduct the experiments on-line, utilizing computer technology, particularly for brief, short-term interventions aimed at transmitting knowledge. In addition, strategies for implementing time-series designs with social indicators or behavioral measures were discussed.

The importance of sampling from relevant populations within countries was stressed, and different sampling modalities, such as stratified random sampling and accidental sampling, were discussed. In particular, we emphasized the importance of making efforts to retain participants in research; and we also considered replications as an alternative to representative sampling to enhance generalizability.

We discussed the value of collecting multiple modes of data, the equivalence of data analytic categories, and the role of ethics in gathering data for transnational research. Moreover, we considered precautions that must be taken in using existing data sets. We also recommended using multiple types of data analytic techniques to increase the researcher's confidence in the results of the research. We further indicated several decisions transnational researchers must make in forming conclusions and deriving implications for their research. Furthermore, we indicated that researchers and utilizers of the research could put the findings of a particular study in the context of other possible studies dealing with the same phenomena by using the internet.

We noted that transnational research is the most difficult type of international research and that it cumulates the barriers and incentives found in supranational and intranational research. We indicated that collaboration and cooperation are paramount in transnational research. Moreover, we suggested that panels of international researchers could serve as an incentive for the countries involved in research to enhance the validity of research results. We also discussed varied perceptions of ethics and of incentives, sociopolitical differences and sensitivities between countries, the costs of field experimentation, and the promise of the conduct of surveys and experiments online.

7

ISSUES AND EXAMPLES
OF TRANSNATIONAL RESEARCH

As in the chapters devoted to issues and examples of supranational and intranational research, we present here examples of five transnational research studies. We describe each study, focusing on these aspects of the research process: problem formulation and knowledge objectives; instrumentation and data collection; sampling, relevant populations, and research design; and data analyses, conclusions, and implications. We specify why we classify each study as transnational; and we present issues discussed or alluded to in the research. In addition, we derive issues that are pertinent to the conduct and utilization of transnational research. In conclusion, we summarize the issues presented in the five studies.

SELECTION OF THE STUDIES

We used these criteria for selecting transnational research studies:

- Excellence of study
- Presentation of a range of research methods
- Studies are from several social work journals
- Studies are from different countries
- Studies evoke pertinent issues in the conduct and utilization of research

The research studies in this chapter were selected from these journals: *Social Work*, *Journal of Social Work Research and Evaluation: An International Publication*, and *International Social Work*. The five studies are focused, respectively, on the United States and Ukraine; Romania and the United States; New Zealand and Canada; 80 countries with unemployment programs; and these countries: Australia, Brazil, Canada, Britain, Germany, Hong Kong, Hungary, Israel, the United States, and Zimbabwe. The studies included these research approaches: a pretest-posttest evaluation design with a 4-month follow-up, a survey, cross-validation of an assessment procedure, a qualitative and quantitative comparative policy analysis of 80 countries, and cross-national comparative surveys of BSW graduates.

STUDY 1: "TEACHING BRIEF INTERVENTION FOR ADOLESCENT DEPRESSION: AN EVALUATION OF A CROSS-NATIONAL APPROACH," BY ROBERT CHAZIN, LISA COLAROSSI, MEREDITH HANSON, IRINA GRISHAYEVEA, AND GEORGE CONTIS (2004)

According to the authors, their article "describes the rationale and content of an advanced training offered to a select group of Ukrainian practitioners previously trained by us. It also provides an outcome evaluation of the training and discusses implications for future cross-national teaching" (Chazin et al., 2004, p. 20).

Study Description

Problem Formulation and Knowledge Objectives

The rationale for their study is as follows.

- Social work has had a continuing concern with the benefits of international collaboration.
- Schools of social work and social workers throughout the world are interested in the effects of globalization on social work practices and policies.
- "The professional literature also reflects social work's international interests and abounds with references that exemplify the profession's strong interest in, and commitment to, global efforts" (Chazin et al., 2004, p. 20).
- Cross-national efforts in areas such as professional development and training need to be subjected to rigorous evaluation in order to expand and export tested knowledge to and from other countries.

As a result, the authors' work

represents a continuation of . . . efforts to describe and evaluate a cross-national training experience. The training was part of multiyear project that brought experts from the United States to help Ukrainian school-based practitioners enhance their capacity to assist children and families coping with a stressful environment. This environment included living with the long-term consequences of the Chernobyl nuclear power plant disaster and coping with Ukraine's difficult social, economic and political transition over the past decade. (Chazin et al., 2004, p. 20)

The authors decided to offer advanced training focused on brief intervention with depressed adolescents in response to these factors:

- In the course of their project they collected data indicating that more than 7,000 adolescents were suffering with depression and a range of psychosocial problems.
- Feedback from the social workers who received training in basic psychosocial intervention indicated "the need for additional training concentrating on direct practice with seriously depressed youth" (Chazin et al., 2004, p. 21).

The authors developed a training model based on the following conceptualization:

Drawing on intervention strategies from two empirically validated therapy models, cognitive-behavioral therapy ... and interpersonal psychotherapy with depressed adolescents ... we created a model we believed particularly relevant for these Ukrainian practitioners. From the interpersonal psychotherapy model we identified particular areas of life stress that would be the focus of intervention (grief reactions, role transitions, interpersonal deficits, problems associated with living in single-parent families, and interpersonal role disputes). To this basic problem list we added problem-solving deficits. From the cognitive-behavioral practice model we incorporated a functional analysis of behavior work sheet, a daily record of dysfunctional thoughts, problem-solving protocols, and intervention planning worksheets.

The model we developed has several characteristics. First, it is client-centered and ecologically oriented in its conceptualization of depression. Second, it draws concepts from two widely practiced models, both of which are empirically supported treatments (Lebow, 2001). Third, the model utilizes a strengths-empowerment perspective and principles to enhance interaction between trainers and participants and decrease the risk of imposing U.S. values without input and concordance. . . . Fourth, it is time-sensitive. This is appropriate both for adolescents who often prefer time-limited counseling and for Ukrainian clinicians who generally have limited time in which to assist large numbers of troubled youth. Fifth, a manual is provided to aid teaching and to ensure uniformity in application. (p. 21)

The authors posited these hypotheses (Chazin et al., 2004, p. 23):

- Knowledge scores immediately after the training would show a significant increase from baseline (pretest) scores. Further, there would be no decrease in this posttraining score when participants were follow-up tested four months later.
- Trainees' reports of how willing they were to use various interventions would increase after the training reports, as compared to their pretraining of how often they used the interventions in the past with adolescents.
- Trainees' beliefs about how effective the interventions were for helping adolescents would significantly increase from pretraining reports to 4-month follow-up reports, after they had an opportunity to use the interventions in their work.
- Controlling for prior intervention use and perceived helpfulness, knowledge increases at posttraining will predict future frequency of use and perceived helpfulness of the intervention.

The knowledge objectives were essentially those of testing correlational hypotheses for a sample of Ukrainian practitioners who received a training module. Correlations were posited between training and measures of knowledge, utilization, and efficacy.

Instrumentation and the Process of Data Collection

Each training participant was asked to complete three questionnaires: a pretest questionnaire regarding knowledge, utilization of interventions, and perceived efficacy, that is, usefulness of the interventions in work with adolescents; a posttest

questionnaire at the end of the 5-day training module; and a follow-up questionnaire 4 months after the posttest questionnaire. The questionnaires were completed
voluntarily and anonymously by the participants, who were assured that no efforts
would be made to identify them and that their participation or lack of participation
in the research would not affect their involvement in the training program. Moreover, the participants were not paid for their participation. The response rate was
100% at pre- and posttesting and 90% at 4-month follow-up.

In addition to measures of knowledge, utilization, and efficacy, participant satisfaction with training was assessed by participants' responses to 13 Likert scale
items ranging from 1, strongly disagree, to 5, strongly agree. Items specifically
referred to issues such as "The professor's presentation of material was clear"
(Chazin et al., 2004, p. 24). Measures for knowledge, utilization, and efficacy were
as follows:

> *Knowledge.* Participants were asked to rate 21 items on a scale from 1 to 5 (1 = strongly
> disagree, 5 = strongly agree). Each item asked about an aspect of adolescent de-
> pression or direct practice intervention. Items included "It is normal for adoles-
> cents to experience extreme and unexplainable mood swings," "When an
> adolescent is using drugs and/or alcohol, depression should always be assessed."
> *Utilization.* Participants' willingness to use various interventions was assessed using
> 13 items on a 5-point scale (1 = never, 5 = very often), which were developed
> based on the content of the training. The pretest questions stem asked partici-
> pants to "Rate how often you do each of the following interventions with adoles-
> cents." The posttest stem stated, "Rate how often you think you will do each of
> the following interventions in your future work with adolescents." At the 4-month
> follow-up, participants were asked how often they now use each of the interven-
> tions. Intervention items included "Provide adolescents information about de-
> pression," "Role play to improve social skills."
> *Efficacy.* The same items from the utilization scale were used with a new stem to assess
> participants' perceptions of usefulness for work with adolescents. For each item,
> participants were asked to "Rate how helpful you have found each of the follow-
> ing activities to be when counseling adolescents" (0 = never used, 1 = never ef-
> fective, 5 = very effective). These questions were asked in the pretest and the
> four-month follow-up. (pp. 24–25)

None of the measures were standardized with respect to reliability and validity.
As noted by the authors, a limitation of the measures is that they are based on the
perceptions of clinicians, rather than on actual clinician and client outcomes.

Sampling, Relevant Populations, and Research Design

The sample they chose was a purposive sample, in that the effectiveness of a training program with clinicians who had basic training in working with adolescents could
be demonstrated. Participants were recruited from "four Ukrainian states to which
families affected by the Chernobyl accident had been relocated" (Chazin et al., 2004,
p. 23). Criteria for selection were that all trainees had to have completed a basic
course; the trainees were currently involved in practice with adolescents; and trainees

should be representative of practitioners in the four Ukrainian states. An exception to those criteria was the inclusion of a few participants who had leadership positions in mental health. The sample of 30 participants included 22 mental health practitioners (20 psychologists and 2 social workers), 7 administrators, and 1 teacher. The authors indicated that psychologists and social workers "reported that their job tasks were the same . . . performing regular counseling assessment, and/or prevention" (p. 24). Relevant populations include those of psychologists, social workers, mental health administrators, and teachers in Ukraine who work with depressed adolescents. For this research, the sample is the population, and results cannot be generalized beyond the sample; however, the research does provide a demonstration of the possibility of effective training.

The research design is that of a one-group pretest-posttest evaluation with a 4-month follow-up. No comparison or control group was employed; nor was the training group used as its own control on measures of effectiveness prior to the pretesting.

Data Analysis, Conclusions, and Implications

Changes from pretests to posttests and 4-month follow-up were analyzed by paired samples t-tests for changes in the unweighted means of the items for knowledge, utilization, and measures of efficacy. There were statistically significant changes from pretest to posttest for knowledge and utilization, and from pretest to follow-up for efficacy. In addition, there were no statistically significant changes from posttest to follow-up; and there were statistically significant changes from posttest to follow-up for utilization. All of the changes were in favorable directions in support of the hypotheses that were posited.

Data were also analyzed by obtaining Pearson product-moment correlations between the measures; and by regression analyses controlling for prior utilization at pretest and by controlling for pretraining efficacy. The authors demonstrated that posttest knowledge is related to posttest utilization (i.e., willingness to use interventions) and to the frequency at which practitioners used interventions at follow-up. Posttest knowledge was predictive of follow-up utilization and future intervention efficacy (4 months follow-up). Overall, participants were satisfied with the training program.

According to the authors,

although significant increases were found, the effect sizes for knowledge development were relatively small. However, the effect of the training on participants' use of the interventions was large, especially at follow-up. This indicates that after the training, participants' expectations of using the interventions increased as they had new tools to use with clients. Then, when they had the actual opportunity to use the interventions in practice (between the posttest and the follow-up), they used them even more than they expected. (Chazin et al., 2004, p. 26)

The authors concluded further that their "multi-level assessment provides a variety of evidence that cross-national training can be both palatable to professionals from developing countries, despite differences in cultural practices and language barriers, and effective in improving interventions to address problems in their country" (Chazin et al., 2004, p. 27). They also believed that their work has implications for the possibility of transporting and transferring knowledge of Western methodology cross-nationally.

Classification of the Study

This study is classified as transnational research for these reasons:

- Previously verified knowledge in another country (regarding cognitive-behavioral therapy and interpersonal psychotherapy with adolescents) was transported to the Ukraine, and evaluated there.
- There was collaboration between U.S. and Ukrainian researchers.
- The problem formulation was based on U.S. and Ukrainian literature and experiences.
- Implications were raised that affect future research that could be carried out in Ukraine as well as in other countries.

Issues Addressed in the Study

Translation of Training Manual and Questionnaires

The use of the training manual and questionnaires in research in the Ukraine depended heavily on the authors' care in attending to issues involved in translation. This is typically the case in transnational research, even if the same language is used in the countries being compared, for there are often idiomatic differences in languages. In this research, the authors followed these procedures in implementing the training intervention (Chazin et al., 2004, p. 22):

> Ukrainian professional colleagues translated the manual. It was then subjected to a backwards translation from Ukrainian to English to ensure that material was translated accurately. Unclear sections were re-worked until they were translated accurately. The manual was distributed to all trainees and discussed on the first training day. . . . All teaching was done through a translator who was present at all times. The translator was a university language professor who was fluent in Russian, Ukrainian, and English. The individual had worked with us in prior training sessions and was familiar with both the teaching and learning styles. In addition to the translator, the project manager was a professional psychologist who was fluent in English, Russian, and Ukrainian. She was present for all sessions and was able to monitor the translation for accuracy. At other times a third bilingual project member was present to monitor and validate the translation.

The authors also indicated that, similar to their translation of the training manual, forward and backward translations of the questionnaires were employed. In addition, they believed this was sufficient to ensure the reliability of translation. Although it adds to the costs of translation and instrument construction, we believe that it increases the face validity of the questionnaires to have their translations reviewed by a panel of several persons who are representative of the target population, that is, the population to whom the questionnaires are directed. In this way, possible ambiguities in the wording of questionnaires as well as the meaning of the response systems can be clarified, preferably in pretesting the instrument prior to its use in the research.

Clinicians' Perceptions versus Clinicians' and Clients' Outcomes

The authors noted the issue of clinicians' perceptions versus client outcomes in their research (Chazin et al., 2004, p. 27):

> Despite the overall positive results of this investigation, some limitations deserve noting. One is using a clinician's own perceptions, on nonstandardized measures, of how effective the interventions were for their clients, rather than an objective measure of client outcomes. It is possible that the training increased their accurate use of, and confidence with, the interventions, which, in turn, increased their helpfulness to clients. However, the participants' responses could also be a function of demand characteristics and selection bias, especially evident in satisfaction scores. The use of a control group and a direct examination of client outcomes would determine more accurately the efficacy of the interventions for clients.
>
> In this instance there are two sources of outcomes: the clinician and the client. First of all, the clinician needs to actually implement the interventions as perceived by the clients as well as by the clinicians. This involves the actual use of interventions by verbal, written, and/or other means of communication. These behavioral observations of clinicians should be highly correlated with the clinicians' perceptions if there is validity of the perceptions. Secondly, client outcomes would refer to the results of interventions implemented with the clients. This can be determined by intervention research focused on evaluating the intended effects of the intervention. Obviously, if clinician and client outcomes are highly correlated with clinicians' perceptions, there would be some evidence validating the measure of clinician's perceptions. This information could be obtained if it is built into the research strategy, or by a separate study of the effectiveness of interventions, or by a more thorough development of the instruments employed in this research.

Issues Arising from the Study

Lack of Standardized Research Instruments

According to the authors, measures of satisfaction, knowledge, utilization, and efficacy were not standardized. Essentially, there was no information as to whether or not the instruments were reliable and valid. Since the authors were interested in measuring changes over time (from pretest to posttest to 4-month follow-up), it would have been important to have knowledge of the stability (test-retest reliability) of the instruments. Otherwise, it is possible that the changes observed are due to unreliability of the measuring instruments. At a minimum, interitem consistency (alpha), test-retest reliability, and content validity of the items could have been investigated in pilot testing of the instruments. However, it might not have been possible to find a sample of participants representative of those included in the study. Hence these procedures could have been built into the research. First, a panel of experts, trainers and practitioners, could reflect on the extent to which the contents of questionnaire items represented the interventions that were in the training modules. Second, additional measurements of the scales of knowledge, utilization, and effectiveness could have been taken 5 days before the pretest measurements. In this manner, stability of the measures could be determined when the training module has not been implemented. In essence, the group of participants would be acting as its own control group. In addition, interitem consistency could be obtained at each of the measurement stages—before the pretest, pretest, posttest, and 4-month follow-up.

Representative Sampling versus Purposive Sampling

The sampling procedure in this study is purposive, in that the sample was deliberately chosen to demonstrate the possibility of teaching interventions to a particular group of mental health practitioners. The sample was chosen from those practitioners who received previous training from the research team. However, the extent to which it is representative of Ukrainian psychologists, social workers, mental health administrators, or teachers is unknown. Without representative sampling, the results of the research are restricted to the sample under investigation and not necessarily generalizable to other relevant populations. The authors asserted that "the ongoing evaluations of our training have demonstrated the potential for success of transferring Western methodology cross-nationally" (Chazin et al., 2004, p. 28). Without representative sampling of practitioners from other countries as well as from Ukraine, one can only conclude that the training appeared to be effective, given the use of nonstandardized measures, with a sample of practitioners in Ukraine especially chosen by the authors. Obviously, much more research would be needed to validate the success of transferring the particular intervention methodologies of cognitive-behavioral therapy and interpersonal psychotherapy with adolescents to practitioners in non-Western countries.

Research Design Alternatives

The authors employed a one-group, pretest-posttest, 4-month-follow-up research design; and they noted that a control group would have been desirable. We believe the issue here is the extent to which other research designs that employ control groups might have been employed. Two possibilities come to mind. First, as was discussed in the issue pertaining to lack of standardized research instruments, the group receiving the training can be used as its own control. This is done by taking measurements before the pretest measurements. One can test for stability by taking measurements over two periods of time without introducing the training. In addition, it is possible to take repeated measurements over time and analyze the changes in a time series of data; however, this would be more feasible for behavioral observations than with perceptual observations that can be influenced by expectancy and memory of the questions asked repeatedly over time.

A second possibility of a control group is that of using a crossover design. For example, approximately half of the group might be randomly assigned to a training group or to a nontraining group. Both groups would be measured at the same time before the training group actually received training. Then, the training group (approximately 15) would receive the 5-day training module; and the nontraining group (approximately 15) would not. After 5 days, when training is completed for the training group, posttest measurements are given to both groups. The nontraining group serves as a control group for the training group. This is followed by administering the training module to the nontraining group. After it has completed the training module, measurements are taken again. This serves as a potential replication. Since the nontraining group was measured twice over a 5-day period before it receives training, it acts as its own control group.

The point that we are making here is that it is important for the investigators to consider whether there are alternative research designs that might be employed in their research. If alternative designs are not feasible, it would be worthwhile for investigators to inform other researchers why this is the case.

STUDY 2: "ROMANIAN ADOPTEES: A CROSS-NATIONAL COMPARISON," BY SCOTT D. RYAN AND VICTOR GROZA (2004)

Ryan and Groza (2004) present a cross-national comparison of Romanian adoptees in Romania and in the United States. They describe the background rationale for their study, and its conceptualization, that lead to the principal questions of their research.

Study Description

Problem Formulation and Knowledge Objectives

The rationale for their study is as follows.

- Since the World War II, a number of developing countries or countries recovering from war or disaster have relied on international adoption, which represents about 15% of adoptive placements in the United States (p. 53).
- Romania, in particular, became notorious in the early 1990s because of media exposure about problems in its child welfare system and the thousands of children languishing in institutions (p. 53).
- Since the fall of communism, there also have been many innovations in Romania trying to deal with the child welfare problems, in particular, increasing the number of children placed for adoption in-country and attempts to develop a foster family care system. . . . To date, little but anecdotal information is available about the experiences of these families and the children they adopt (p. 53).
- Ryan and Groza believe it is beneficial to make cross-national comparisons of vulnerable children. Researchers can study similarities and differences in adoption across cultures; the consequences of children separated from their original culture; and possible solutions to common cross-national problems.

The authors use a theoretical framework based on families as systems of resources and stressors. They focus on resources, that is, a strength perspective, rather than on stressors: "resources for adoptive families include those from the community, those from the service system, those that the child as a subsystem brings to the family, and those that the historical family system brings to the new adoptive family system" (Ryan & Groza, 2004, p. 55).

By focusing on an ecological perspective, the authors indicate that family adoptive life experiences contain more stressors and different types of experiences compared to other family systems. They focus on the child's behavior, the preplacement setting, and the parent-child relationship as resources to derive these questions for their research:

- What are the similarities and differences among Romanian children adopted by Romanian families and Romanian children adopted by American families?
- What is the relationship between the adoptive country and parent-child relationship satisfaction on postadoption child behaviors?
- Is the total time in a preplacement setting a better indicator of postadoption child behavior than developmentally specific staging?
- What are the implications for strengthening and supporting the families that adopt these children (Ryan & Groza, 2004, p. 58)?

The knowledge objectives inherent in these questions are quantitative descriptions comparing Romanian children adopted by Romanian families with Romanian children adopted by American families, and correlational knowledge about the relationships between children's behaviors and predictive variables such as parent-child satisfaction and total time in a preplacement setting.

Instrumentation and the Process of Data Collection

Data collection was implemented separately for a sample of those Romanian children adopted in Romania and for an international sample of Romanian children adopted in the United States. In Romania,

> data collection occurred in two stages. In the first stage, all the families from the satellite office in the northwest part of the country (n = 8), a random sample of half of the families (n = 41) from a satellite office on the east coast, and all the families who were associated with the central office (Bucharest) but who lived outside the city (n = 23) received mail questionnaires from the central office. Included in the questionnaires were envelopes for mailing the survey back to the central office. The returned questionnaires had no family identification. Thus, the investigators did not know family names, nor was the agency able to trace individual responses. A total of 72 surveys were mailed to the adoptive families, of which 43 were returned, to make a response rate of 60 percent.
>
> The second stage of data collection in Romania involved contacting half of the adoptive families living in Bucharest (n = 53). Twenty-five families of the 53 contacted agreed to be interviewed face-to-face; the interviews were structured and contained the same questions as in the mailed survey. (Ryan & Groza, 2004, p. 59)

In the United States, there were two waves of data collection. Data were collected on 475 children residing in 399 families in the first wave. This represented "about 16 percent of all adoptions from Romania between 1990 and 1993" (p. 59). Of those families, 330 were recontacted to collect data a second time, as well as 10 additional families that were involved in the second year of the project. The second wave obtained information about the placement history of the children before adoptions and developmental changes in the children; data were collected on 230 children living in 209 families.

These instruments were employed in the surveys: the Child Behavior Checklist (CBCL) and the Parent-Child Relationship Scale. Ryan and Groza (2004, p. 60) staid:

> The portion of the CBCL used was the list of 113 behavior problems with the 1991 scoring for the CBCL (Achenbach, 1991). The CBCL provides measures containing five subscales assessing internalizing problems plus a summative Internalizing Scale, and four subscales assessing externalizing problems plus a summative Externalizing Scale. The checklist has been extensively validated and utilized in numerous research studies.

The parent-child relationship scale cumulates responses to seven questions, each of which ranges from 1, least like the trait in question, to 4, most like the trait in question. Hence scores can range from 7 to 28, with higher numbers representing parent-child satisfaction. The questions ask about getting along, spending time together, communication, impact on family, closeness, trust, and respect. Ryan and Groza (2004, p. 6) indicate that

> it was determined by factor analysis that the seven questions loaded on one factor, explaining 64.65 percent of the variance and all of the questions loading with a minimum factor load of .7 (range .71–.87). The scale has an alpha = .90, and ranged from .74 to 4.00 (M = 1.31, SD = .49).

Sampling, Relevant Populations, and Research Design

Sampling was described in the previous section on data collection. For the in-country adoption sample, there was an attempt to secure representative sampling by selecting potential participants randomly and by including all participants in selected areas. The response rate was 60%. In the second wave of data collection, random sampling was again attempted, but there was a 47% response rate. The sample of Romanian children adopted in the United States was a convenience sample. The response rate of children living in 209 families in the second wave of data collection was 63%.

Relevant populations are all of the Romanian children placed in adoption in various years, Romanian children adopted in Romania, Romanian children adopted in the United States, and Romanian children adopted in other countries. Relevant populations could also be specified by year of adoption, length of time in an adoptive family, characteristics of families that adopted Romanian children, and so forth.

The characteristics of American and Romanian samples were compared. According to the authors,

A total of 298 adoptive families responded to the surveys, with 230 families residing in the US and 68 living in Romania. . . . The majority of respondents from both the US and Romania were the adoptive mothers (73.5% and 82.4%, respectively) with no statistical differences in the rates of respondent relationship. . . . The primary respondents from the US were significantly older (4.16 years) than those from Romania. . . . Of those individuals with partners, the partner's age was significantly older for US families. Partners in the US averaged almost 43 years of age . . . while Romanian partners were almost three years younger. . . . Romanian families had significantly fewer children in the home. (Ryan & Groza, 2004, pp. 62–65)

These and other findings reported by the authors point to the fact that on certain variables, such as age, the samples from both countries are not comparable, leading to the possibility that more behaviorally difficult and hard-to-place children might have been placed in the United States in comparison to those placed in Romania.

The research design is that of a comparative survey design. Those variables compared pertain to child's demographics and placement history, child's current developmental and behavioral status, and time in specific placement.

Data Analysis, Conclusions, and Implications

Tests for statistical differences between means for the United States and Romanian sample were conducted for variables pertaining to parent-child relationship status, child's demographics and placement history, and child's current developmental and behavioral status. In addition, multivariate, regression analyses were conducted to study, while controlling for several factors, the "time spent in specific pre-placement settings regardless of the developmental time period, as well as the effect of the parent-child relationship, on the child's behavior" (Ryan & Groza, 2004, p. 69). Moreover, the child's preplacement history was examined in relation to child behaviors.

These are typical of the results presented in the study:

- Parents from both countries overwhelmingly responded that they got along very well with their child (Ryan & Groza, 2004, p. 62).
- All the Romanian respondents spent time with their child every day . . . which is significantly more than their U.S. counterparts (pp. 62–63).
- Of Romanian adoptive parents, 100% reported feeling very close to the child. This is significantly more than the almost 80% of U.S. families who also reported feeling very close to the child (p. 63).
- Children adopted in the United States were, on average, almost one year older than their Romanian counterparts when adopted (p. 65).
- Children residing with families in the United States were significantly older by almost 3.5 years (p. 65).
- Children living in the United States also scored significantly higher on all of the CBCL scales and subscales, which means that they exhibit more difficult behaviors than the children living in Romania (p. 66).
- The test age of the child was a significant predictor for several of the models, especially in those scenarios examining externalized behaviors such as

delinquency and aggression. Thus, for every yearly increase in the child's age the child's behavior worsened (p. 69).

The authors concluded that the families from the United States and Romania were structurally different. Adoptive parents in the United States, and their partners, were older than Romanian parents. In addition, Romanian children adopted by U.S. families were older than Romanian children adopted by Romanian families; these children also spent more time in institutions prior to being adopted.

These are implications that the authors derived from their research:

- Practitioners can help prospective adoptive parents by discussing some of the challenges they face in adoption.
- There appears to be a significant relationship between parental dissatisfaction and problematic child behavior; this should be explored in further research.
- Knowledge about preadoptive placement settings and developmental issues in children may help practitioners to prepare prospective adoptive parents for adoptive placements.

The quantitative descriptions and comparisons between the United States and Romanian samples are restricted to those samples, and should not necessarily be generalized to other populations. This is due to the fact that the samples of each country are illustrative, but not necessarily representative. Implications 1 and 3 should be regarded as hypotheses and reserved for further research, since they were not tested in the research study.

Classification of the Study

These are the reasons for classifying this study as transnational research:

- Samples from two different countries were selected and compared.
- Literature from more than one country was employed to frame the research problem.
- Literature from more than one country was employed to consider the conclusions and possible implications for further practice and research.

Issues Addressed in the Study

Incomplete Records and Low Response Rates

Procedures utilized in research for locating potential participants and for selecting samples, to some extent, depend upon available lists and records of addresses and possibly phone numbers. The authors were interested in drawing a random sample of families in Bucharest, and they indicated:

At the same time of the study for the years under observation, there were 106 adoptive families living in Bucharest. Half the families (n = 53) from the list living in Bucharest were asked to participate in in-home interviews. However, the families were not randomly selected because complete addresses were not available for almost half of the families. . . . Of the 53 families contacted from Bucharest, 25 agreed to be interviewed, making a response rate of 47 percent. Although the overall response rate for mailed surveys was acceptable by scientific standards, the low response rate for Bucharest was problematic from a social science standard. (Ryan & Groza, 2004, p. 59)

The issue here has to do with the degree of representativeness that is sought for what relevant population. If the relevant population is the 106 adoptive families and a complete list of their addresses is not available, what alternatives are available for the researchers? The first alternative is to spend extra effort in attempting to locate the families, perhaps by snowball sampling on the part of those professionals who worked with the families, as well as other families who might have known their whereabouts. Second, if there are records of characteristics such as age, size of family, family composition, and so on regarding the families, the characteristics of the total population of 106 can be compared with the characteristics of the sample. The purpose of this would be to determine the extent to which the obtained sample of 25 is representative of the 53 contacted, as well as of the 106 families on available variables.

With respect to the response rate, the lower it is, the less likely it is that the obtained sample is representative of the population from which it is drawn. The investigator, if interested in representativeness, should indicate, if possible, the extent to which the obtained sample is representative; that is, the sampling distributions should not be significantly different on available variables. Still another alternative is to reexamine the purpose of the study. Instead of representing the population, the purpose may be to illustrate in an exploratory fashion characteristics of those adoptive families that were available; or the definition of the relevant population may be reconsidered.

When the response rate is low, the investigators may consider to what extent it might be possible to increase participation. Perhaps incentives such as payment, gifts, or exchanges for food, and so on, might be employed; or the investigators may seek to be as flexible as possible in arranging interviews. Of course, the participants continue to have the right to refuse their participation. For the purpose of future research with similar participants, it would be important for the researchers to attempt to secure information as to why participants declined to engage in the research. Such information could be instructive for the planning of future research with similar populations.

Missing Data

Often in data analysis, data are incomplete. Data may be complete for all participants for one variable and not for another. This means that the number of participants may vary as a function of different variables being analyzed. To exaggerate the phenomenon, suppose there are 100 participants. Further suppose that one is interested in determining the average number of previous placements in foster care settings for the participants. However, information on only 50 is available. The result is that the sample is reduced significantly and may not be representative of the original 100.

The investigators were aware of such a possibility and indicated their solution to the problem (Ryan & Groza, 2004, p. 61):

> There were a significant number of cases with at least one independent variable missing. Utilizing a listwise method of data analysis would have resulted in a severely reduced sample size. To utilize all available data a method of data imputation was chosen to estimate the missing data.... Utilizing the SPSS program Missing Value Analysis 7.5, an expectation maximization (EM) technique was used with inferences assumed based on the likelihood under the normal distribution. (Hill, 1997)

Issues Arising from the Study

Further Data Analyses

Additional data analyses can help to shed light on possible discrepancies or distortions that may exist in the data. In this study, for example, there were 230 U.S. participants and 68 Romanian participants. The authors examined the characteristics of these participants, concluding that there were statistically significant differences in the ages of participants and in the number of children in the home. Subsequent analyses indicated that the adoptive children in the U.S. sample were older and displayed more behavior problems. It is possible that the differences in results regarding behaviors of the adoptive children were due to the U.S. sample receiving older children with more difficulties prior to being adopted than Romanian children adopted by Romanian families. In other words, there may have been a selective bias in the samples. Additional data analyses may help to discern whether this is the case. One possibility is to match characteristics of the Romanian sample, for example, on age of adoptive parent and age of child, with those of the American sample. The samples might be matched in such a way that there are 68 participants in each sample. If this is possible, then analyses can be conducted to compare results of the 68 in each sample.

Further Research

This study was based on comparisons of responses obtained by cross-sectional surveys. Among the findings it was observed that adoptive children in the U.S. sample were older and had significantly more behavior problems. In addition, the authors reported that

> those children living in Romania scored significantly less on measures of withdrawal, thought, attention, aggression and overall externalized behavior. The test age of the child was a significant predictor for several of the models, especially in those scenarios examining externalized behaviors such as delinquency and aggression. Thus, for every yearly increase in the child's age the child's behavior worsened. (Ryan & Groza, 2004, p. 69)

Since cross-sectional surveys cannot show causality among variables or the relationships among variables over time, it would be instructive to select a sample of participants and follow them up in a longitudinal research format. Repeated interviews could be conducted over time to discern what changes in children's behavior are made as a function of adoptive care. In addition, such a study might corroborate the inferences made from the cross-sectional surveys.

STUDY 3: "THE STANDARDIZED ASSESSMENT OF CHILD WELL-BEING IN CHILD PROTECTION WORK," BY JAMES G. BARBER AND PAUL DELFABBRO (2000)

The authors report on a demonstration project conducted for the Children, Young Persons and Their Families Services (CYPFS) of New Zealand. Their aim was to develop a standardized procedure for assessing the well-being of children.

Study Description

Problem Formulation and Knowledge Objectives

The rationale for conducting the study was as follows.

- In view of the centrality of child well-being in the clinical decisions of child welfare service providers, there is surprising lack of vigor in the way well-being is normally assessed in the field. In Australia and New Zealand, for example, standardized instruments have only recently come into operation in statutory services, and most of the existing instruments deal with objective aspects of the child's circumstances known to be associated with reabuse, such as whether or not the child's primary caregiver uses drugs or has a previous history of violence. . . . Not only do such measures overlook the affective dimension of well-being, but they almost never include the child's perspective (Barber & Delfabbro, 2000, p. 111).
- Among the best known of the child well-being instruments currently available to service providers are the Child Well-Being Scales (CWBS) developed by Magura and Moses (1986). The CWBS consists of 43 separate scales, which are designed to measure four areas: parenting role performance, familial capacities, child role performance, and child capacities. Despite their obvious appeal in child welfare assessments, the CWBS has received mixed reviews in relation to its reliability and validity. . . . Moreover, the CWBS suffers from conceptual and methodological shortcomings that limit its usefulness in clinical decision-making (pp. 111–112).
- What service providers need . . . is a standardized assessment procedure that applies the standards of the community from which the client derives; and to accomplish this, not only must the assessment instruments be normed against the relevant community but also, as far as possible, the scores that are assigned should be independent of the values and standards of the practitioner (p. 112).

The authors' approach was intended to provide a useful procedure for clinical assessment by including six separate sources of information: the child, the child abuse perpetrator, the perpetrator's partner, a family or friend key informant, a professional key informant (such as a doctor or teacher), and the worker's own observations. These six instruments "were combined into a single instrument on which social workers recorded the sources of information used in completing each section of the questionnaire" (Barber & Delfabbro, 2000, p. 113).

The authors' purpose was to develop a methodological procedure that could be used for assessing the well-being of children in New Zealand. To accomplish this, the researchers compared the well-being scores of children receiving services from CYPFS with normative information from two nonclinical populations in Canada and Australia that had available data sets that could be used for secondary analyses (i.e., as normative data). For purposes of this article, the authors focused on comparisons between a CYPFS sample of children and a normative sample from Canada. The aim of the study was, therefore, to produce methodological knowledge that could be demonstrated to be useful by comparing clinical with nonclinical samples. The resulting knowledge could be conceptually generalized for use in New Zealand.

Instrumentation and the Process of Data Collection

The researchers used four basic measures for obtaining data and reporting results: The Child Behavior Check List, the Control Problems Check List, the Sexual Activity/Abuse Inventory, and Information Quality. According to the authors,

> the child's behavior was assessed using the 15 items comprising the conduct disorder subscale of Boyle & Colleagues (1987) Child Behavior Checklist (CBC). In total, the CBC contains four subscales measuring somatic illness, emotional disorder, hyperactivity, and conduct disorder . . . conduct disorder refers to a "persistent pattern of physical violence against persons or property and/or severe violation of social norms" (Boyle et al., 1987, p. 826). Responses to each item are scored on a 3-point scale from 0, Never or not true to 2, Often or very true. Thus, total scores on the conduct disorder subscale can range from 0 to 30. (Barber & Delfabbro, 2000, p. 114)

Boyle et al. reported high levels of agreement of workers' ratings with psychiatrists' diagnoses for all of the subscales of the CBC (87% agreement) and an alpha of .86, representing a high degree of interitem consistency, for the conduct disorder subscale. The CBC was administered to the 64 children and adolescents in the New Zealand sample. Data on the same measure were available from the normative Canadian sample. The process of data collection for the Canadian participants involved the following procedure. Students were selected from 95 Canadian schools to represent different age groupings of children and adolescents.

> Following identification of the students, mailing labels containing parents' names and addresses were prepared by each school district. Each of these parents was dispatched a letter describing the study and indicating that their child had been selected to participate. The letter explained the content and purpose of the questionnaire in general terms and their participation was voluntary. A final list of participating students was then compiled and questionnaires were dispatched to them. (pp. 113–114)

The Control Problems Check List was used to ask caseworkers to estimate how often in 1 week the child went to school, slept at home, left home without permission, and took alcohol or drugs. Scores ranged from 0 to 28; lower scores indicated more control problems. There was a reported alpha of .71 and construct validity in correlating with a parenting checklist. Social workers also completed a Sexual Activity/Abuse Inventory, indicating sexual activities and the parties or perpetrators involved in each sexual activity. No information on reliability or validity was provided. In addition, information quality was assessed for reliability by referring to the extent to which six sources of information were employed, the social workers' ratings of the extent of the agreement of the various sources, and social workers' confidence in the information those sources provided. None of these measures were available for the comparison sample of Canadian respondents.

Sampling, Relevant Populations, and Research Design

The CYPFS sample was a convenience sample that consisted of 64 children and adolescents receiving services from CYPFS social workers. Some characteristics of the sample were:

> The mean age of the sample was 13.5 ... with a range of 2–18 years. ... Twenty-four (38%) of these clients were European, 33 (52%) identified themselves as Maori, and 6 (10%) identified with other ethnic groups. Thirty-seven (58%) of the children were living at home and 27 (43%) were living elsewhere. (Barber & Delfabbro, 2000, p. 113)

The authors reported that

> the Canadian sample of nonclinical youth comprised 985 junior and senior high school students drawn from 95 Canadian schools. One school was randomly selected from each of the nine school districts in the province of Alberta. Within these schools individual students were selected by stratified random sampling according to age from 12 through 17 years. ... Individual school districts were responsible for drawing the sample based on a required sample size. In a few cases where individual sampling was not possible, a classroom sampling method was adopted. In these cases one or more classes that were not mandatory for all students within the schools were randomly selected, thereby enhancing the representativeness of the sample. (Barber & Delfabbro, 2000, p. 113)

The relevant populations for the New Zealand sample are junior and senior high school students in New Zealand, students under the care of CYPFS, and the sample itself, which is a clinical sample. Although not included in the study, a normative, nonclinical sample could have been chosen from junior and senior high school students in New Zealand. In comparison, the relevant populations for the Canadian sample include junior and senior high school students in Canada, and those students who were under the care of services in Canada comparable to CYPFS services provided in New Zealand. The immediate relevant populations for the study are those under the care of CYPFS in New Zealand and junior and senior high school students in Canada.

The research design is survey research at one point in time of CYPFS children and their workers, and secondary data provided from a survey in Canada prior in time to the New Zealand survey. The results of both surveys were compared on hyperactivity, emotion disorder, conduct disorder, and somatic illness—all subscales of the Child Behavior Checklist.

Data Analysis, Conclusions, and Implications

Means of the subscales of the CBC were tested for statistically significant differences between independent samples for the New Zealand and the Canadian samples. These are the results of those comparisons:

> While both the CYPFS and normative samples obtained similar scores on the hyperactivity and emotional disorder subscales, the CYPFS sample scored significantly higher on conduct disorder than the Canadian sample, t (1044) = 7.85, p. < .001, but significantly lower on somatic illness, t (1044) = 7.28, p < .001. All four subscales were positively correlated in the CYPFS sample, with coefficients ranging from a minimum of r (51) = 0.33, p < .05 between conduct disorder and somatic illness, to a maximum of r (62) = 0.74, p < .001 for hyperactivity and conduct disorder. (Barber & Delfabbro, 2000, p. 115)

With respect to results for only the CYPFS sample, these are representative findings:

- While most of the children in the sample went to school and slept at home most of the time, leaving home without permission and drug and/or alcohol consumption occurred at the rate of approximately twice per week in the CYPFS sample as a whole (Barber & Delfabbro, 2000, p. 118).
- Maori children were significantly more likely to leave home without permission than the rest of the sample, Ç² (1) = 4.07, p < .05. Not surprisingly, leaving home without permission was positively related to scores on the conduct disorder subscale of the Child Behavior Checklist (CBC), r (32) = 0.57, p < .001, and those with conduct disorder scores in the clinical range were significantly less likely to attend school compared with the rest of the sample (p. 118).
- Analysis of the nine children who were involved in at least one type of sexual activity revealed that they were more likely to be girls. . . . All other characteristics were very similar to the rest of the sample (p. 119).

The authors also reported the mean number of information sources, confidence ratings, and the level of agreement among sources, as well as information quality, as determined by formula, which will be discussed later as an issue arising from the study. In addition, Barber and Delfabbro reported on the sources that social workers consulted for each section of the questionnaire, as well as predictors of confidence ratings, as determined in regression analyses. These findings were only reported for the CYPFS sample.

The authors did demonstrate the possibility of using their procedures; however, they appropriately concluded that the procedures could not become operational in

New Zealand until norms for the New Zealand population are developed for all the instruments employed in this research. In addition, the authors pointed out that it is necessary to "identify thresholds for significant subpopulations, especially the Maori and Pacific Islander groups" (Barber & Delfabbro, 2000, p. 122). Essentially, the major implication of their research is that the procedure is promising but should be pursued more specifically in relation to the development of norms for the New Zealand population, including its subcultural groupings.

Classification of the Study

This study is classified as transnational because:

- Comparisons were made between New Zealand and Canadian populations on the CBC. For the other instruments where only data were presented for the New Zealand sample, we regard that research as supranational.
- Literature from New Zealand, Canada, and other countries was used to formulate the research problem and discuss implications.
- Literature from several countries was used in choosing and developing instruments for the research.

Issues Addressed in the Study

Choosing Normative Samples

In constructing clinical instruments, it is the custom to sample a clinical population and then compare it against a nonclinical population. In this research, a sample of children in supervisory care were compared with children and adolescents not in care, who were in junior and senior high school in Canada. The authors then developed a procedure to estimate clinical cutoff scores for each subscale of the CBC:

> A further analysis considered the characteristics of those with the highest scores on each subscale. Selection was based on norms established on the CBC by Boyle & Colleagues (1987) who presented details of the percentage of young people in the general population diagnosed with each of the four disorders. These percentages were matched with the data obtained from our normative Canadian sample to produce an estimated clinical cutoff score for each subscale. For example, since Boyle & Colleagues (1987) estimate that 7.21% of the general population experience clinically significant conduct disorder, the top 7.21% of cases from the Canadian distribution of scores were identified and the conduct disorder scores which cutoff, or lay at the lower boundary of this group, became the threshold score distinguishing between clinical and nonclinical cases. Since Boyle & Colleagues (1987) also found significant gender differences in the prevalence of each disorder, the estimated cutoff score for the CYPFS sample was weighted according to the number of males (n = 39) and females (n = 23) in the sample. (Barber & Delfabbro, 2000, pp. 116–118)

The issue here is centered on the choice of normative samples. Why should New Zealand supervised children be normed against Canadian, or even Australian, British, or U.S. children? Typically, as the authors indicate in their conclusions, the normative sample should be from the same country and reflective of its cultural variation, for example, Maoris and Pacific Rim children in New Zealand. Of further empirical interest, it would be instructive to obtain comparative means on these different countries where English is the predominant language. Moreover, it would be of further interest to provide comparative information from other countries to the CYPFS sample.

Cross-sectional Survey Research versus Qualitative Longitudinal Research

The authors undertook a regression analysis to explore

> the relationship between the number of sources consulted and the level of agreement (independent variables) and confidence ratings (dependent variable).... The results of the analysis ... show that confidence ratings were negatively related to the number of sources consulted, but positively related to the level of agreement. (Barber & Delfabbro, 2000, p. 120)

The authors (p. 120) speculated about the results as follows.

> These results suggest one of two possible interpretations. The first is that the more people the social worker consults, the greater the likelihood of disagreement or inconsistency between resources. The second is that caseworkers who consult more sources are those who experience greater difficulty in obtaining reliable information about the child and respond by seeking out more sources of information: sources that become increasingly remote from the child and are therefore unable to provide useful information.

The authors argued for the second interpretation. However, it is clear that the information involves a causal link among variables, and the different interpretations are unable to be resolved by cross-sectional survey research. It appears that more study would be required of a longitudinal nature to examine the workers' decision-making processes and the reasons for their decisions regarding the use of information sources and their confidence in them.

Issues Arising from the Study

Secondary Data versus Original Data

Both secondary and original data are useful in different research strategies. In this research, the authors obtained original (primary) data from the CYPFS sample and secondary data for comparisons with the Canadian sample. It was not clear as to when the Canadian data were provided. Obviously, the further the distance in time between the original collection of data for both samples, the greater the possibility of sources of error through time. Would, for example, Canadian data on conduct disorder of children and adolescents produce the same results in samples of data collected 5 or 10 years apart? If there would be no changes over the years, then secondary data would be appropriate for making comparisons with currently obtained data. On the other hand, if the results of secondary data, that is, data on the Canadian sample collected in the past, are not correlated with Canadian data collected in the present, the use of secondary data for comparison against a current sample of data collected on CYPFS youth would be questionable. In such an instance, the collection of original data from the normative sample would be preferred.

Information Quality as a Measure of Reliability

The authors developed a formula that produces a weighted summary measure of reliability (Barber & Delfabbro, 2000, p. 119):

$I = [S^* A^* (C / 100)] / 18$
where
I is the index of information quality.
S is the number of sources consulted (range = 1–6).
A is the level of agreement between sources (range = 1–3).
C is the caseworker's confidence in the information provided (range = 1–100).
Thus, reliability of information increases as I approaches 1".

The inherent assumption in this formula is that there is equivalence in the different sources of information. The sources of information are the child, the perpetrator of the abuse, the partner of the perpetrator, personal observation, a family or friend key informant, and a professional key informant. Moreover, it is assumed that accuracy increases as there is agreement among the sources. In addition, it assumes that the addition of sources will lead to greater reliability. It is quite possible that only one of the sources is correct (i.e., provides valid or accurate information); if so, then whether or not there is agreement with the other sources would be irrelevant. Therefore, we believe that this formula, which may be correct, should be validated in research that examines the use and agreement of information from sources when the information from sources varies in terms of accuracy.

STUDY 4: "A GLOBAL PERSPECTIVE ON SOCIAL SECURITY PROGRAMS FOR THE UNEMPLOYED," BY JOHN DIXON (2001)

The author noted that "the rich diversity of statutory social security provisions embedded in unemployed programs that are in evidence on a global basis has only recently begun to be explored" (Dixon, 2001, p. 405).

Study Description

Problem Formulation and Knowledge Objectives

Studying international social policy, this inspired him to engage in policy analyses with two major objectives:

- To seek descriptive information on the frequency of various countries involved in different "global patterns of statutory social security provision for the unemployed and its method of financing" (p. 205)

- "To rank unemployment programs in 80 countries . . . using a comparative design feature methodology that enables an assessment to be made of each country's statutory intention with respect to social security provision for the unemployed" (p. 205)

Essentially, the author seeks to provide quantitative descriptive information of the number out of 80 countries engaging in various statutory provisions, coverage requirements, and benefit-eligibility criteria and entitlements, and to provide quantitative rankings of the 80 countries.

Instrumentation and Data Collection

The perspectives for gathering and analyzing data are based on these considerations (Dixon, 2001, p. 205):

- The value premises adopted are derived from the conventions International Labor Organization (ILO) on minimum social security standards for unemployment protection provision.
- The unemployment design feature data used in this study come very largely from the 1995 edition of the United States Social Security Administration's *Social Security Programs Throughout the World—1995* (US SSA, 1996).

To explore the data for objective number 1, the author made qualitative, narrative appraisals of different patterns of design features related to unemployment programs. There was no verification of the reliability of his descriptions and frequency counts.

For objective number 2, regarding the ranking of 80 countries, Dixon developed a comparative evaluation methodology that evaluates

design features of all social security programs, social security financing arrangements and social security administrative arrangements. . . . What is being assessed are program design features, not program cost, efficiency, effectiveness or performance. . . . To operationalize this comparative evaluation methodology involved the articulation of a comprehensive set of 64 design features and the systematic attachment of a subjective score to the inclusion or exclusion of particular design features that make an unemployment program "more" or "less" acceptable. (2001, pp. 415–416)

The author discussed four value premises that define programs that are more or less acceptable with respect to universal coverage or not; minimal versus maximal restrictions regarding eligibility requirements; cash entitlements versus benefits on other bases and lack of cost-of-living increments; and incentives to encourage welfare-to-work measures as opposed to disincentives. On the basis of these value premises, a ranking score was developed for unemployment programs (Dixon, 2001, p. 417):

$$R \text{ (unemployed)} = 0.3 \, (100—C_d + (b) + (100—E_d + E_b) + (100—B_d + B_b) + S_b)$$

where C_d is the sum of all primary strategy coverage design shortcoming deductions (such as for excluding from coverage low income of farm employees); C_b is the sum of all primary strategy coverage design merit bonuses (such as for including in coverage the self-employed); Ed is the sum of all primary strategy benefit-eligibility design shortcoming deductions (such as for disqualifying applicants because they have no dependents); Eb is the sum of all primary strategy benefit-eligibility merit bonuses (such as, for applying an asset test); Bd is the sum of all primary strategy benefit design shortcoming deductions (such as for providing only lump sum benefits); Bb is the aggregate primary strategy benefit merit bonuses (such as for providing special-need, training and relocation allowances); and Sb is the merit bonus assigned to any supplementary strategies (such as for extending population coverage or for supplementary benefits).

The author used these scores for ranking the 80 countries. No reliability data were provided regarding the extent to which other policy analysts might have agreed with these scores.

Sampling, Relevant Populations, and Research Design

The relevant population is 80 countries that have unemployment programs. In this instance, the sample is the population, since all of the countries are included in the analysis. The research design is based on a content analysis of documentation regarding the 80 countries, which is essentially the author's abstraction and appraisal of the information included in source documents.

Data Analysis, Conclusions, and Implications

The data were examined qualitatively by referring to design features of unemployment programs and quantitatively by calculating ranking scores for each of the 80 countries. Qualitative comparisons of the countries were made with respect to objective number 1, and quantitative rank orderings were compared with respect to objective 2.

Dixon analyzed social security strategies (social assistance, social insurance, social allowances, mandatory public savings, employer liability, and mandatory personal savings) in relation to the primary social security goal, primary sources of funding, coverage, primary benefits eligibility, and primary forms of benefits for objective number 1. Illustrative global patterns are as follows.

- Most of the 80 countries with unemployment programs have adopted social insurance as their primary (that is, the dominant or most important) policy strategy (51 countries), followed by employer liability (12 countries), social assistance (Australia, Brazil, Finland, Hong Kong, Mauritius, New Zealand, Sri Lanka, and Tunisia), social allowances (Chile, Estonia, Luxembourg, Slovakia, and Sweden), mandatory public savings (national provident funds) (Nepal and Zambia), and mandatory personal savings (Colombia and Guatemala) (Dixon, 2001, p. 407).
- In all countries, coverage is concentrated on all or most of those in paid formal employment, although it is extended by some countries to all residents

of working age, which is variously defined, but typically is 16 years to the minimum age for old-age program eligibility (21 countries, including 15 postsocialist countries) (p. 408).

- The categories into which applicants must fit to gain unemployment benefits are twofold: being of working age and being without gainful employment. Three eligible unemployed categories have been defined: those suffering a loss of employment (all countries), those seeking their first job (22 countries), and those seeking to reenter the workforce (15 countries) (p. 409).
- Minimum unemployment or waiting period requirements are sometimes specified; maximum payment periods for unemployed benefits are indicated in more than 70% of the countries; minimum contribution periods are specified in 35% of the countries; minimum employment period requirements are specified in 25%; a minimum residency requirement of 1 year is specified for social assistance programs in Hong Kong and New Zealand; and minimum earning requirements are specified in Norway and the United States (pp. 410–411).
- Unemployment programs, whether primary or supplementary, are largely contributory (61 countries), although entirely government-financed programs are not uncommon (23 countries), nor are entirely employer-financed benefits (18 countries) (p. 413).

The results of rankings with respect to objective 2 were presented in a table. Australia and Finland were the top-ranked countries, with scores of 125; Tunisia was the lowest ranked country, with a score of 80; Germany and Sweden were ranked 10th, with a score of 113; the United Kingdom was ranked 30th, with a score of 90; Hong Kong, Malta, and Argentina were ranked 40th, with a score of 85; and Tanzania and Hungary were ranked 50th, with a score of 75.

Among the conclusions made by the author are these (Dixon, 2001, pp. 419–420):

- The provision of unemployment benefits has been addressed by most countries with the adoption of the social insurance strategy.
- The twentieth century saw the gradual global spread of unemployment programs. They can no longer be perceived to be limited to a group of industrialized countries.
- The Australian model . . . is worthy of greater scrutiny by those countries seeking to improve their unemployment benefit provision.

Classification of the Study

This study is classified as transnational because:

- It uses literature from more than one country to frame the research problem.
- Eighty countries were analyzed with respect to their provisions for unemployment programs.
- Literature was used to consider conclusions of the author's analyses.

Issues Addressed in the Study

Reliability and Validity of Ranking Methodology

The 80 countries were rank ordered on the basis of subjective scores that involved the inclusion or exclusion of design features regarding the acceptability of unemployment programs. The intent of the author was to rank order the programs regarding their relative degrees of acceptability in terms of their intentions, not their implementation and outcomes. Dixon pointed out that he was concentrating only on the intentions of the programs.

There are two issues here that might affect the validity of the subjective ranking scores. First, the reliability of the selection of design features might be in question. Would different policy analysts, using the definitions of acceptability, agree with those assertions with respect to the data recorded for the 80 countries? Agreement in this regard would reflect an affirmation of the content validity of the design features. Such information might be obtained in subsequent methodological studies about the comparative evaluation strategy.

Although the author was not interested in studying implementation of the design features and its effects for this particular study, it might be worthwhile to study the extent to which rank orderings of program intentions are correlated with rank orderings of design futures that were actually implemented. A high rank-order correlation would provide an indication of predictive validity. A low correlation would indicate that the phenomena of intentions and actual implementation are different, and would provide important information to utilizers of this knowledge.

Issues Arising from the Study

The Reliability of Themes and Frequency Counts

The investigator abstracted narrative themes from the sources of data regarding unemployment programs. It is quite possible that other investigators viewing the same materials would independently derive the same themes. Nevertheless, it adds to the rigor of the investigation by documenting the reliability of themes selected. This can be done by having one or more investigators select themes from the same sources and calculate their percentage agreement with the author of this research, for example.

A second potential source of unreliability pertains to the count of countries that are tabulated with respect to the selected themes of unemployment programs. A systematic content analysis could be employed in this regard. A high percentage agreement would help to provide evidence for the rigor of the study. Results like the following, although they may be accurate, might be more acceptable, with reliability of the themes, as well as reliability of the frequency counts:

> That an unemployed person must be available for, and willing to seek work is another general qualified criterion applied in most countries. Registering as an unemployed person with an appropriate administrative agency, involving regular, periodic reporting, is a requirement in 52 countries. Disqualification can also occur because

an unemployed person refuses either to take "suitable" work (14 countries, largely in western Europe) or "any" work (three countries), again largely in Europe. Refusing training, in some instances, also results in either disqualification (in nine countries, six of which are post-socialist) or an extended waiting period (in 11 countries, again largely in Europe). (Dixon, 2001, p. 410)

STUDY 5: "IS THERE A GLOBAL COMMON CORE TO SOCIAL WORK? A CROSS-NATIONAL COMPARATIVE STUDY OF BSW GRADUATE STUDENTS," BY IDIT WEISS (2005)

According to the author, a basic question for international social work is whether "social work is a global profession with a common core of values, theoretical foundations, and modes of practice . . . or whether it is a context-contingent profession that differs in essential ways from country to country" (Weiss, 2005, p. 101).

Study Description

Problem Formulation and Knowledge Objectives

The author develops a rationale for the study by noting the interplay of similarities and differences in international social work:

- "The need of the profession to cope with similar demographic trends, especially worldwide aging, and with similar problems, such as poverty, violence, ethnic conflict, and AIDS, has encouraged sharing knowledge and international cooperation" (p. 102).
- Differences in the profession have occurred as a result of diversity in social, political, cultural, and economic contexts.
- Social workers in all countries deal with similar problems such as poverty, children and families, the aged, and so on.
- Not all countries have adopted ethical codes of conduct; yet among those countries that do have ethical standards, there is variation in emphasis and interpretation from country to country.
- "With regard to patterns of practice, social work appears to be an enormously diverse profession, with social workers involved in many fields and with many types of clientele, social services, problems, and functions (Hokenstad, Khinduka, & Midgley, 1992). Yet there is considerable variety in the types of services in which social workers are employed, their fields of practice, and the domains and boundaries of the practice" (p. 102).
- "International commonalities and differences have also been identified in the status and training of the profession. Social workers in all countries have sought official recognition and legitimization for the profession, yet the results of these efforts have been uneven" (p. 102).
- "Commonalities and differences have been identified with regard to the goals of social work in a global context. On the one hand, the profession worldwide subscribes to the dual aims of improving the well-being of in-

dividuals in distress and promoting social justice and reform. On the other hand, substantial differences emerge in the manner in which these goals are emphasized in the dominant practice models" (p. 103).

- "There is little empirical support for claims regarding the similarities and differences in social work around the world and only scant evidence on the domains in which social workers around the world coalesce. To improve the knowledge base and to generate a more empirically based understanding of the phenomenon of global social work, a cross-national study of the professional ideologies and professional preferences of social work graduates in 10 countries was undertaken" (p. 103).

Conceptualizing profession ideology as "a belief system about the causes of human needs and problems, ways of dealing with these problems, and the values that serve as a basis for the modes of response (Hasenfeld, 1983)," Weiss examined the professional ideology of graduating BSW students in 10 countries toward three variables: causes of poverty, preferred ways of dealing with poverty, and the goals of social work. The knowledge objective sought was that of quantitative descriptions within countries regarding the three variables.

Instrumentation and the Process of Data Collection

The researchers in this study "contacted social work scholars in each country, who distributed the questionnaires to all graduating BSW students in their respective schools. The researchers were chosen on the basis of their experience in cross-national research, professional standing, and proficiency in English" (Weiss, 2005, pp. 103–104). The questionnaires were in English; and the researchers in Brazil, Germany, and Hungary were asked to translate the questionnaires into their own languages. The countries receiving questionnaires were Australia, Brazil, Britain, Canada, Germany, Hong Kong, Hungary, Israel, the United States, and Zimbabwe. The instruments in the study were initially developed on the basis of published research pertaining to the three variables; then a panel of senior staff members in schools of social work in Britain, Israel, and the United States judged the extent to which questionnaire items reflected the study variables. Consequently, changes were made in the questionnaires. The three instruments were as follows.

- "*Attitudes about the causes of poverty* were measured by a 17-item scale, with each item naming a possible cause of poverty. Respondents were asked to rate their agreement with each item on a five-point Likert scale (ranging from 1 = strongly disagree to 5 = strongly agree)" (Weiss, 2005, p. 104). A principal components factor analysis with varimax rotation produced three factors: social causes, psychological causes, and lack of motivational responsibility. Cronbach's alpha was .76 for social causes, .81 for psychological causes, and .82 for lack of motivation.
- "*Perceptions of best ways to deal with poverty* were measured by a 15-item scale, with each item naming a possible way of dealing with poverty. Respondents were asked to rate the degree to which they agreed that each was a good

way for the state to deal with poverty on a five-point Likert scale (ranging from 1 = strongly disagree to 5 = strongly agree" (p. 104–105). A principal components factor analysis produced these factors: extending state social welfare programs, with an alpha of .76; providing psychological treatment, with an alpha of .83; and minimizing state assistance to the poor, encouraging them to enter the labor market, with an alpha of .82.

- "*Importance attributed to social work goals* was measured by a nine-item scale listing social work goals and asking respondents to rate the importance they attributed to each on a five-point Likert scale (ranging from 1 = very little importance to 5 = very great importance)" (p. 105). A principal components factor analysis with varimax rotation produced three factors: enhancing individual well-being, with an alpha of .75; promoting social justice, with an alpha of .77; and social control, with an alpha of .65.

Sampling, Relevant Populations, and Research Design

The author employed a diverse group of countries in the selection of the sample. It consisted of 781 graduating BSW students from 10 countries: Australia (n = 62), Brazil (n = 95), Canada (n = 34), Britain (n = 64), Germany (n = 141), Hong Kong (n = 42), Hungary (n = 101), Israel (n = 138), the United States (n = 78), and Zimbabwe (n = 26). Three schools were sampled in Brazil and four were sampled in Hungary. In the remaining countries, samples were obtained from one school each (Weiss, 2005, p. 104).

Response rates to the questionnaires distributed in each country were: Australia, 42 percent; Brazil, 88 percent; Canada, 52 percent; Britain, 94 percent; Germany, 41 percent; Hong Kong, 60 percent; Hungary, 80 percent; Israel, 83 percent; the United States, 77 percent; and Zimbabwe, 73 percent (p. 104).

The relevant populations are graduating BSW students from all of the countries that have social work schools. The 10 schools chosen were from industrialized and developing countries. The selection of the countries and of the schools sampled within each country resulted in convenience samples for each of the countries. Whether the samples are representative of all of the students enrolled in the countries selected for the study is not clear; since random sampling procedures were not employed, it is inferred that the samples are not necessarily representative.

The research design was that of a comparative cross-sectional survey. Means and standard deviations of variables related to the causes of poverty, ways of dealing with poverty, and goals of social work were compared for the 10 countries.

Data Analyses, Conclusions, and Implications

The statistical procedures employed were as follows.

Between-cohort differences were analyzed using one-way MANOVAs, followed by univariate ANOVAs and Sheffé paired comparison tests to locate the source of the differences. Within-cohort differences were analyzed using ANOVAs with repeated measures, followed by paired comparison tests, using the Student-Newman-Keuls test (SNK). (Weiss, 2005, p. 105)

The results regarding the causes of poverty indicated that the students in all 10 countries reported that social causes were more important than psychological causes, which in turn were more important than lack of motivation. With respect to preferred ways of dealing with poverty,

> paired comparison tests according to SNK showed that all the student groups ranked extended social welfare highest. They also showed that, with the exception of the Brazilian and Zimbabwean cohorts, who showed equal preference for the other two approaches, all the cohorts ranked psychological treatment second and minimizing state support third. (Weiss, 2005, p. 106)

Results regarding the goals of social work indicated that social control was the least important goal for all 10 countries. Students in Australia, Brazil, Canada, and the United States thought social justice was the most important goal, while those in Britain, Germany, Hong Kong, Hungary, and Israel believed individual well-being was the most important goal. Israeli students had the highest average scores for social justice, 4.51 (5 is most important, and 1 is least important); individual well-being, 4.70; and social control, 4.24. In contrast, Hong Kong students had the lowest average score for social justice, 3.91; Brazil had the lowest average score for individual well-being, 3.85; and Australia had the lowest average score for social control, 3.37.

The author believed that "the findings provide support for the claim that a common core is shared by social workers across different countries and contexts" (Weiss, 2005, p. 108). However, she also said that there were differences in emphases:

> The most distinctive and internally consistent patterns were found in the Brazilian, Hong Kong, and Australian cohorts. The Brazilian cohort is distinguished from the others by the less weight that it gave to the psychological and individual aspects of the profession. It exhibited less support for psychological and motivational explanations of poverty, the least support of any of the cohorts for psychological treatment as a way of dealing with poverty, and the least support for enhancing individual well-being as a goal of the profession. (p. 108)

The author made the implication that more research is needed to examine the forces that lead to similarities and differences among the social work profession internationally. Moreover, she indicated that there should be caution in generalizing the results of the study, since the students in the study are not necessarily representative of BSW graduating students in the world.

Classification of the Study

This is a transnational study because:

- It involved the collaboration of researchers from Britain, Israel, and the United States.

- It used literature from more than one country to frame the research problem.
- It used literature from more than one country to consider the meaning of the results.
- Samples were obtained and compared on variables for 10 countries.

Issues Addressed in the Study

Representativeness of the Sample

The sampling was accidental and convenient for the investigators of the study, who selected researchers from 10 countries to distribute questionnaires. The author noted in her conclusions that there should be caution in attempting to generalize these results. Nevertheless, it might have been instructive to consider what steps might have been taken to enhance generalizability.

One procedure is to compare characteristics of the samples of students in each country with all of the students who were graduating from BSW programs at the time of the study. This, of course, depends upon whether data exist in each country regarding demographic variables such as age, gender, and so forth. If such data do exist, data from the samples would be compared with data on the study populations within each country. If there are no statistical differences between data in the samples and the populations, the samples could be said to be representative on those variables for which there was available information.

A second procedure would involve representative sampling. For example, countries with BSW social work programs would be identified and listed. Countries might be stratified into industrialized and developing countries. Countries would be randomly selected from each stratum. Within each country, the number of schools would be listed, and schools would be randomly selected. And within each school students would be randomly selected, say, to represent at least 50% of the school's population. Data on demographic variables would be compared, where available, between the resulting samples and the populations from which they were drawn. Such comparisons would serve to validate the sampling procedures, providing some evidence of generalizability.

Instrument Construction and the Process of Pretesting

The author describes an excellent use of pretesting in the construction of the instruments for the study. After changes in the questionnaires were made by a panel comprised of six senior staff members in schools of social work in Britain, Israel, and the United States,

> a pretest of the questionnaires was conducted among 75 students in the BSW and MSW programs at an Israeli university. For each questionnaire, a principal components factor analysis with varimax rotation was conducted, yielding three factors with eigen values greater than 1 for each questionnaire item. Items that loaded less than .5 in the relevant factor were either removed or reformulated in accordance with student suggestions to make them clearer. The fourth stage was the cross-national

validation of the questionnaires. Principal components factor analyses with varimax rotation were carried out separately in the four national cohorts with more than 85 participants (Brazil, Germany, Hungary, and Israel). These analyses yielded much the same factors found in the pretest, with only a few differences in the items contained in the factors. Two items that loaded less than .5 in two or more national cohorts were removed. In the final stage, another set of principal components factor analyses with varimax rotation were conducted for all of the respondents in a single block. The internal consistency of each of the factors was examined for each national cohort separately. Because reliability was acceptable in all the cohorts, with Cronbach alphas above .70 in most of them, the reliability of each factor in all the questionnaires was calculated for the entire sample. (Weiss, 2005, p. 104)

Issues Arising from the Study

Translation of Questionnaires

The questionnaires were in English, and all of the researchers were asked to adapt the questionnaires to the cultures represented in their 10 countries. Moreover, the researchers in Brazil, Germany, and Hungary were required to translate the questionnaires into Portuguese, German, and Hungarian, respectively. The issue is whether or not more rigorous procedures should have been employed. To have the same meaning for all of the items in the questionnaires is what is necessary for making cross-national comparisons. The meaning of some of the questions may vary, even in different countries that have the same language as their primary language, due to various cultural contexts. Therefore, procedures of pretesting for all of the countries regarding the meanings of the questionnaire items might have been employed. Furthermore, systems of translation, back-translation, and panel review by experts in each country might have enhanced the rigor of the study.

Comparisons of Students and Instructors

It appears to be an assumption that graduating BSW students in each country will represent the ideologies of social work education in that country. This assumption can be validated with further research that would:

- Obtain ratings of instructors from the schools in which the students were enrolled
- Obtain ratings of graduating students enrolled in those schools
- Compare average ratings of instructors and students by testing whether the distributions of scores for instructors and students are equivalent, that is, there are no statistical differences between the groups

SUMMARY

We have presented five studies that are illustrative of transnational research. We described all of the studies with reference to problem formulation and knowledge objectives; instrumentation and the process of data collection; sampling, relevant populations, and research design; and data analyses, conclusions, and implications. The reasons for classifying each study as transnational research were also presented.

For each study, we discussed issues that were considered by the authors. In addition, we presented issues that were derived from critical analysis of the studies. The issues addressed in the studies were translation of training manual and questionnaires; clinicians' perceptions versus clinicians' and clients' outcomes; incomplete records and low response rates; missing data; choosing normative samples; cross-sectional survey research versus qualitative longitudinal research; reliability and validity of ranking methodology; representativeness of the sample; and instrument construction and the process of pretesting. Issues arising from the studies were lack of standardized research instruments; representative sampling versus purposive sampling; research design alternatives; further data analyses; further research; secondary data versus original data; information quality as a measure of reliability; the reliability of themes and frequency counts; translation of questionnaires; and comparisons of students and instructors. We discussed the issues within the contexts of the five transnational studies we described.

8

SUMMARY AND CONCLUSIONS

In this final chapter, we review the purpose of the book and its subpurposes. Then we define international social work research, presenting our perspective of different types of research: supranational, intranational, and transnational social work research. We review similarities and differences between national research and the three types of international research we have posited, and we briefly discuss social work problems confronted by international research. This is followed by a discussion of the context in which we presented and analyzed issues in the conduct and utilization of international social work research—a consideration of knowledge objectives, their generalizability, and aspects of the research process: problem formulation, instrument construction, data collection, sampling, research design, data analysis, conclusions, and implications. We conclude with a thematic, content analysis of research issues, as well as barriers and incentives, that were presented in the preceding chapters.

PURPOSE OF THE BOOK

This book was intended to present a perspective on international social work research, issues involved in the conduct and utilization of international social work research, and examples of international social work research studies. We believe we have accomplished this overall purpose in chapters 1–7. Moreover, this book sensitizes the reader to the prospects and potential for international social work research. Not only can it be used as a sequel to basic texts in social work research but also it can be employed as supplementary reading to texts on international social work.

In addition to the overall purpose, we discussed five subpurposes that are unique to this book:

- The two social work streams of international social work and social work and social work research were juxtaposed as international social work research.

- A broad definition of international social work research was provided. We indicated that international social work research involves the use of literature from two or more countries to frame the research problem, and specifies implications of the research for two or more countries. We noted that, in general, international social work research involves different languages, customs, traditions, and emphases in using social research methods to develop knowledge for social work.

- We presented a unique typology of international social work research to serve as a guiding framework for assessing and conducting such research. Our typology encompasses some concepts already in existence, but goes further in providing a new perspective on what international social work is, how it differs from national research, and how it may be classified. We noted that the commonality in all international research is the extensive use of literature from two or more countries and the development of implications for two or more countries. Within that umbrella, we typologized international social work research as supranational, intranational, and transnational.

- We focused on social work research as distinguished from social science research or social work practice. Moreover, we presented and expanded this definition of social work research: the use of social research methods for producing and disseminating knowledge that is pertinent to policies and practices that affect and/or are implemented by social work organizations, practitioners, and educators. Social work research aims to describe and explain phenomena relevant to social work. Social research methods include all of those procedures and conceptual approaches for obtaining credible, reliable, and valid observations for specifying concepts and quantitative and qualitative relationships among variables, and for making inferences and generalizations about social phenomena. A variety of concepts, techniques, and procedures are employed in social research, such as the following: research designs for case studies, surveys, correlational studies, and quasi and true experiments; participatory research, action research, and ethnographic field studies; qualitative data gathering and analytic techniques; single-subject designs; statistical techniques, such as multivariate and bivariate analyses; graphic techniques and the development of mathematical models; instrument construction; and techniques for generalizing causal inferences.

- We presented in-depth examples of international social work research studies from national and international journals to illustrate and explore relevant methodological issues involved in the international research process.

TYPOLOGY OF INTERNATIONAL SOCIAL WORK RESEARCH

Building on the preceding definition of social work research, we defined international social work research as social work research that is relevant to international social work. It aims to develop knowledge that is pertinent to any of Healy's (2001, p. 13) four areas of action: "internationally informed domestic practice and related policy advocacy, participation in and utilization of international exchange, international practice, and international policy formulation and advocacy." The knowledge sought for international social work depends on the state of current knowledge available for the social work problem under investigation, and the research methods used depend upon the level of knowledge sought, financial and ethical considerations, the sociopolitical environment, and expertise in the use of research methods. What is common in all international research is the extensive use of literature from two or more countries to formulate research problems and objectives, and the development of implications for two or more countries. International social work research is distinguished from national (noninternational) research, in that national social work research is research directed at native populations within a country with no attempt to use literature from other countries to frame the research problem, or to discuss implications for international social work.

We typologized these three types of international social work research: supranational, intranational, and transnational research. Supranational research is concerned only with research and research participants from one country. It may be focused on research in any country. Intranational research occurs when a population from another country (that is, international migrants) is studied within a country, and literature from both countries is used with implications for two or more countries. Transnational research is comparative research between populations of two or more countries; literature across populations is used, and implications are made for each population.

Similarities and Differences Among National and International Social Work Research Types

National research and supranational research are similar with respect to these characteristics:

- They follow steps in the research process from problem formulation, sampling, and research design to instrument construction, data gathering, analyses, and conclusions.
- They may be engaged in cross-cultural research, that is, seeking to generalize across subcultural groups within a native population.
- They seek to apply research findings to the population where the research is conducted.

In contrast to national research, supranational research is characterized by these considerations:

- It uses literature from two or more countries.
- It generalizes substantive knowledge across countries or specifies differences between countries in formulating the research problem.
- It seeks to generalize implications across countries.
- It may conceptualize the generalizability of methodological knowledge across countries in formulating the research problem.

Intranational research has all of the characteristics of supranational research, plus these:

- It studies two or more countries, for example, the migrant population or populations, as well as the population of the host country.
- It may study populations within the country of origin in addition to those who migrated from the country of origin to live in another country.
- Migration may be studied over time, including postmigration patterns such as repatriation in the country of origin.

Transnational research has all of the characteristics of supranational research and intranational research. In addition, these unique characteristics may be emphasized:

- Qualitative comparisons may be made between countries with respect to programs, policies, laws, social resources, social needs, and/or social interventions, and so on.
- Quantitative comparisons may be made with respect to social indicators, and/or to international standards regarding social and health needs, and so on.
- Quantitative comparisons may be made with respect to common stimuli, for example, professional reactions to a case vignette.
- Correlational and causal research designs may be employed within two or more countries that are being studied; and comparisons may be made qualitatively or quantitatively between countries.

SOCIAL WORK PROBLEMS IN INTERNATIONAL SOCIAL WORK RESEARCH

In general, any social work problem can be considered for international research. In chapter 1 we referred to a content analysis of articles in international social work journals, indicating that these were salient topics: social work education, social work practice, child welfare, immigrants, international social work, poverty and development, women's issues, and mental health treatment and services (Potocky-Tripodi & Tripodi, 2005). In chapter 2, we indicated that social work problems that occur within and between countries should be studied internationally; for example: drug trafficking, human trafficking, substance abuse, HIV/AIDS, physical health, domestic violence, elder abuse, child abuse, mental health, child welfare, and so forth.

In chapter 4 we pointed out that intranational research, to a large extent, focuses on research that deals with refugees and immigrants. Problems such as these are involved in such research: economic adaptation, legal rights in the new country, language acquisition, domestic violence, health care access, differential treatment of minority clients, depression, somatization, guilt, anxiety, posttraumatic stress disorder, substance abuse, marital conflict, intergenerational conflict, and so forth (Potocky-Tripodi, 2002). Refugees and immigrants present any and all of the problems that social workers deal with, as well as problems that are specific to migration and displacement experiences.

Transnational research confronts problems that social work educators and practitioners confront within and between countries. In chapter 6 we listed problems such as these that are considered in transnational research:

- The transportation of social work knowledge validated in one country to other countries with respect to social interventions, education, policy development, and methodological knowledge regarding the transmission and utilization of substantive information.
- The identification and treatment of problems that occur across countries, such as domestic violence, bullying, child abuse, elder abuse, and other forms of delinquent and criminal behavior.
- The study of poverty, welfare, welfare reform, and the development of policies, programs, and services to reduce or eliminate poverty.
- The study of cross-cultural phenomena regarding ethnicity, gender, sexual orientation, and minority groups; and their similarities and differences within and between countries in research on poverty, social policies, mental health, child welfare, and so on.
- The cross-validation of instruments for collecting data in international social work research.
- Comparisons of laws, policies, programs, practices, and services that deal with social work problems across countries.
- Comparisons of social workers' responses to standardized cases, vignettes, and other protocols regarding the assessment, prevention, and treatment of biosociopsychological problems.

ISSUES IN CONDUCTING AND UTILIZING INTERNATIONAL SOCIAL WORK RESEARCH

The Research Process

To discuss issues involved in the various types of international social work research, we provided the context of the research process, knowledge objectives and criteria for achieving them, and the generalizability of knowledge objectives and criteria for assessing generalizability. Notions about these phenomena are common for all three types of international social work research, and provide a context for a systematic discussion of issues involved in the conduct and utilization of social work research.

In chapter 2 we described four interrelated models of research: quantitative research, qualitative research, program evaluation, and single-subject design. After reviewing those models of the research process, we decided to use relatively standard categories of the research process for discussing issues in international social work research: problem formulation; instrument construction and data collection; sampling and study populations; research design; and data analysis, conclusions, and implications. These aspects of the research process were described in detail. It should be pointed out that these categories are interrelated, often overlapping, and do not necessarily follow a strict order. For example, issues of research design and data analysis might be considered along with theoretical notions and hypothesis development in the initial stages of problem formulation; notions of sampling may be considered in instrument construction; and so forth.

Knowledge Objectives and Their Generalizability

We further provided in chapter 2 a fundamental perspective for assessing national or international research: a discussion of the knowledge objectives of social work research and criteria for achieving them; and a discussion of the generalizability of knowledge objectives and criteria for assessing generalizability. Knowledge objectives of research were presented as (1) the development and operationalization of concepts, (2) qualitative and quantitative descriptions of concepts, (3) the formation of hypotheses, (4) the testing of correlational hypotheses, and (5) the testing of cause-effect hypotheses. The criterion/criteria for achieving objective (1) were specified as concept translatability; for (2), measurement accuracy (reliability and validity) and/or the existence of credible qualitative relationships; (3), hypothesis researchability; (4), statistical evidence of correlations and measurement accuracy; and (5), time order of independent and dependent variables, control of extraneous variables, and evidence of a correlational relationship.

We concurred with Shadish et al. (2002) regarding the difficulties in setting achievable standards for generalizing social work knowledge; and we discussed four types of generalization and procedures that could be employed for inferring generalizabilty. The types of generalization discussed were conceptual generality, representativeness (sample to population), replication, and external validity control (in experimentation). Criteria for inferring generality that were discussed included qualitative judgment, representativeness (sampling) procedures, replication criteria, and experimental procedures.

Summary of Issues from Chapters 2, 4, and 6

We discussed methodological issues regarding the conduct and utilization of research in the various aspects of the research process for each type of international social work research in chapters 2, 4, and 6. Table 8.1 presents the themes we emphasized. The reader should note that the aspects of the research process are arbitrary demarcations, and they do overlap in the actual conduct of research. Furthermore, the reader should understand that intranational social work research subsumes the issues presented in supranational research; and transnational social work research subsumes the issues involved in intranational research. In addition, it is to be noted that these are illustrative issues and are not necessarily exhaustive; they represent a content analysis of the themes we covered in chapters 2, 4, and 6.

In problem formulation for supranational research, we stressed the importance of using the literature from two or more countries, and we focused on different procedures for doing so: narrative review, metaevaluation, and metaanalysis. And we specified procedures for summarizing from the literature the achievement of knowledge objectives and their generalizability, including notions of evidence-based practice (Gibbs, 2003). Intranational and transnational social work research deal with the same issues as does supranational research in problem formulation. We emphasized the use of content analysis, cultural competency, and international migration policies in intranational research, specifying procedures that can be employed. And we stressed the notion of international competency (between nations) as well as cultural competency (between cultures) for transnational researchers.

For instrument construction and data collection, referring to table 8.1, we emphasized cross-validation, the construction of culturally appropriate instruments and basic qualitative and quantitative comparative strategies.

We presented notions of probability and nonprobability sampling procedures for recruiting and retaining research participants, and we discussed the notion of relevant populations. A variety of research designs were presented, and we emphasized survey procedures, longitudinal research, participatory research, and comparative experimental and quasi-experimental designs. In data analyses and conclusions, we provided principles for assessing the implementation of recommendations made in international social work research, and we stressed the importance of considering knowledge objectives achieved and their generalizability with respect to recommendations. We noted that recommendations are often at the level of hypotheses and need to be evaluated if they are to be implemented.

Summary of Issues Addressed in and Arising from Examples of International Social Work Research

We presented descriptions of research studies that were illustrative of supranational, intranational, and transnational social work research in chapters 3, 5, and 7, respectively. After describing each study with respect to the aspects of the research process, we presented issues in the conduct and utilization of research that were suggested by the authors. In addition, after critically analyzing each study, we presented issues we derived from the studies. Examples of issues we discussed in examples of supranational research are, first, issues addressed in the studies—the cultural context of the research, ethics and informed consent, cultural awareness, conceptualization of empowerment, the importance of conducting a pilot study, and so on, and, second, issues arising from the studies—translation and back-translation, the use of computerized programs to develop categories, a priori versus a posteriori evaluation, the reliability and validity of content analysis, and so on.

Examples of issues we discussed with respect to studies of intranational research are, first, issues addressed in the studies—group equivalence in experimental studies, attrition in panel studies, training and monitoring of staff in field research, group interviewing versus individual interviewing, and so on, and, second, issues arising from the studies—implications as hypotheses to be tested, representativeness of key informants, analyzing complex interactions, cross-sectional versus panel studies, incorporating qualitative research in quantitative research studies, and so on. And examples of transnational research issues are, first, issues addressed in the studies—translations of tracking manuals and questionnaires, clinicians' perceptions versus clinicians' and client' outcomes, choosing normative samples, incomplete records and low response rates, and so on, and, second, issues arising from the studies—lack of standardized research instruments, secondary data versus original data, information quality as a measure of reliability, research design alternatives, and so on.

Table 8.2 summarizes the number of issues addressed in and arising from the studies that we discussed, in relation to aspects of the research process for each type

Table 8.1 Summary of Issues in Research Emphasized by Type of International Social Work Research and Aspects of the Research Process

| Research process | Types of international social work research | | |
	Supranational	Intranational	Transnational
Problem formulation	• Literature review • Narrative review • Meta-evaluation • Meta-analysis • Summarizing knowledge and its generalizability	• Content analysis • Cultural competency • International migration policies	• International competency
Instrument construction and data collection	• Cross-validation	• Construction of culturally appropriate instruments: three models	• Basic comparative strategies • Qualitative and quantitative review of previous research: narrative review, content analysis, metaanalysis • Compare social indicators • Compare responses to common stimuli • Comparison against a standard
Sampling	• Sampling strategies for different knowledge objectives	• Relevant populations	• Sampling from two or more countries
Research design	• Knowledge objectives and research designs	• Longitudinal research • Participatory research	• Comparative research designs
Data analyses, conclusions, and implications	• Utilization of research • Recommendations for deriving implications for two or more countries	• Implementation and evaluating implementation • Recommendations as hypotheses	• Uses of data archives • Fitting statistical models

Note. Intranational research also subsumes issues considered for supranational research, and transnational research subsumes issues covered by intranational research. Issues refer to considerations involved in the procedures for conducting and utilizing research.

Table 8.2 Number of Issues Addressed in and Arising from Examples of International Social Work Research

| | Types of international social work research | | | | | |
| | Supranational | | Intranational | | Transnational | |
Research process	Issues addressed in studies	Issues arising from studies	Issues addressed in studies	Issues arising from studies	Issues addressed in studies	Issues arising from studies
Problem formulation	7	3	0	3	0	0
Instrument construction and data collection	6	10	5	2	5	5
Research design and sampling	0	2	3	2	4	2
Data analyses, conclusions, and implications	1	4	1	6	0	4

Note. Intranational research also subsumes issues considered for supranational research, and transnational research subsumes issues covered by intranational research. Issues addressed in the studies refer to methodological and substantive considerations by the authors of studies reviewed; issues arising from the studies refer to methodological and substantive considerations derived from a critical analysis of the studies.

of international social work research. The bulk of the issues and derivative issues we discussed were focused on instrument construction and data collection, followed by data analyses, conclusions, and implications. A variety of issues were presented and discussed in relation to the possibility of improving international social work research.

BARRIERS AND INCENTIVES TO INTERNATIONAL SOCIAL WORK RESEARCH

Table 8.3 includes a summary of the barriers and incentives for national research, as well as the three types of international research. Barriers accumulate as one goes from national to supranational, supranational to intranational, and intranational to transnational research. Hence transnational research is the most difficult type to execute; and these studies are less likely to occur in the social work literature. The barriers we list in table 8.3 are illustrative and not necessarily comprehensive, but they are the kinds of obstacles that social work researchers must overcome. Among the barriers for national (noninternational) social work research are costs of time and labor, environmental constraints, difficulty of access to research participants, lack of continued participation, ethical constraints, and so on. In addition to these potential barriers, supranational social work research must deal with the lack of availability and accessibility of international literature, translation accuracy and costs,

Table 8.3 Summary of Barriers and Incentives Discussed by Types of Social
         Work Research

| | Types of social work research | | | |
	Domestic	Supranational	Intranational	Transnational
Barriers	• Costs of time and labor • Environmental constraints • Access to research participants • Lack of continued participation • Ethical constraints	• Availability and accessibility of literature • Translation accuracy and costs • Costs in reviewing literature	• Sociopolitical constraints • Lack of collaboration • Lack of time • Difficulties in recruitment and retention • Lack of cross-cultural instruments • Lack of resources to meet participants' needs	• Geopolitical constraints • Extra costs involved in time, travel, and collaboration.
Incentives	• Research grants • Contribution to knowledge • Personal gratification • Professional achievement • Helping members of population in need • Cash or gifts as incentives for participants	• Contributions to international knowledge • Collaborations between agencies, investigators, and universities	• Sharing of resources between agencies and universities	• Use of technology for surveys and experiments on-line, to cut travel and other costs, and to conduct research on more than one country from primarily one country.

Note. Supranational research subsumes barriers and incentives for national research; intranational research subsumes barriers and incentives for supranational research; and transnational research subsumes barriers and incentives for intranational research.

and extra costs involved in reviewing literature. Barriers become increasingly problematic as representatives of other countries are involved. In addition to the potential barriers listed for supranational social work research, barriers for intranational social work research include sociopolitical constraints, lack of collaboration, lack of time, difficulties in recruitment and retention, lack of cross-cultural and cross-national instruments, and lack of resources to meet participants' needs. In addition, transnational research involves extra costs in time, travel, and collaboration, and must deal with geopolitical constraints.

Incentives involve the means and strategies to overcome barriers to research. As with our listing of barriers, incentives are illustrative but not necessarily exhaustive. Moreover, incentives are cumulative, that is, transnational research subsumes the incentives for the other types of research; intranational social work research subsumes incentives for supranational and national social work research; and supranational research subsumes incentives involved in national research. These incentives may be overlapping for each of the research types. We have indicated, for each type, relative emphases of the incentives. For national social work research, we listed these incentives: research grants, contribution to knowledge, personal gratification, professional advancement, helping members of the population in need, and cash and gifts as incentives for participants. In supranational research, in addition to incentives listed for national research, we emphasized contributions to international knowledge and collaborations between social agencies, investigators, and universities. The sharing of resources by social agencies and universities was emphasized for intranational research. Finally, for transnational research, we advocate the use of computer technology in conducting comparative surveys and experiments online. We believe this will reduce travel and other costs, and the research could be conducted primarily from one country.

THE POTENTIAL OF INTERNATIONAL SOCIAL WORK RESEARCH

We believe the potential for increasing the production and dissemination of knowledge from international social work research is great. There are several reasons for this view. First, due to the forces of internationalism and globalization, social work problems encountered within any country increasingly have their causes, effects, and/or counterparts elsewhere in the world. Thus, adopting a global perspective enhances the likelihood of effectively addressing these problems. Second, our definition of international social work research broadens the scope of previous conceptualizations, thus broadening the opportunities for such research. And finally, as we have discussed, international social work research can be carried out primarily in one country. Supranational social work research involves the use of literature that can be accessed through the internet. Intranational social work research focuses on studying a migrant population from another country that resides within one country. And transnational research can be conducted online (comparative surveys and experiments) primarily from one country, with communications conducted by e-mail. Given these possibilities and opportunities, we call on all social work researchers to think globally, even when acting locally.

REFERENCES

Achenbach, T. (1991). *Manual for the child behavior Checklist/ 4–18 and 1991 profile.* Burlington, VT: Department of Psychiatry, University of Vermont.

Afifi, A. A., & Clark, V. (1990). *Computer-aided multivariate analyses* (2nd ed.). New York: Van Nostrand Reinhold.

Agbayani-Siewert, P. (2004). Assumptions of Asian American similarity: The case of Filipino and Chinese American students. *Social Work, 49,* 39–54.

Alaggia, R., Chau, S., & Tsang, K. (2001). Astronaut Asian families: Impact of migration on family structure from the perspective of the youth. *Journal of Social Work Research and Evaluation: An International Publication, 2,* 295–306.

Alvelo, J., Collazo, A. A., & Rosario, D. (2001). Comprehensive assessment tools for Hispanics: Validation of the multi-problem screening inventory (MPSI) for Puerto Ricans. *Research on Social Work Practice, 11,* 699–724.

Auslander, G. K. (2000). Social work research and evaluation in Israel. *Journal of Social Work Research and Evaluation: An International Publication, 1,* 17–34.

Bagati, D. (2003). Microcredit and empowerment of women. *Journal of Social Work Research and Evaluation: An International Publication, 4,* 19–35.

Barak, M. E. M., Findler, L., & Wind, L. H. Cross-cultural aspects of diversity and well being in the workplace: An international perspective. *Journal of Social Work Research Evaluation: An International Publication, 4,* 145–169.

Barber, J. G., & Delfabbro, P. (2000). The standardized assessment of child well-being in child protection work. *Journal of Social Work Research and Evaluation: An International Publication, 2,* 111–123.

Beiser, M., Dion, R., Gotowiec, A., Hyman, I., & Nhi, V. (1995). Immigrant and refugee children in Canada. *Canadian Journal of Psychiatry, 40,* 67–72.

Ben-Ari, A. (2004). Sources of social support and attachment styles among Israeli Arab students. *International Social Work, 47,* 187–201.

Blythe, B., Tripodi, T., & Briar, S. (1994). *Direct practice research in human service agencies.* New York: Columbia University Press.

Bowers, A., Guadalupe, J. L., & Bolden, E. (2003). Faith, hope, and mutual support: Paths to empowerment as perceived by women in pverty. *Journal of Social Work Research and Evaluation, 4*(1): 5–18.

Boyle, M. H., Offord, D. T., Hoffman, H. G., Catlin, G. P., Byles, J. A., Crawford, J. W., Links, P. S., Rae-Grant, N. I., & Szatmari, P. (1987). Ontario child health study: 1. Methodology. *Archives of General Psychiatry, 44,* 926–831.

Bronson, D. E. (2000). Progress and problems in social work research and evaluation in the United States. *Journal of Social Work Research and Evaluation: An International Publication, 1*, 125–137.

Burnette, D. (1998). Conceptual and methodological considerations in research with non-white ethnic elders. In M. Potocky & A. Y. Rodgers-Farmer (Eds.), *Social work research with minority and oppressed populations: Methodological issues and innovations* (pp. 71–91). New York: Haworth Press.

Buttell, F. P., & Pike, C. K. (2003). Investigating the differential effectiveness of a batterer treatment program on outcomes for African American and Caucasian batterers. *Research on Social Work Practice, 13*, 675–692.

Campbell, D. T., & Stanley, J. C. (1966). *Experimental and quasi-experimental designs for research.* Skokie, IL: Rand McNally.

Carpenter, J., Schneider, J., McNiven, F., Brandon, T., Stevens, R., & Wooff, D. (2004). Integration and targeting of community care for people with severe and enduring mental health problems: Users' experiences of the care programme approach and care management. *British Journal of Social Work, 34*, 313–333.

Chambon, A. S., McGrath, S., Shapiro, B., Z., Abai, M., Dremetsikas, T., & Dudziak, S. (2001). Interpersonal links to webs of relations: Creating befriending relationships with survivors of torture and of war. *Journal of Social Work Research and Evaluation: An International Publication, 2*, 157–171.

Chazin, R., Colorossi, L., Hanson, M., Grishayeva, I., & Contis, G. (2004). Teaching brief intervention for adolescent depression: An evaluation of a cross-national approach. *Journal of Social Work Research and Evaluation: An International Publication, 5*, 19–30.

Christopher, K. (2002). Single motherhood, employment, or social assistance: Why are U.S. women poorer than women in other affluent nations? *Journal of Poverty, 6*, 61–80.

Cook, T. D., & Campbell, D. T. (1979). *Quasi-experimentation: Design and analysis issues for field settings.* Chicago: Rand McNally.

Cornelius, L. J., Booker, N. C., Arthur, T. E., Reeves, I., & Morgan, O. (2004). The validity and reliability testing of a consumer-based cultural competency inventory. *Research on Social Work Practice, 14*, 201–209.

Corrigan, P. W., & Salzer, M. S. (2003). The conflict between random assignment and treatment preference: Implications for internal validity. *Evaluation and Program Planning, 26*, 109–121.

Cotter, R. B., Burke, J. D., Stouthamer-Loerber, M., & Loeber, R. (2005). Contacting participants for follow-up: How much effort is required in longitudinal studies? *Evaluation and Program Planning, 28*, 15–21.

Crisp, B. R. (2000). A history of Australian social work practice research. *Research on Social Work Practice, 10*, 179–194.

Crisp, B. R. (2004). Evidence-based practice and the borders of data in the global information era. *Journal of Social Work Education, 40*, 73–86.

Dixon, J., & Joyner, M. (2003). Family abuse: A cross-national review. *New Global Development: Journal of International and Comparative Social Welfare, 16*, 1–3.

Dixon, J. (2001). A global perspective on social security programs for the unemployed. *International Social Work, 44*, 405–422.

Dominelli, L. (2003). *Globalization and citizenship: New issues, challenges and opportunities.* 2003 John F. Roatch Global Lecture Series on Social Policy and Practice.

Drachman, D. (1992). A stage-of-migration framework for service to immigrant populations. *Social Work, 37*, 68–72.

English, R. (Ed.). (2003). *Encyclopedia of social work* (19th ed.). *2003 Supplement.* Washington, DC: NASW Press.

Engstrom, D. W., Minas, S. A., Espinoza, M., & Jones, L. (2004). Halting the trafficking of women and children in Thailand for the sex trade: Progress and challenges. *Journal of Social Work Research and Evaluation: An International Publication, 2,* 193–206.

Estes, R. J. (1984) *Comparative social welfare research.* Retrieved December 21, 2004, from http://caster.ssw.upenn.edu/~restes/isw/chapter6.html.

Faul, A. C., & van Zyl, M. A. (2003). Work-based social welfare reform in the United States and Africa: The answer to self-sufficiency for poor women? *Journal of Social Work Research and Evaluation: An International Publication, 4,* 95–106.

Folkman, S., & Lazarus, R. S. (1988*).* Coping as a mediator of emotion. *Journal of Personality and Social Psychology, 54,* 466–475.

Gadzekpo, L. (2004). Gender, bureaucracy, and development in Ghana: An examination of the civil service. *Social Development Issues, 26,* 51–63.

Gellis, Z. (2001). Using a participatory approach to mobilize immigrant minority family caregivers. *Journal of Social Work Research and Evaluation: An International Publication, 2,* 267–282.

Gellis, Z. P. (2003). Kin and nonkin social supports in a community sample of Vietnamese immigrants. *Social Work, 48,* 248–258.

Georgiades, S., & Potocky-Tripodi, M. (2000). Public perceptions of social welfare services in Cyprus. *Journal of Social Work Research and Evaluation: An International Publication, 1,* 139–151.

Gibbs, L. E. (2003). *Evidence-based practice for the helping professions.* Pacific Grove, CA: Brooks/Cole-Thomson Learning.

Gillespie, D. E. (1995). Ethical issues in research. In R. L. Edwards (Ed.), *Encyclopedia of Social Work* (19th ed., pp. 884–893). Washington, DC: NASW Press.

Glaser, B. G., & Strauss, A. L. (1967). *The discovery of grounded theory: Strategies for qualitative research.* Chicago: Aldine.

Global Social Work Congress. (2004). *Registration brochure.* Adelaide, Australia: Author.

Godenzi, A. (2004). *Draft proposal for a project on international social work activities.* U.S. National Association of Deans and Directors International Task Force.

Greif, G. L. (2004). How international is the social work knowledge base? *Social Work, 49,* 514–516.

Grinnell, R. M., & Unrau, Y. A. (Eds.). (2005). *Social work research and evaluation: Quantitative and qualitative approaches.* New York: Oxford University Press.

Gutierrez, L. (2003). Participatory and stakeholder research. In. R. A. English (Ed.), *Encyclopedia of social work* (19th ed.). *2003 Supplement* (pp. 115–124). Washington, DC: NASW Press.

Harman, H. H. (1960). *Modern factor analysis.* Chicago: University of Chicago Press.

Harper, K. V., & Lantz, J. (1996). *Cross-cultural practice: Social work with diverse populations.* Chicago: Lyceum Books.

Hasenfeld, Y. (1983*).* *Human service organizations.* Englewood Cliffs, NJ: Prentice Hall.

Healy, L. M. (2001). *International social work: Professional action in an interdependent world.* New York: Oxford University Press.

Hersen, M., & Barlow, D. H. (1976). *Single case experimental designs.* New York: Pergamon Press.

Hill, M. (1997). *SPSS missing value analysis 7.5.* Chicago: SPSS.

Hokenstad, M. C., Khinduka, S. K., & Midgley, J. (Eds.). (1992). *Profiles in international social work.* Washington, DC: NASW Press.

Hokenstad, M. C., & Midgley, J. (Eds.). (1997). *Issues in international social work: Global challenges for a new century.* Washington, DC: NASW Press.

Hokenstad, M. C., & Midgley, J. (Eds.). (2004). *Lessons from abroad: Adapting international social welfare innovations.* Washington, DC: NASW Press.

Hurdle, D. E. (2002). Native Hawaiian traditional healing: Culturally based interventions for social work practice. *Social Work, 47,* 183–192.

Jergeby, U., & Soydan, H. (2000). Social work research and evaluation: A Swedish perspective. *Journal of Social Work Research and Evaluation: An International Publication, 1,* 59–69.

Jergeby, U., & Soydan, H. (2002). Assessment processes in social work practice when children are at risk: A comparative, cross-national vignette study. *Journal of Social work Research and Evaluation: An International Publication, 3,* 127–144.

Jinkerson, D. L., Cummings, O. W., Neisendorf, B. J., & Schwandt, T. A. (1992). A case study of methodological issues in cross-cultural evaluation. *Evaluation and Program Planning, 15,* 273–286.

Joyner, M. (2000). Conceptual struggles and policy complexities: Family abuse research in a cross-national context. *New Global Development: Journal of International and Comparative Social Welfare, 16,* 94–171.

Kazi, M. A. F. (2000). Evaluation of social work practice in England. *Journal of Social Work Research and Evaluation: An International Perspective, 1,* 101–109.

Kazi, M. A. F., Blom, B., Moren, S., Perdal, A., & Rostila, I. (2002). Realist evaluation for practice in Sweden, Finland, and Britain. *Journal of Social Work Research Evaluation: An International Publication, 3,* 171–186.

Ki, A.Y-T.W. (2004). Economic exclusion and social isolation: The social impact of unemployment on urban workers and their families in China. *Social Development Issues, 26,* 25–37.

Kim, J., & Mueller, C. W. (1978). *Factor analysis: Statistical methods and practical issues.* Newbury Park, CA: Sage.

Knudsen, D. D. (1992). *Child maltreatment: Emerging perspectives.* Dix Hills, NY: General Hall.

Koch, M. (2004). European reactions to global challenges: The cases of the Netherlands, the UK, Sweden, Spain, and Germany. *New Global Development: Journal of International Comparative Social Welfare, 20,* 15–22.

Koren, P. DeChillo, N., & Friesen, B. (1992). Measuring empowerment in families whose children have emotional disabilities: A brief questionnaire. *Rehabilitation Psychology, 37,* 305–321.

Kosberg, J. I., Lowenstein, A., Garcia, J. L., & Biggs, S. (2002). Challenges to the cross-cultural and cross-national study of elder abuse. *Journal of Social Work Research and Evaluation: An International Publication, 3,* 19–31.

Lane, J.-E. (1990). Data archives as an instrument for coparative resaerch. In E. Oyen (Ed.). Comparative methodology: Theory and practice in international research (pp. 187–202). Newbury Park, CA: Sage.

Lebrow, J. (2001). Therapy by the numbers? *Psychotherapy Networker, 25,* 74–76.

Lin, N. (1989). Measuring depressive symptomatology in China. *Journal of Nervous and Mental Disease, 177,* 121–131.

Link, B. (1987). Understanding labeling effects in the area of mental disorders: An assessment of the effects of expectations of rejection. *American Sociological Review, 52,* 96–112.

Link, B. (1989). A modified labeling theory approach to mental disorders: An empirical assessment. *American Sociological Review, 54,* 400–423.

Littell, J. (2004). News from the Campbell Collaboration. *SSWR News, 11*(1), 10–11.

Long, J. S. (1983). *Confirmatory factor analysis.* Newbury Park, CA: Sage.

Lyons, K. (1999). *International social work: Themes and perspectives.* Aldershot, England: Ashgate.

Magura, S., & Moses, B. S. (1986). *Outcome measures for child welfare services: Theory and applications.* Washington, DC: Child Welfare League of America.

McCubbin, H. I., Olson, D., & Larsen, A. (1991). Family crisis oriented personal evaluation scales. In H. McCubbin and A. Thompson (Eds.), *Family assessment inventories for research and practice* (pp. 272–275). Madison: University of Wisconsin Press.

McCubbin, H. I., & Patterson, J. M. (1983). The family stress process: The double ABCX model of adjustment and adaptation. In H. I. McCubbin, M. R. Susman, & J. M. Patterson (Eds.), *Social stress and the family: Advances and developments in family stress theory and research* (pp. 7–37). New York: Haworth Press.

McDonald, L., & Timoshkina, N. (2004). Examining service needs of trafficked women from the former Eastern Bloc: The Canadian case. *Journal of Social Work Research and Evaluation: An International Publication, 5,* 169–192.

McRoy, R. G. (1995). Qualitative research. In R. L. Edwards (Ed.), *Encyclopedia of Social Work* (19th ed., pp. 2009–2015). Washington, DC: NASW Press.

Menard, S. (1991). *Longitudinal research.* Newbury Park, CA: Sage.

Michalski, J. H. (2001). The challenges of resettlement among male, government-assisted Iraqi refugees in Canada. *Journal of Social Work Research and Evaluation: An International Publication, 2,* 207–226.

Midgley, J. (1995). International and comparative social welfare. In R. L. Edwards (Ed.), *Encyclopedia of Social Work* (19th ed., pp. 1490–1499). Washington, DC: NASW Press.

Midgley, J. (2004). International social welfare: The challenge of international social work. *Social Welfare at Berkeley, 10, Summer 2004.* Berkeley: School of Social Welfare, University of California.

National Association of Social Workers (NASW). (2004). *Issue fact sheet: International social work.* Washington, DC: Author.

Noble, J. H., Jr., and Ahearn, F. L., Jr. (2001). Critical assumptions in providing aid to forced and voluntary migrants in Managua, Nicaragua. *Journal of Social Work Research and Evaluation: An International Publication, 2,* 125–141.

Norusis, M. J. (1995). *SPPS advanced statistics guide.* Chicago: McGraw-Hill.

Nurius, P. S., & Tripodi, T. (1985). Methods of generalization used in empirical social work literature. *Social Service Review, 59,* 239–257.

Nutter, B., & Hudson, J. (2000). Social work research and evaluation in Canada. *Journal of Social Work Research and Evaluation: An International Publication, 1,* 49–58.

O'Neill, J. V. (2003). Nearly all members linked to Internet. *NASW News, 48,* 9.

Ogg, J., & Munn-Giddings, C. (1993). Researching elder abuse. *Aging and Society, 13,* 389–413.

Ortega, D. M., & Richey, C. A. (1998). Methodological issues in social work research with depressed women of color. In M. Potocky & A. Y. Rodgers-Farmer (Eds.), *Social work research with minority and oppressed populations: Methodological issues and innovations* (pp. 47–70). Binghamton, NY: Haworth Press.

Oyen, E. (1990a). Comparative content analysis for biographies, or history, sampling, data archives, time series. In E. Oyen (Ed.), *Comparative methodology: Theory and practice in international social research.* Newbury Park, CA: Sage.

Oyen, E. (1990b). The imperfection of comparisons. In E. Oyen (Ed.), *Comparative methodology: Theory and practice in international social research* (pp. 1–18). Newbury Park, CA: Sage.

Padgett, D. K. (1998). *Qualitative methods in social work research.* Thousand Oaks, CA: Sage.

Palley, H. A., & Forest, P. G. (2004). Canadian fiscal federalism, regionalization, and the development of Quebec's health care delivery system. *New Global Development: Journal of International and Comparative Social Welfare, 20,* 87–96.

Panos, P. T., Pettys, G., Cox, E. E., & Jones-Hart, E. (2004). Survey of international field education placements of accredited social work education programs. *Journal of Social Work Education, 40,* 467–478.

Patel, M. (2002). A metaevaluation or quality assessment of the evaluations in this issue, based on the African evaluation guidelines, 2012. *Evaluation and Program Planning, 25,* 329–332.

Polack, R. J. (2004). Social justice and the global economy: New challenges for social work in the twenty-first century. *Social Work, 49,* 281–290.

Popper, K. (1959). *The logic of scientific discovery.* London: Hutchinson.

Potocky, M., & Rodgers-Farmer, A. Y. (Eds.) (1998). *Social work research with minority and oppressed populations: Methodological issues and innovations.* Binghamton, NY: Haworth Press.

Potocky-Tripodi, M. (2002). *Best practices for social work with refugees and immigrants.* New York: Columbia University Press.

Potocky-Tripodi, M., & Tripodi, T. (2005). The future of global social work. *Advances in Social Work, 6,* 33–42.

Potocky-Tripodi, M., & Tripodi, T. (Eds.) (1999). *New directions for social work practice research.* Washington, DC: NASW Press.

Potocky-Tripodi, M., & Tripodi, T. (Eds). (2001). Special issue: Research on refugees and immigrants. *Journal of Social Work Research and Evaluation: An International Publication, 2(2).*

Potocky-Tripodi, M., & Tripodi, T. (Eds). (2004). Human trafficking [Special issue]. *Journal of Social Work Research and Evaluation: An International Publication, 5(2).*

Ringel, S., Ronell, N., & Getahune, S. (2005). Factors in the integration process of adolescent immigrants: The case of Ethiopian Jews in Israel. *International Social Work, 48,* 63–76.

Roffman, R. A., Picciano, J., Wickizer, L., Bolan, M., & Ryan, R. (1998). Anonymous enrollment in AIDS prevention telephone group counseling: Facilitating the participation of gay and bisexual men in intervention and research. In M. Potocky & A. Y. Rodgers-Farmer (Eds.), *Social work research with minority and oppressed populations: Methodological issues and innovations* (pp. 5–22). Binghamton, NY: Haworth Press.

Ross-Sheriff, F. (2001). Immigrant Muslim women in the United States: Adaptation to American society. *Journal of Social Work Research and Evaluation: An International Publication, 2,* 283–294.

Rubin, A. (1995). Survey research. In R. L. Edwards (Ed.), *Encyclopedia of Social Work* (19th ed., pp. 2385–2391). Washington, DC: NASW Press.

Rubin, A., & Babbie, E. R. (2005). *Research methods for social work.* Pacific Grove, CA: Wadsworth.

Ryan, S. D., & Groza, V. (2004). Romanian adoptees: A cross national comparison. *International Social Work, 47,* 53–79.

Seidl, F. W. (1995). Program evaluation. In R. L. Edwards (Ed.), *Encyclopedia of Social Work* (19th ed., pp. 1927–1932). Washington, DC: NASW Press.

Seipel, M. O. (2003). Global poverty no longer an untouchable problem. *International Social Work, 46,* 191–207.

Shadish, W. R., Cook, T. D., & Campbell, D. T. (2002*). Experimental and quasi-experimental designs for generalized causal inference.* Boston: Houghton Mifflin.

Shek, D. T. L. (2002a). Assessment of family functioning in Chinese adolescents: The Chinese version of the family assessment device. *Research on Social Work Practice, 12,* 502–524.

Shek, D. T. L. (2002b). Guest editor's foreword. *Research on Social Work Practice, 12,* 485–489.

Shin, S. (2004). Effects of culturally relevant psychoeducation for Korean American families of persons with chronic mental illness. *Research on Social Work Practice, 14,* 231–239.

Shlonsky, A., & Gibbs, L. (2004). Will the real evidence-based practice please stand up?

Teaching the process of evidence-based practice to the helping professions. *Brief Treatment and Crisis Intervention, 4*(2), 137–153.

Smith, M. S. (2002). Program evaluation. In A. R. Roberts & G. J. Greene (Eds.), *Social workers' desk reference* (pp. 757–763). New York: Oxford University Press.

Soliman, H. (2004). A proactive solution to the drug problem in Egypt: An evaluation of a drug training program. *Social Development Issues, 26,* 95–107.

Springer, D. W., Abell, N., & Nugent, W. R. (2002). Creating and validating rapid assessment instruments for practice and research: Part 2. *Research on Social Work Practice, 12,* 786–795.

Tangeberg, K. M. (2003). Gender, geography, culture, and health: Emerging interdisciplinary approaches to global HIV/AIDS services. *Journal of Social Work Research Evaluation: An International Publication, 4,* 37–48.

Teasley, M. L. (2004). Perceived levels of cultural competence through social work education and professional development for urban school social workers. *Journal of Social Work Education, 41,* 85–98.

Teune, H. (1990). Comparing countries: Lessons learned. In E. Oyen (Ed.), *Comparative methodology: Theory and practice in international social research* (pp. 187–202). Newbury Park, CA: Sage.

Thomas, E. J. (1981). Developmental research: A model for interventional innovation. In R. M. Grinnell, Sr. (Ed.), *Social work research and eEvaluation* (pp. 590–605). Itasca, IL: F. E. Peacock.

Thyer, B. A. (2002). Principles of evidence based practice and treatment development. In A. R. Roberts & G. J. Greene (Eds.), *Social workers' desk reference* (pp. 739–742). New York: Oxford University Press.

Tran, T., & Aroian, K. J. (2000). Developing cross-cultural research instruments. *Journal of Social Work Research and Evaluation: An International Publication, 1,* 35–48.

Tripodi, T. (1974). *Uses and abuses of social research in social work.* New York: Columbia University Press.

Tripodi, T. (1981). The logic of research design. In R. M. Grinnell, Jr. (Ed.), *Social work research and evaluation* (pp. 198–225). Itasca, IL: F. E. Peacock.

Tripodi, T. (1983). *Evaluative research for social workers.* Englewood Cliffs, NJ: Prentice-Hall.

Tripodi, T. (1994). *A primer on single subject design for clinical social workers.* Washington, DC: NASW Press.

Tripodi, T. (2000). The contemporary challenge in evaluating social services: An international perspective. The 1999 Peter Hodge Memorial Lecture Hong Kong. *Journal of Social Work Research and Evaluation: An International Publcation, 1,* 5–16.

Tripodi, T. (2002). Single-subject designs. In A. R. Roberts & G. J. Greene (Eds.), *Social workers' desk reference* (pp. 748–751). New York: Oxford University Press.

Tripodi, T., Fellin, P., & Epstein, I. (1978). *Differential social program evaluation.* Itasca, IL: F. E. Peacock.

Tripodi, T., Fellin, P., & Meyer, H. J. (1983). *The assessment of social research: Guidelines for use of research in social work and social science* (2nd ed.). Itasca, IL: F. E. Peacock.

Turner, R. H. (1990). A comparative content analysis of biographies. In E. Oyen (Ed.), *Comparative methodology: Theory and practice in international social research* (pp. 134–150). Newbury Park, CA: Sage.

Twenge, J. M., Zhang, L., & Im, C. (2004). It's beyond my control: A cross-temporal meta-analysis of increasing externality in locus of control, 1960–2002. *Personality and Social Psychology Review, 8,* 308–319.

United States Social Security Administration (US SSA). (1996*). Social security programs throughout the world—1995.* Washington, DC: U.S. Government Printing Office.

Videka-Sherman, L. (1995). Metaanalysis. In R. L. Edwards (Ed.), *Encyclopedia of Social Work* (19th ed., pp. 1711–1719). Washington, DC: NASW Press.

Weiss, I. (2005). Is there a global common core to social work? A cross-national comparative study of BSW graduate students. *Social Work, 50,* 101–110.

Yegidis, B. L., & Weinbach, R. W. (2001). *Research methods for social workers.* Boston: Allyn and Bacon.

Young, L., Johnson, K. W., & Bryant, D. (2002). Conducting a therapeutic community training experiment in Peru: Research design and implementation issues. *Journal of Social Work Research and Evaluation: An International Publication, 3,* 89–102.

Zeira, A., Astor, R. A., & Benbemishty, R. (2003). School violence in Israel: Findings of a national survey. *Social Work, 48,* 471–483.

INDEX